PENGUIN BOOKS

CATCHING COLD

'Davies's exhaustive research and fluent prose makes compelling, if somewhat terrifying, reading, while his predictions will have you scouring the pages of the book of Revelations' *Arena*

'A rattling good story which, in the telling, illuminates the investigative power of modern genetics and the agony and ecstasy of modern scientific research' *Literary Review*

'A lucid and entertaining book' *The Times Literary Supplement*

'Fast paced and readable' *Daily Mail*

Acclaim for Pete Davis's *All Played Out*:

'Exhilarating . . . full of drama, full of its own reckless and compelling logic' *Independent*

'This could well be the best book ever written about football' *Time Out*

For *This England*:

Succulently well written . . . Davies's sketches of people and places are a joy. The pace and tension as it reaches its climax leave you on the edge of your seat. This book is a treat from page one. By the end, it's a triumph' *Guardian*

'Engrossing and impassioned . . . a wonderfully readable account' *Mail on Sunday*

Pete Davies is the author of a number of critically acclaimed, bestselling works of non-fiction, including *All Played Out*, *I Lost My Heart to the Belles* and *This England*. His latest book, *The Devil's Music: In the Eye of the Hurricane*, is published by Michael Joseph.

He lives in West Yorkshire.

CATCHING COLD

*1918's forgotten tragedy and the scientific
hunt for the virus that caused it*

PETE DAVIES

PENGUIN BOOKS

PENGUIN BOOKS

Published by the Penguin Group
Penguin Books Ltd, 27 Wrights Lane, London W8 5TZ, England
Penguin Putnam Inc., 375 Hudson Street, New York, New York 10014, USA
Penguin Books Australia Ltd, Ringwood, Victoria, Australia
Penguin Books Canada Ltd, 10 Alcorn Avenue, Toronto, Ontario, Canada M4V 3B2
Penguin Books (NZ) Ltd, Private Bag 102902, NSMC, Auckland, New Zealand

Penguin Books Ltd, Registered Offices: Harmondsworth, Middlesex, England

First published by Michael Joseph 1999
Published in Penguin Books 2000
10 9 8 7 6 5 4 3 2 1

Set in 11.75/15.5 pt Monotype Sabon
Typeset by Rowland Phototypesetting Ltd,
Bury St Edmunds, Suffolk
Printed in England by Clays Ltd, St Ives plc

for Tim and Jenny

CONTENTS

Acknowledgements ix

1 The Incident in Hong Kong 1

2 Some New Kind of Plague 39

3 On the Edge of Life 65

4 The Frozen Coast 104

5 Stressed to the Max 134

6 Respect and Dignity 157

7 The Language of Life 194

8 $3,000 and a Shovel 224

9 Marvellously Humiliating 250

10 Plug Drugs 274

Further Reading 305

ACKNOWLEDGEMENTS

I am grateful to Rowland White for having the idea in the first place, and for the deft editorial touch he deployed to rein me in whenever I got too excitable. As ever, thanks also to my agent Rachel Calder, and to all at Tessa Sayle.

Dr William Liddell and Dr Rob Brett were kind enough to read the manuscript, making many pertinent comments, and correcting me on matters medical and molecular wherever necessary. Both also answered my numerous questions, as did Drs Jane Smith and Steve Johl. Any errors that may remain are mine alone.

I am grateful above all to the many scientists and public health officials involved in this story – in England, Holland, Hong Kong, Canada, the United States and elsewhere – many of whom gave me considerable amounts of their hard-pressed time. I doubt they'll all like the end-product, or agree entirely with everything in it, but if they did they wouldn't be scientists. I hope, however, that they'll believe it to be a fair and accurate account of a complex, fascinating and vitally important subject that deserves a lot more public attention than it normally gets.

Finally, thanks as always to Rebecca, Joe and Megan for tolerating so patiently my too-frequent absences.

1 THE INCIDENT IN HONG KONG

Hong Kong's Central Market is on Queen's Road, a few minutes' walk from the hub of the Territory's capital around Statue Square and the Star Ferry Pier. On three floors of a nondescript grey building you'll find clothing, fruit and vegetables, meat, fish and chickens. These last two are sold on the ground floor, from separate aisles of concrete stalls under a tangle of strip-lights and ventilation ducts.

For all the Territory's hectic modernity, most Chinese still view fresh food as one of life's essentials, and many shop for it daily before they go to work. As a result, when I got to the market at nine-thirty one morning in June 1998, much of the day's business was already done. Seafood – live crabs, tuna steaks, king prawns and slinky eels – still lay on beds of ice; on the other aisle, however, the chicken merchants were packing up.

Birds jostled and squawked, crammed tight in cages made of metal or plastic. Plucked and gutted for restaurants, others floated in wooden tubs, tied in bunches at the neck or feet with lengths of reed. The tile floor was sopping wet where it had been washed down, and here and there lay greasy piles of red and yellow entrails. Even packing up, the place was vivid to the senses – but you'll not find any poultry market in Hong Kong as vibrant today as they were until the last days of 1997.

Before then you'd have found chickens, ducks, geese,

quail, pigeons and pheasants squeezed higgledy-piggledy together in wooden cages in a honking mayhem of beak and feather. Among those birds in 1997, however, a virus load was building up that led to one of the most frightening outbreaks of disease this century, carrying within it the potential to kill millions upon millions of people.

The first sign of trouble came in March 1997, when chickens started dying on a farm near Yuen Long, in Hong Kong's rural New Territories. On a second farm, and then a third, they started dying in droves – in all, nearly 7,000 birds succumbed – and the disease that was killing them was flu.

When a pathogenic strain of influenza takes hold in chickens, it's an ugly business. The virus spreads through the bloodstream to infect every tissue and organ; the brain, stomach, lungs and eyes all leak blood in a body-wide haemorrhage until, from the tips of their combs to the claws on their feet, the birds literally melt. During an outbreak in Pennsylvania in 1983, as birds keeled over and died within a couple of days of contracting the infection, one researcher described them as being reduced to 'bloody Jell-O'.

Apart from being thoroughly unpleasant, for the farmers involved it's economically disastrous. To put an end to it in Pennsylvania, the US Department of Agriculture eventually had to slaughter some twenty million chickens. In the spring of 1997, therefore, the agricultural authorities in Hong Kong took the only possible course of action; on the farms affected, every bird not already dead was destroyed. Not that many were left; the disease was so bad that on two of the three farms, it had killed virtually every bird already.

The virus responsible was isolated by Hong Kong's

Department of Agriculture and Fisheries, and passed to Kennedy Shortridge for identification. Fifty-seven years old, Shortridge is a tall, bluff, cheerful Queenslander who'd been in Hong Kong for twenty-five years; now Chair Professor of Microbiology at the Territory's University, he'd been studying multifarious strains of flu in birds and animals nearly all the time he'd been there. When he saw what this strain was, however, he decided straight away that he wasn't going near it.

There are countless types of flu virus; some are harmless, others are lethal, but either way they're characterized according to the nature of two proteins on their outer skin. One, called haemagglutinin, is shaped like a spike; the other, neuraminidase, looks like a long-stemmed mushroom. To date, flu strains with fifteen different forms of haemagglutinin have been found, and with nine different variants of neuraminidase – so viruses are labelled H1N1, H2N2, and so forth.

The new Hong Kong virus was an H5N1 – and virologists know that when an H5 turns nasty in chickens, it can turn very nasty indeed. To handle it, therefore, you need containment conditions involving an appropriately high level of bio-security. Ken Shortridge's lab is housed in the University's Pathology Building, part of the Queen Mary Hospital compound at Pok Fu Lam, overlooking the western approaches into Victoria Harbour; in due course, the events of 1997 in Hong Kong would see the facilities there significantly upgraded. In the spring, however, Shortridge readily accepted that they weren't sufficiently secure. 'The last thing I wanted,' he says, 'was for this virus to escape.'

He called Rob Webster in Memphis, Tennessee. Nine

years Shortridge's senior, Webster is a small, trim, bluntly spoken New Zealander who's worked in the United States for the best part of thirty years. Chair Professor at the Department of Virology and Molecular Biology at the St Jude Children's Research Hospital, Webster runs the World Health Organization's Collaborating Centre for Influenza Viruses of Lower Animals and Birds; he's described by one virologist who's worked for him as 'the Pope of Bird Flu'. In characteristically un-papal language, Webster's term for H5 and H7 strains of flu says it all; he calls them simply 'the nasty bastards'.

On and off, he and Shortridge had worked together for many years; when Shortridge called him now, says Webster, 'I said we should get right on it. Whenever there's an H5 outbreak anywhere in the world, you want to characterize the damn thing.'

You want to find out what it is – and quickly – because killer strains of flu don't exist in nature. The natural reservoir for influenza viruses is aquatic wildfowl; the viruses live in the birds' intestinal tracts, happily co-existing in a state of evolutionary stability, and the infections are asymptomatic – the birds don't get sick. Indeed, there's only ever been one recorded incident of a flu virus killing a species in nature, when a South African scientist described a die-off of terns forty years ago. This means that whenever a new flu virus turns up in domestic animals (be it chickens, pigs or horses), what you've got is a mutation, or more likely a series of mutations, that's jumped at least one species barrier. In short, it's a freak – so you need to figure out fast what it's up to.

Shortridge and Webster arranged to have the virus

shipped to Ames, Iowa, where the US Department of Agriculture has a high-security lab. The highest level of containment is Bio-Security Level 4, used for working with viruses like Ebola; there are only a handful of such labs around the world. Precautions include maintaining negative air pressure; the pressure's always lower inside the lab than outside, so if there's a leak, the air (and any viruses in it) get sucked in, not blown out. The air inside is recirculated twenty-five times an hour anyway, through filters that should net the smallest virus, while all liquid wastes are cooked for hours at a soaringly high temperature before they leave the lab.

The facility at Ames was one rung down from that, BSL3+; in essence, the only difference is that you don't wear a barrier suit. In this lab, a virologist named Dennis Senne tested Hong Kong's H5 on chickens, and watched it killing every one of them. Analysing the genetics of the virus, meanwhile, Webster found similarities with the strain that had wrought havoc in Pennsylvania fourteen years earlier.

It wasn't stable, either; Webster would say later, 'This thing was evolving like crazy.' At the time, however, they could at least feel sure that it didn't threaten human beings. All the dogma, all the received wisdom, all the evidence said that people didn't get sick with an H5.

In 1918, in the worst medical catastrophe in history, influenza killed probably the best part of forty million people; the virus that did that was an H1N1. In 1957, the Asian flu that raced around the world – killing perhaps a million people – was an H2N2. The viral offspring of this century's second pandemic strain held sway for eleven years; then, in 1968, Hong Kong flu appeared and took over, and it's been with us ever since. It's an H3N2 – and variants of those three

Hs, from 1 to 3, were the three types scientists thought we needed to watch out for.

H5 was a different issue. It was bad for birds, and it was bad economically for the farmers who reared them; periodically it flared up here or there around the world in highly virulent forms, causing deadly outbreaks of fowl plague. It killed turkeys in Great Britain in 1991, it killed chickens all over Mexico soon afterwards – but wherever it turned up, humans didn't catch it.

There was, perhaps, a scintilla of doubt. In 1992, Ken Shortridge had published the results from extensive sampling of people, birds and animals in Hong Kong, Taiwan and southern China, in Jiangsu Province and the Pearl River Delta. Particularly among farmers in the last two places, he'd found antibodies in their sera suggesting they'd been exposed to flu strains sporting every single haemagglutinin subtype then known.

This suggested to him that in an area where people lived in close proximity to countless numbers of domesticated ducks, human exposure to all the different avian subtypes of flu – including H5 – did occur. Exposure, however, is not the same as illness; there wasn't any record of deaths from these infections. Obviously, Shortridge couldn't preclude it – as he says, 'In the little villages out there, who knows what's happened?' Still, it seemed likely that any infections would have been asymptomatic; most tellingly, after all, wherever there'd been explosive outbreaks in chicken flocks (as in Pennsylvania, or in Hong Kong's New Territories now) no farmer had fallen ill.

There was, in short, no record anywhere of people dying with an H5. In half a century of increasingly rigorous

6

surveillance around the world, the first three Hs were the only ones humans had ever got. Indeed, if a new candidate was to be proposed for the next pandemic (and scientists are unusually united in agreeing that whatever causes the next pandemic, sooner or later there certainly will be one), Shortridge thought in 1992 that the most likely strain was H4, simply because he'd found so much more of it around in the wild than any of the other types.

In Ames and Memphis, therefore, the scientists studying the new H5 from Hong Kong thought they were looking at a problem concerning agriculture and economics. At that stage, Webster told *Time* magazine, 'It was merely interesting.'

On 9 May 1997, a three-year-old boy fell sick in Hong Kong. At first, it seemed he had an ordinary upper respiratory illness – a sore throat and a fever. His regular physician said it looked like a bread and butter case; how many children with a cough and a temperature does a doctor see? After five days, however, this particular cough and temperature weren't going away, and his parents took the boy to a community hospital.

When the staff there worked him up, they couldn't identify what was wrong with him, but the admitting physician felt sufficiently uncomfortable about the case to transfer him to the Queen Elizabeth Hospital in Kowloon. Again they worked him up, and again, nothing specific was found – just that the boy was having increasing difficulty breathing, and becoming progressively more ill.

He was put into intensive care; his illness worsened and complicated. He had hypoxaemia; oxygen wasn't getting round his body. The respiratory failure was consistent with viral pneumonia; consistent with another condition called Reye's Syndrome, he became unresponsive, mentally lifeless. On top of that, his blood started going haywire; he was having trouble with his clotting, losing the factor that stops you bleeding.

Despite mechanical ventilation and a wide spread of antibiotics, the boy died twelve days after he'd fallen ill. The cause of death was noted as acute respiratory failure, liver and kidney failure, and 'disseminated intravascular coagulopathy'. In effect, his blood had curdled.

On 20 May, the day before he died, Wilina Lim received a specimen of fluid from the boy's windpipe. A slight, pale woman of forty-eight with a busy, quick-talking manner, Lim came originally from Indonesia; at seventeen she'd gone to Australia and studied medicine at Sydney University. She'd worked in Hong Kong since 1981, and was now chief virologist in the Department of Health; her lab was just around the corner from where Ken Shortridge worked at the Queen Mary compound, on the seventh floor of the Clinical Pathology Building, with a view from her office of the freighters and junks rounding the north-west shore towards the harbour.

In this lab, on any normal day, Lim might receive eighty different samples of blood and tissue for analysis. Across the water from where the child lay dying in Kowloon, her staff went to work on this particular specimen, and confirmed three days later that the infectious agent was an influenza virus. The next thing to be done, in the standard course of action, was to discover what kind of influenza – in the jargon of the trade, to type it.

The Incident in Hong Kong

If you fell sick with flu in 1997, most likely you fell sick with an H3N2, a descendant of the last pandemic strain that emerged in Hong Kong in 1968, and which was, coincidentally, first isolated by Lim's predecessor in the very same lab. Alternatively, there was a slimmer possibility that you'd fallen victim to an H1N1; that brand resurfaced in 1977, believed by most scientists to have been let loose by mistake from a laboratory freezer in either Russia or China.

Lim had reagents for H1 and H3; her lab tried them out, and came up blank. Over the following days, they double-checked. They did serology, fluorescence tests, electromicroscopy – and still they got nothing. All the same, Lim wasn't unduly concerned; like flu in general, H3 is busy mutating all the while, so she just figured the reagents she had didn't fit this particular strain. The next move, therefore – again, a standard course of action – was to send it to people who had a lot more reagents than she did.

Like terrorism – and more than a few scientists have described influenza as a terrorist, single-minded, travelling light, always switching disguises – this protean virus is under constant, world-wide surveillance. At the apex of the network stand four WHO Collaborating Centres, in London, Tokyo, Melbourne and Atlanta. London is the oldest of them, while the Influenza Branch at the Centers for Disease Control and Prevention (CDC) in Atlanta is the biggest. Nearly 100 other national laboratories around the world watch out for new viruses, and feed anything unusual up to the top four; Wilina Lim's lab is one of these flu monitors.

In mid-June, stumped, she freeze-dried samples of her virus and sent them to London and Atlanta. She also sent a sample to Holland, to a wiry, nervy, bespectacled and rather charming virologist named Jan de Jong. De Jong had worked for twenty-five years at the Dutch National Institute of Public Health and the Environment in Bilthoven, a small town near Utrecht, and he was something of a collector. Although he and Lim had never met, he'd first been in touch with her over ten years before, asking her to send him anything out of the ordinary, and she'd been shipping him her more interesting samples ever since.

At this stage, she had no cause to be worried; interesting viruses crop up all the time, and besides, no one had told her that the boy had died. So she continued on about her work, the weeks went by, and she heard nothing back. Then, on Friday, 8 August, she got a phone call from de Jong. He'd booked a flight, he told her, and was arriving in Hong Kong on Sunday. He didn't say why he was coming, and again she had no cause to be perturbed; she was just looking forward to meeting him at last.

On the Monday morning, she picked him up from the Kowloon Ramada, and they set off towards her lab in Pok Fu Lam. In the car beside her de Jong said, 'Do you have any idea what virus you sent me?'

Lim told him she assumed it was an H3, a strain that had evolved and changed to the extent that her reagents couldn't spot it.

De Jong said, 'It was an H5.'

Lim was astounded. She told me later, 'I was completely not prepared for this.'

Jan de Jong is retired now; possessed of the compulsive curiosity that fires any scientist worth the name, however, he hasn't stopped working. He has what the Dutch call ironically 'a zero appointment' at Holland's National Influenza Centre in Rotterdam – in other words, he doesn't receive a salary. The quality of these national flu labs around the world varies considerably, and since he's not being paid, that might add a little weight to it when he says with a gentle smile that the Dutch lab 'is one of the best, of course'.

In the summer of 1997, still working at that point in Bilthoven, de Jong had no reason to fear a pandemic. He got Lim's virus in late June, he spent ten days propagating it, he went to work trying to type it with the standard reagents – and like Lim before him, he came up blank. He tried testing it with antisera to any number of old variants of H1 and H3; he tried testing it with human flu strains, and with flu strains from pigs. 'We tried again and again,' he says, 'because we didn't believe it could be anything else.'

By the end of July, he still had no reaction at all. For the experts, says de Jong, 'There's an important difference between not at all, and a little bit. Usually there's at least some tiny little bit of reactivity, and a good technician will see that but in my whole life I never saw any virus that didn't react *at all* with *any* antisera. So then I was confident, and I knew we had to hurry very much.'

De Jong sent the virus from Bilthoven to the National Influenza Centre in Rotterdam. The Centre is part of Erasmus University's Institute of Virology; it's housed on the seventeenth floor in the functional white tower of the Hoboken Complex, a few blocks back from the graceful span of the Erasmusbrug over the Nieuwe Maas. Rising between a children's hospital and a teaching hospital, the tower is a compendium of the medical disciplines; in the virologists' corner of it, spartan concrete corridors stand stacked with filing cabinets under a jumble of exposed ventilation ducts.

Here, Professor Ab Osterhaus and his staff study viruses, from measles in people to distemper in seals, and in the process one of Osterhaus's team, a dark-haired, handsome fellow of thirty-seven named Eric Claas, had twice been to Memphis to work for Rob Webster.

Over the years, principally using antisera from rabbits and ferrets, Webster had built up a panel of reagents to every type of flu strain yet known. Claas had brought this panel back to Rotterdam, and stashed them away in the freezer; there'd never been any cause to use them. Now he fished them out, he ran tests you couldn't argue with – and within a week, he knew he was looking at an H5N1.

He couldn't believe it. He says now, 'I thought, that's impossible. So you repeat the tests, you confirm the findings, you *know* it's H5 – and it amazed me a lot.'

On Thursday, 7 August, de Jong came to Rotterdam for a regular flu meeting. Osterhaus and Claas gave him the news and, says de Jong, 'We were all very shocked about it.' The general reaction from Claas and Osterhaus was that this had to be a mistake – that the H5 had surely resulted from some kind of laboratory contamination in Hong Kong. Claas knew his tests were right, and he knew the contamination couldn't have occurred at de Jong's lab in Bilthoven – Bilthoven didn't have any H5. But they also knew Ken Shortridge's lab was close to Lim's, and that Shortridge worked with avian viruses – so had someone maybe walked it across to Lim's place from there? Or had it somehow got loose from an egg in Lim's lab? There was only one way to know for sure. Jan de Jong had to get on a plane.

De Jong didn't think Lim would have slipped up. True, this was only a single virus from a single case; this wasn't like the emergence of the H3N2 in 1968, when you suddenly had hundreds of cases, and you could be more confident that it wasn't a mix-up. On the other hand, says de Jong, 'I believed it was true. I knew Doctor Lim for ten years, and I knew she was a very competent woman with a good laboratory. But Osterhaus said someone should go there, and of course he was right, because we can all make mistakes. So I agreed to go and look around, to see how well the lab was run – and also, of course, I liked the idea of meeting her in person.'

He called Lim, but he didn't say it was H5 – partly, he says, 'because we wanted to publish it very quickly. We knew the virus had also gone to Atlanta and London, and we felt a bit that we were in a race.'

On the one hand, they wanted feathers in their caps for pipping London and Atlanta to a major result. On the other, they needed to get the news out fast – faster, certainly, than the slow-grinding mills of academic publication would allow. As de Jong puts it, 'A bird virus should take hundreds of mutations before it can adapt to grow happily in human cells, but this one had infected the child extensively. So we wanted to publish it – but we had to alert people, beyond our personal interest, that this needed looking at.'

While de Jong prepared to depart for Hong Kong, the Dutch faxed London, Atlanta, and the WHO in Geneva. Wilina Lim, meanwhile, had already been in touch with Atlanta herself – not because she was specifically concerned about the H5 (she didn't know it was H5 at that point) but because it was one of three viruses she'd sent to CDC, and she wanted to know if they'd got around to looking at them yet.

They hadn't, for a variety of reasons. Nancy Cox, the head of the Influenza Branch, had been on holiday. Kanta Subbarao, only recently installed as the acting head of the molecular genetics section in Cox's branch, had been working on other projects. Besides, as the Dutch readily recognized, Atlanta receives a constant stream of viruses and requests to study them; as Eric Claas puts it, 'I can imagine the logistics might cause some delay there.'

The news was a bombshell in Atlanta – and there was egg on a few faces as well. With the quality of its people and the weight of its resources, CDC doesn't often get caught out; it also has a mightily efficient PR machine, whose initial output led to a spot of low muttering in Rotterdam that the Americans were cross and disappointed and had promptly set about trying to minimize the work the Dutch had done. It's noticeable, for example, in a CDC press release about this first case of H5, issued as late as the end of December at the peak of the outbreak, that no mention is made of the Dutch being the first to identify the virus.

CDC, however, had a more immediately pressing problem than any blot on their reputation. Like Lim and de Jong before them, they didn't have any reagents for H5. Spurred by Lim's call in early August to get out the virus and go to work on it, they couldn't get the answer to what it was, because they didn't have the equipment to ask the right questions.

The Centers for Disease Control and Prevention are based in an imposing fortress of brick and concrete in Atlanta's leafy suburb of Druid Hills. If the exterior is impressive, however, there are no frills when you get inside the Influenza Branch; along plain corridors of painted breeze-block, people work out of cramped offices spilling over with files and folders. Kanta Subbarao, thirty-eight years old with silvered hair, a pleasant, quietly spoken woman from the industrial town of Kanpur on the Ganges, works in this busy warren of labs and offices; she has a cubbyhole whose most prominent feature is two colour images on the wall of the molecular evolution of the current human flu strain. One of them looks disconcertingly like a nuclear mushroom cloud.

Confronted with the news from Rotterdam, Subbarao had to get some H5 reagents fast. They were in the process of setting up a panel of those tools, she says, 'because we realized we needed them for any pandemic threat in the future. But we didn't actually have them on hand.'

She got in touch with her avian virology colleagues at the Department of Agriculture in Athens, eighty miles to the east, and they drove over with the primers straight away. There was, she says, 'a certain amount of panic. We were very fortunate that we had their expertise nearby, and a willingness on their part to share it with us, and to give us an idea of how to proceed. But there was a certain amount of . . . I don't know. Disbelief. It was pretty exciting, but it was scary. There was a certain amount of dread.'

CDC confirmed the Dutch finding in three days. This was a new flu virus that had infected a human being – a flu virus all eight of whose gene segments were avian, not human – and any element of competitive dispute about that news had to be set aside, because the import of it was simply too big. As Eric Claas puts it, 'We knew this might be the start of something very, very dangerous. This might be the next pandemic.'

In Hong Kong, de Jong called Osterhaus; the organization of Lim's lab, he reported, was impressive, and the H5 was not a contaminant. Osterhaus in turn called Rob Webster in Memphis; Webster's first thought, like the Dutch before him, was that this surely had to be a mistake.

'Over the years,' says Webster, 'I've learnt that scepticism is much healthier than rushing out and proclaiming something bizarre. You get more information if you make everyone *prove* what they have – if you put them on the line.'

On the other hand, of course, Webster knew about the chicken outbreak – he already had the virus from the birds in his lab – and if anyone in the world was going to put two and two together here, Rob Webster was, because he'd been arguing for over two decades that this was how influenza pandemics began.

Webster talked with Claas, and began to believe that the Dutch finding could be right; the news from CDC clinched it. Inside CDC, meanwhile, the phones were also humming. One of Subbarao's colleagues was an epidemiologist called Keiji Fukuda; when the H5 was confirmed Fukuda was in San Francisco, while his boss Nancy Cox was in Montana. A conference call was immediately organized between these two, Atlanta, Hong Kong and Holland – and Fukuda remembers that call all too clearly.

A tall man with distinguished streaks of grey just appearing in the close-cropped hair above his ears, Fukuda has a thoughtful and relaxed manner. When I met him, trainers and a basketball lay on the bottom shelf of his cluttered office, and a navy uniform hung on the back of the door, 'because I'm a member of the Public Health Service, and it's part of the pact'. Behind the calm demeanour and the quiet, dry wit, however, Hong Kong's H5 sparked a vein of what Fukuda himself calls 'substantial anxiety'.

He says of that conference call, 'All of us were immediately aware of the potential implications. Everyone clearly understood that if this was a real virus, then this could be the beginning of the next pandemic, and that made the conversation very serious. It made all of our guts tighten considerably. I've been involved in a number of investigations, but in terms of infectious diseases, there are very few comparable events to an influenza pandemic. Most infectious diseases have regional or local implications; even a really devastating disease like malaria is confined to warmer areas. There's probably no other disease like influenza that has the potential to infect a huge percentage of the world's population inside the space of a year, and to cause a lot of deaths all over the world.'

With three other people from CDC, Fukuda arrived in Hong Kong a couple of days later, and went to work with the Territory's Department of Health. By now the staff there had got news of the fowl plague outbreak in the New Territories, and they knew something had to be happening to the birds; amidst a flurry of investigative activity, one of the things they looked at hardest was whether the dead child had had any contact with chickens.

They looked into whether he'd been to any markets with his parents, or with the maid who looked after him while his parents were at work. They looked into picnics, outings, visits to other family members – and they found that at the boy's playschool there'd been a pet corner, with chicks and ducklings. Before the boy had fallen ill the birds had died, but no one knew why. Swabs taken from the classroom turned up no trace of the virus, and to this day, no one can say for sure how that boy caught his fatal disease – but the playschool's innocent nature corner stands as the most likely source.

Keiji Fukuda was in Hong Kong for three weeks; during that time his team, together with the local authorities, took 2,000 throat swabs and blood samples. They wanted specimens from the boy's close contacts, his family, neighbours and schoolmates; for control purposes, they also took specimens from other people wholly unconnected to the child. Their objective was to discover if anybody else had been ill; to find out if the H5 was spreading.

From 2,000 samples, they found antibodies in only nine people suggesting exposure to H5N1. No member of the boy's family had been infected; out of 261 playschool staff, pupils and their parents, one child was found with H5 antibodies. Among fifty-four health care workers who'd been involved in the case, one doctor showed positive; she recalled that when she'd examined the boy, she'd come into contact with the tears in his eyes.

Otherwise, one out of sixty-three neighbours was found positive, and one out of seventy-three lab staff. More disturbingly, five out of twenty-nine poultry workers proved to have been exposed to H5. None of these nine positive cases, however, had been ill – and nine out of 2,000 people picking up an asymptomatic infection was no kind of pandemic.

By the time Keiji Fukuda returned to Atlanta his anxiety, if not dispelled, was at least somewhat diminished. He was beginning to hope and feel that it had been a freak event, and that the next pandemic was not imminent after all.

His hope and feeling were widely shared, from Hong Kong to Holland. For Jan de Jong, the fact that the child had died didn't mean that this virus was going to cause any global outbreak. From time to time, an entirely unadapted flu virus from a bird or an animal just does kill someone, without the problem ever spreading any further. In Holland in the mid-eighties, for example, a pig farmer was desperately ill with an unadapted strain of swine flu; it took him twelve days on a respirator to recover, and he could easily have died, but it remained an isolated event.

So now, said de Jong, this child had almost certainly picked up the virus by direct contact, probably from chicken droppings; he'd got some on his shoe, perhaps, then he'd tied his laces, wiped his nose, and been tragically unlucky. There was, however, no evidence that this thing would or could spread any further than that, and Eric Claas agreed. 'One case only,' he says, 'that's an incident, no more. It couldn't have been rapidly expanding, or there'd have been more cases already.'

There weren't – but that didn't mean it couldn't still happen. 'This was something quite different,' says Wilina Lim. 'It wasn't something that seemed to have spread but even so, because the child died and this was something that had never been documented, it was very worrying.' Lim, after all, had seen what this virus could do in her lab. It reproduced much faster than ordinary flu strains, and in cells that ordinary flu strains couldn't live in, and if you grew it in eggs, it killed them. This virus, said Lim, was like an alien.

In October, together with de Jong, Claas, Osterhaus

and Webster, Lim put her name to a letter in *Nature* titled simply, 'A Pandemic Warning?' If you disentangle the restrained, sober and necessarily stilted language of their trade, the message was plain: Watch this space. Lim was given the necessary reagents to detect any more H5 – and the next case turned up three weeks after their letter was published.

The second case was a two-year-old boy from Kennedy Town, on the north-west corner of Hong Kong Island. He fell ill on 6 November with a fever, a sore throat, a cough and a runny nose, and although he wasn't too poorly, he was admitted to Queen Mary the next day as a precaution, because it was known that he had a weak heart. He recovered in two days and was discharged – but not before a specimen from his nose and throat had gone to Lim's lab.

They tested as usual for H1 and H3, got no reaction, pulled out the H5 primers and got a positive. Because they'd had H5 in the lab since August, they double-checked to be sure it wasn't a contaminant, and came up with the same result. Lim called the Department of Health, and she called CDC.

By the time of the second investigation, says Keiji Fukuda, 'We weren't thinking about laboratory contamination any more. The real question now was, What's going on? Is this the start of a large number of cases? Where's the virus coming from? How many infected people are there?'

With the time-lag involved for Lim to run her tests before she put out the news, it was early December when Fukuda returned to Hong Kong. The Department of Health officials who met him at the airport had more news for him;

there was a third case now. A thirty-seven-year-old man from Kowloon had gone down on 17 November with chills, muscle pains and a general malaise, and had been admitted to Queen Elizabeth a week later; he was still in hospital when Fukuda arrived.

Nor was he the only one. On 20 November, a girl of thirteen from Ma On Shan in the New Territories fell sick with headaches, a cough and a fever. She went into the Prince of Wales Hospital six days later, and was there for nearly a month. Four days before Christmas, she would die of pneumonia and multiple organ failure. In Kowloon, meanwhile, on 24 November, a man of fifty-four fell ill; he died of pneumonia in the Queen Elizabeth twelve days later. By the time Fukuda returned, the outbreak was well under way.

Wilina Lim reported the third and fourth cases on 6 December, and from there, she says, 'That month was terrible. It wasn't clear where these viruses were coming from, but these people were getting sick, there were new cases day by day and we were really under a lot of stress, we were worrying that this virus was spreading all over the place. And the workload – coming into something like this, suddenly everyone was panicking. Everyone with the most minor illness was going to the doctor wanting tests, scared they had bird flu; specimens were just *pouring* into the laboratory.'

Lim was working seven days a week – then, towards the middle of the month, her daughter said she had a sore throat. 'She's sixteen,' says Lim, 'it was a Saturday, and usually on Saturday she goes to a piano lesson. Now, piano isn't something she's particularly keen on, so if she has the opportunity not to go to a lesson, well . . . normally I'd say, you have to go. But that day, I told her to ring her teacher and say she wasn't coming. She said that wasn't like me, but I told her, you stay in bed – because there was that worry. I was frightened. A lot of people were.'

Inevitably, much of the world's media attention, both at the time and in the aftermath, focussed on the big names. When you have a figure of Rob Webster's repute fly into town, that's going to catch the attention. When you have the power and authority of the CDC on the case – their team complete with a public relations officer – that's where reporters are going to take their notepads and dictaphones.

At the eye of the storm, however, stood the Hong Kong Department of Health, based in the featureless white tower of Wu Chung House on Queen's Road in Wanchai. By Harry Ramsden's fish'n'chip restaurant you take an escalator up from the street to the main lobby, and on the twenty-first floor you'll find Dr Paul Saw, the Department's deputy director. A fit, trim man looking too young to be near retirement, Saw bears more than a passing resemblance to Mr Sulu out of *Star Trek* – and he makes it plain that Hong Kong's H5 was an event as alien as anything you might find in that series.

The scale of the Territory's alarm can be gauged by one simple fact. In December 1997, Hong Kong bought two million doses of an antiviral drug called amantadine. Developed to combat flu in the late sixties, amantadine was one of the first antivirals; while doctors differ over its efficacy, the general consensus is that, at least to a certain extent, it helps a lot more often than not. But Paul Saw didn't want to use it – not in the way the politicians wanted him to, anyway.

The politicians wanted him to buy six and a half million doses, enough to give the drug to every citizen of Hong Kong, and they wanted him to start giving it out straight away. 'I was,' says Saw, 'sort of directed – but I said, there's no way you could make me do that.'

He didn't want to do it, firstly, because amantadine can tend in some cases to have other effects besides the suppression of influenza. Loss of concentration, an inability fully to control your movements – do you want, asked Saw, to risk having air traffic controllers like that? Or truck drivers, or armed policemen? With mass therapy, he said, 'There's going to be a *lot* of social dislocation.'

Secondly, he didn't want to do it because it simply wasn't good public health practice. If you distributed amantadine indiscriminately, the H5 would evolve a way to beat it in no time, and then you'd have deprived your clinicians (in the absence of any vaccine) of the only drug with the potential to save lives.

Even so, in the face of those powerful arguments – between fear as new cases mounted up, and pressure from what Saw calls 'not very well-informed people who were in a position to come and kick you' – Hong Kong bought two million doses anyway.

Then there were the media. Hong Kong has two English newspapers and over thirty Chinese ones, and competition is intense, leading to all manner of sensational stories. Six months after the return of the Territory to the People's Republic, there was the additional factor that the local press were more than keen to demonstrate that they continued to exercise free speech – and bird flu was an ideal vehicle to do that. If people privately conceded that on some matters regarding Beijing, a certain degree of self-censorship now operated, on flu there was no need to be coy; you can blame a lot on Communism, maybe, but you can't blame it for a virus.

Wilina Lim stopped reading the papers after she saw a report that there were chickens running around loose in her lab. Events were upsetting enough, she said, without having to contend with that sort of stuff as well. Meanwhile in Wanchai, Saw and his colleagues were facing twenty or more camera crews every morning, and seventy or eighty reporters. It was, he says mildly, 'Not something I'd like to do very often. They want to know *everything*, from the very first moment. Whenever they ask a question and we can't answer it, because it's part of the ongoing investigation, they think we're covering up. But honestly, honestly, *honestly* – we just didn't have the information.'

Besides the media, there were panicked politicians to contend with, and all the visiting specialists to be accom-modated and shown around. Rob Webster had a team moving in with Ken Shortridge, there was the CDC, there was an outfit from Japan – and while their assistance was welcome, it added to the load. They were working until midnight and beyond seven days a week, Christmas was just a day at work like any other – and all the while, news of more real or potential cases kept coming in.

Saw couldn't say what the worst day was; he reckoned every day was as bad as any other. But towards the end of the month, he did begin to fear that the world was standing on the brink of another 1918. The cases were building up, in the main they were desperately serious, there was no way to know when it would peak – and, most chillingly, unlike ordinary flu, the disease wasn't only taking the very old and the very young. As had happened in 1918, it was cutting down people in the prime of their lives.

When I spoke to Saw six months later, he said that from a public health official's professional point of view, Hong Kong's H5 had been the ultimate challenge. But from a personal point of view, he said, 'I've had enough for a lifetime.'

There were three pandemics of influenza in the eighteenth century, four in the nineteenth, and there have been three more so far in the twentieth as it draws to its end. After living through those weeks of fear and fever in Hong Kong, Keiji Fukuda now says of the next one, 'I don't think anybody's prepared. I don't think even people in the field really have a good understanding of what it could be like. There's a big difference between reading about a disaster, and actually being in it. For me, having had the smallest taste of how it could be . . . well, it's been really very sobering. Anything that may have seemed at all interesting or exciting about a pandemic doesn't feel that way now. It just feels spooky.'

The sixth case was a woman of twenty-four from Tsuen Wan, on the south coast of the New Territories. Headaches, dizziness and fever set in on 4 December, she went into hospital three days later and became so ill that she was on a respirator for months; she didn't go home until April.

On the day she was admitted, two more people fell sick. There was a five-year-old girl from the island of Ap Lei Chau, just off Aberdeen on the south side of Hong Kong Island; there was a six-year-old girl from Kowloon. Both were in hospital for most of December. So was the four-year-old boy from Tsuen Wan who became ill on the tenth of that month, and the two-year-old boy who started running a fever on Ap Lei Chau two days later.

Another case showed up in Tsuen Wan on 15 December, when a girl of nineteen became feverish and started coughing up a whitish sputum. She was in hospital for nearly three months; discharged in March, she was readmitted eleven days later, and had to stay in for three more weeks. The second time they let her go home, she lasted another eleven days, then she was back a third time for another fortnight. By the summer, the authorities could only say that her condition was stable.

On 16 December, three people fell ill – one in Kowloon, and two from different towns in the New Territories. A baby boy, one year old, got better in a few days; a little girl, three years old, was in hospital twice, but was discharged by the end of December. The third of these cases, a woman of sixty, died two days before Christmas.

On 17 December a young woman from Yuen Long, twenty-five years old, fell ill with fever, coughing, headaches and pains in her joints; she died in the middle of January, with acute respiratory distress and pneumonia. At about the same time, a woman of thirty-four fell sick in Kowloon, her kidneys failing, her lungs filling with fluid; she too would die in January.

Two days before Christmas, a girl of fourteen fell ill in Kowloon; on top of the regular flu symptoms she had histiocytosis, a clustering of the cells in her bone marrow into granular lumps. Another case appeared five days later, a three-year-old boy – so by 28 December, including the first case back in May, eighteen people in Hong Kong had now fallen victim to a strain of influenza that, in theory, human beings shouldn't have been catching at all. Of those eighteen, six were either dead already or dying – and a disease with a mortality rate of one in three is a disease fit to scare anybody.

Keiji Fukuda says Christmas Day was the worst. On that day, he says, 'We heard about several potential new cases, and it really felt like things were just going up and up. I was worried that this thing was spinning out of control.'

The biggest fear was what virologists call a reassortment event. The one straw everyone in Hong Kong could cling to was that the epidemiological pattern of the H5 outbreak strongly suggested that human-to-human transmission of the virus wasn't possible. In each case, it was still a wholly avian virus that was causing the disease – a virus all of whose genes came from bird flu. As such, it wasn't well adapted to people, and the only way you were going to get it was by direct contact – most likely, faecal–oral.

In case after case, the continuing frantic investigation found contact with chickens, usually a matter of days before the first onset of symptoms. Many of the victims had been to markets, and they'd either bought chickens (in one case, chicken feet) or they'd shopped for something else next door to a chicken merchant; one had actually worked in a market, on her family's vegetable stall. So they'd been desperately unlucky in two ways. Firstly, they'd picked up the virus from chicken droppings. Then secondly, there was something about them, something as yet unknown, that rendered them susceptible to infection.

The H5 outbreak was unprecedented because the receptor cells in the human respiratory tract – the cells which the flu virus can attack – are very different to the receptor cells in birds. Prior to Hong Kong, therefore, it had been widely held that for a bird virus to get into people, it needed first to acquire some human characteristics. It needed to mutate, and to do that it had to pass through a mammalian mixing vessel.

The prime candidate for this role of viral blender was the pig. Pigs have receptor cells that can be infected by both human and avian strains of flu. What had been thought to happen in both 1957 and 1968, therefore, was that a human flu virus and an avian flu virus had met up in a pig, swapped their genes about, and produced a hybrid that was part-bird, part-human and all deadly – because no human immune system on earth had ever met it before.

The proof was in the genes. The H2N2 Asian flu of 1957 had five human gene segments, with three from an avian strain; the ratio in the Hong Kong flu eleven years later was six human, two bird. Once you've got that mix, you have the potential for a pandemic – because the combination can confer both high virulence and easy transmission.

In 1997, this hadn't happened in Hong Kong – but what if it did? Everyone involved was acutely aware that by February, the Territory would be entering a peak period in its seasonal flu cycle. If the H5 was still circulating then, at a time when the human H3N2 was also doing the rounds in big numbers, you wouldn't need a pig to shake up the viral cocktail – the two strains could meet and mix in a person instead. And if that came to pass, eighteen cases would be a drop in the ocean. If that came to pass, you could catch the hybrid virus just by breathing – and you could start counting the cases in millions.

As public health officials contemplated that doom-laden prospect, scientists were puzzling over another enigma. In the spring, this flu strain had killed thousands of chickens. But if people were catching it from chickens now, why weren't any of the birds getting sick?

The answer, in Rob Webster's typically pithy phrase, was that in December 1997, 'Nature was really doing a job on the people of Hong Kong.'

Rob Webster is a chirpy, combative individual from a far-away little place called Balclutha, sixty miles south of Dunedin in Otago, way down at the foot of New Zealand's South Island. He began his career in the Agriculture Department of Otago University, moved to the Australian National University in Canberra, and from there went to work in the United States.

One of his pivotal contributions was made in Canberra in the early seventies, with an Australian virologist called Graeme Laver. These two showed that the haemagglutinin protein in the 1968 pandemic flu virus from Hong Kong was closely related to the same protein in a virus isolated years before from a duck in the Ukraine. The reassortment hypothesis – the notion of an avian strain swapping genes with a human strain so it could cross the species barrier – had been around before, but now Webster and Laver had proved it.

While it seems a solid case, however, it's not universally accepted – or at least, the importance of it isn't. Even in 1998, post-H5 in Hong Kong, I've had one well-respected English virologist say to me airily, 'I think personally there's too much attention paid to bird flu altogether.'

It's the kind of remark that really irks Rob Webster. Speaking of the fact that CDC hadn't had his panel of reagents, he says tetchily, 'You know, there always has been a great deal of scepticism that animal flu has anything whatever to do with human flu. This is why they call me the maverick – because all my life I've believed it was the case. All my life, I've believed that human flu comes from avian flu – maybe through the pig, maybe direct – but the reaction's always been, Oh, you guys. Silly bloody Webster, he's off chasing birds all round the world, he's having fun, and it really doesn't mean a hell of a lot. But all of a sudden it became *vitally* important to know, didn't it?'

Nancy Cox of the CDC told him about the second case, and then the third; she was on her way home for Thanksgiving, but she made time to stop at the airport to call and let him know. Ken Shortridge called too, and they agreed that Webster had to go to Hong Kong.

He arrived in early December; he had lunch with Shortridge and his Australian assistant, and together they worked out a plan of action. First and foremost, they had to find out where the virus was coming from; that meant intensive sampling in the Territory's live bird markets. To do that, they'd have to upgrade Shortridge's lab, and they'd have to put together an international team to work in it. And to do all that, they'd need money – because, as Webster says, 'For God's sake. You don't do these sorts of things out of your back pocket. This is megabucks.'

Hunting money, Shortridge went to the University and the Department of Health, and secured grants from both sources. The Hong Kong people, says Webster, 'were absolutely fantastic. They worked clean through Christmas developing containment labs, they flew in equipment from all round Asia – they really moved their butts to get us those labs.'

Meanwhile, back in his hotel after lunch with Short-ridge, Webster had written a grant application to the US National Institutes of Health (NIH). He submitted that to Washington, then flew back to start rounding up people and supplies. The grant, of around $60,000, wasn't large in the global scheme of American medical research – but it was none the less the fastest-reviewed grant in the history of NIH, and Webster got his approval in a week. Normally it'd take months, you'd be crawling round the bureaucracy getting State Department permission to work in Asia – but in the circumstances, he says, 'They realized this was a very significant event. They really moved.'

Like the scientists, the different funding agencies wanted to find the source of the virus – and to develop a non-pathogenic version of it too, so they could make a vaccine. They wanted that, says Webster, 'like, tomorrow'.

After the money, the people. In Hong Kong, Webster had already spent four hours in his hotel racking up a giant phone bill, calling colleagues all round Asia and America to tell them, 'I need your best young virologists in Hong Kong. *Now.*'

He called Yoshi Kawoaka at the University of Madison in Wisconsin; he knew Kawoaka was good, because he'd trained him in Memphis himself. He called in people from Japan; from his own lab, he took a Chinese PhD who'd worked in Hong Kong with Shortridge, and who knew the local ropes. As the days went by, the different members of the team flew in with their kit and supplies, joining

Shortridge's staff amidst a turmoil of workmen in the lab. There were so many practical considerations – for example, the simple matter of where you find enough eggs to culture thousands of samples. Fortunately, the area where Shortridge kept his animals already had negative pressure; they installed safety cabinets, sorted out reagents, and on 22 December they were ready to start sampling in the markets.

'It was frightening,' says Shortridge, 'it was absolutely frantic. We were in this phase of what could have been the start of a pandemic, and we were handling the virus at source, the virus from the animal. We were careful, obviously, we took a bit longer than we'd have liked to get things operating, and we wore gowns and gloves – the aseptic handling techniques had to be as good as they could possibly be. So there was no need to be neurotic about it – but when you're growing it, the concern is that it's highly concentrated, and then maybe you can have an aerosol.'

By this he means that you could, perhaps, catch the virus out of the air – so they wore masks, too. In 1918, however, the populations of entire cities had worn masks for weeks, and it hadn't done them any good. I said to Shortridge now, 'Even if the masks had better filters than they'd had eighty years ago, they wouldn't necessarily protect you.' He smiled and said, 'No. But it makes you feel better.'

From early December, says Shortridge, 'It was fairly obvious the chickens had to go. But at that stage, the psyche of Hong Kong society wouldn't have accepted it. We had to reach a certain point, almost of no return, until it was obvious to everybody.'

They took samples in the markets every morning and afternoon, and spent their evenings inoculating eggs. Ordinarily, hunting virus samples is like going through grains of sand on the shore, but within a couple of days, the team had H5 isolates from chickens, ducks and geese. As the information emerged, Shortridge fed it into daily meetings with the politicians and the Departments of Health and Agriculture – and those meetings, he says, 'were very intense. It could get a bit niggly. There were many sleepless nights, I can assure you.'

Then, on a farm in the New Territories and in the Cheung Sha Wan wholesale market in Kowloon, more birds started dying.

The scientists had the media all over them. 'You wanted to keep them happy,' says Shortridge, 'you could appreciate their concern – but they were getting very sensational. We reached the point where Rob Webster and I were reported to be out sampling chickens in places we'd never been, like Shenzhen across the border – places we would never go, places it's none of our business to go and do that. It really didn't help.'

Amidst mounting panic, the decision to slaughter Hong Kong's poultry was taken at the highest levels of the Territory's Government on 27 December, and announced the following day. They'd decided, in Webster's phrase, 'They were going to use the chippy-chopper.'

The Hong Kong public, and the market system in particular, went berserk. The following morning, Monday, 29 December, the day the cull was due to start, Webster, Shortridge and their team went to the wholesale market in Kowloon. In the street outside, says Webster, 'It was a media zoo. Hundreds of reporters thrusting microphones in your face – I've never seen anything like it.'

Inside, behind closed gates, the market was quiet as a tomb. The virologists fanned out to take their samples – and to this day, Shortridge finds it hard to believe what they saw there. Chickens were standing up, apparently normal, pecking at their food – then slowly they'd keel over and die, with blood trickling out of their cloacae. 'It was,' he says, 'really scary. It was really chilling.'

Outside, Webster was surrounded by a bawling throng of reporters; eventually, the authorities sent in a yellow Jeep to rescue him from the scrum. A couple of miles away they ran him round the back of a building, transferred him to another car, and sent a decoy out in the Jeep to throw off the chasing pack on their motorbikes. Then they took Webster to Castle Peak.

They didn't want the press out there, because that was where hundreds of people were being instructed by officials from the Department of Agriculture in the business of gassing chickens. All manner of government workers, right through to men who'd normally be tending flowers and shrubs in the public gardens, sat in groups for a few short hours' training in mass slaughter.

On that day and the two days following, they killed around 1,200,000 chickens and 400,000 other birds. They cleaned out every bird from every market; they slaughtered every chicken on every farm, and every other bird that had had any sort of contact with them. They buried them in mass graves, and they shut the border to stop any more birds coming over from China.

Eight months later, in August 1998, I was sitting with

Rob Webster on a bleak Arctic mountainside 600 miles from the North Pole, on the Norwegian archipelago of Svalbard, and I asked him if they'd done the right thing when they killed all those chickens in Hong Kong.

If they hadn't been killed, he said, 'I would predict that you and I would not be sitting here talking now. Because one of us would be dead.'

Rob Webster's noted for a tendency to apocalyptic statements – he's the kind of character who, when he tells you people call him 'the maverick', gives you the distinct impression that's a hat he's happy to wear. In Hong Kong, however, the central thinking behind his life's work had been dramatically demonstrated in action; in the circumstances, a bias towards the dramatic would seem to be justified.

By August 1998, moreover, he'd been studying the H5N1 intensively for months, and the rate of evolution in that virus was as high as he'd ever seen. He said, 'It would probably have taken weeks, maybe months, to acquire whatever mutations are needed for transmitting between people – but it would have done it. And if it had got away, my God . . .'

He gave a sharp exhalation of breath. Then he said, 'I am convinced that this virus was probably like 1918. It was wholly avian, yes – but it had human aspects that we've never seen before.'

Keiji Fukuda says, 'When you look at the people who died, one was fifty-four, one was sixty, one was a child of three – but the other three were basically healthy young adults. These are not the kinds of people you normally see dying from influenza, you don't normally see them dying in these sorts of percentages when they're hospitalized, and most of them died from illnesses generally consistent with viral pneumonia – so it's *very* similar to the picture we saw in 1918. It's disturbingly similar – and that's what gave this added sick feeling in all our stomachs.'

The elimination of the virus load in the birds of Hong Kong was therefore absolutely necessary, as were all the other measures taken subsequently. No chickens were let back into the Territory from China until 7 February; ducks and geese weren't reintroduced into the markets until May, and when they were, the different species of bird were all now kept strictly segregated. All the old wooden cages in which they'd previously been kept – and on which the birds' virus-laden droppings could fester – were destroyed and replaced with plastic or metal pens. On both sides of the border, meanwhile, birds for import were subjected to regular and intensive sampling.

By August 1998, no new H5N1 had shown up. The eighteenth and last human victim of the outbreak had fallen ill on 28 December, the same day the slaughter was announced. That there'd been no more cases since then couldn't be a coincidence – and on the face of it, the international flu surveillance system had worked. Those involved had stood on the cusp of a pandemic, and it looked like they'd stopped it.

None the less, from Atlanta to Holland, from Memphis to Hong Kong, no scientist or doctor could guarantee with any certainty that the virus had been beaten; months later, all of them remained nervous. In April Fukuda told me, 'My guts are still tight. There'll be some considerable anxiety for months to come.'

In June, when I asked Paul Saw in Wu Chung House

if it was over, he said, 'Nobody would dare to say that. Nobody in his right mind would *dare* to guarantee it. We've done everything we can to keep it at bay. But we remain . . . we remain anxious.'

A week later in Rotterdam Jan de Jong told me, 'There are two possibilities. It may still be in Hong Kong going unnoticed, giving only mild symptoms so that people don't go to their doctors. Or more probably, it's in China. In mainland China the situation may still be going on, and nobody can know. That's where the problem is, because the H5 must have been there. They were importing chickens from there, and it was found in imported chickens. You can certainly speculate that those chickens were infected after they came to Hong Kong – but it's not very likely.'

Ken Shortridge agrees. 'It's quite possible,' he says, 'that the virus is still out there. So far as Hong Kong is concerned, it looks very much as if it's been eliminated – but in the wider geographical area, it could be smouldering away. And if it is, there's nothing Hong Kong can do about it.'

Under the auspices of the WHO, the CDC are making a major push to improve flu surveillance in the People's Republic. Monitoring well over a billion people and all their poultry in China, however, is a very different task from monitoring six and a half million people in a contained and efficient place like Hong Kong. When it comes down to it, we simply don't know whether the virus is still out there, what it's doing if it is, and exactly how much danger that might represent. This, however, is the essence of influenza. It is, by its very nature, fundamentally unpredictable.

Towards the end of the outbreak in Hong Kong, Paul Saw's boss Margaret Chan held a dinner party for all those who'd been involved. There were speeches, and Rob Webster was asked to say a few words – so he got up and told them that his Christmas present to Chan was that, henceforth, they would refer to H5N1 as 'The Incident in Hong Kong'. He said that if he could send her a Christmas card twelve months later to the same effect, then he'd be satisfied it really had just been an incident, and they could start being reasonably sure that it hadn't gone any further.

But what if it does go further? I asked Paul Saw what a major pandemic would be like and he said, 'I can't imagine. I can imagine the panic – but the number of people that would be stricken down? No, I can't imagine it. What we've seen here is only eighteen cases, whereas a real pandemic . . . it would be terrible. I went through the '68 pandemic, I went down with it, and it was *horrible*. It's not the same aches and pains you get from your normal flu, the experience is totally different, I was just knocked out. And I remember, you could see the queues of people at every doctor's office; I think in a three- or four-week period, one-third of the people here were sick. You'd go into offices, see the vacant desks – and that wasn't a very serious one. A really major one . . . no. I wouldn't even dare to think.'

We do know, however, what a major flu pandemic would be like, because in Paul Saw's mind, and in the minds of all those who lived and worked through the incident in Hong Kong, lay the shadow of 1918.

2 SOME NEW KIND OF PLAGUE

The men of the 57th Pioneer Infantry of Vermont began their journey to France on the night of 27 September 1918. Leaving their camp in New Jersey, they set out for a ferry landing on the Hudson to board ship for New York. It should have been one hour's march, but the soldiers had a disease taking hold among them, and stricken men began falling out of rank.

Some were left where they lay; others, struggling to keep up, cast off their equipment on the road. The march was forced on; trucks and ambulances came behind to gather up the sick. Those who made it to the landing had two hours on the ferry downriver; on arrival, during a final inspection on the harbour pier, more men dropped where they stood. Those still fit boarded the troopship *Leviathan*; before she set sail, a further 120 men were taken off sick.

The 57th were part of 9,000 army personnel bound for France on the *Leviathan*; the ship's crew numbered 2,000 more. She left New York on 29 September; by the following morning every bunk in the sick bay was taken, and other men lay prostrate in their regular berths. Within thirty-six hours 700 were sick, and the first man had died.

The hospital quarters overflowed. Men lay in their fever on the decks; more than 1,000 extra sick berths were requisitioned, forcing some of those not yet afflicted to relocate into a part of the ship so poorly ventilated that it had previously been condemned as unfit for human habitation. Still there wasn't enough room; more men fell ill by the hour. The sick list climbed to 2,000; the weather was bad, and seasickness added another layer to the misery. Blood and vomit lay splashed on the decks; more men began to die. Mounting fear and horror induced an act of mutiny, when a group of soldiers who were still fit refused to go below decks to wash off the filth-smeared floors, or to bring out the bodies.

It was worst at night. The official report describes scenes that 'cannot be visualized by anyone who has not actually seen them. Pools of blood from severe nasal haemorrhages were scattered throughout the compartments, and the attendants were powerless to escape tracking through the mess, because of the narrow passages between the bunks. The decks became wet and slippery, groans and cries of the terrified added to the confusion of the applicants clamouring for treatment, and altogether a true inferno reigned supreme.'

One soldier died on 2 October; three died the next day, seven the next, ten the next, and twenty-four the day after. As the death toll mounted, the ship's war diary recorded a new horror – it was impossible to embalm the bodies fast enough, and they were beginning to decompose. During the troop convoys that autumn, many bodies were buried at sea; the living watched the dead fall away from the plague ships, fifteen a day or more from each transport, day after day. Some went to their ocean graves unidentified and unknown; they hadn't been issued with dog tags yet, or their tags were blank, and in their delirium they were unable even to tell anyone who they were.

On 7 October, the *Leviathan* docked in Brest; thirty-one

men died that day. The following day fourteen more died out of 280 who'd stayed on board, too sick to be landed; 969 other patients went to hospital ashore. For those still standing (though many of these were also ill) it was a four-mile march to their barracks through pouring rain and howling wind. During the march the US Navy Medical Corps, along with volunteers from the YMCA and the Knights of Columbus, picked up 600 more men who couldn't manage those four miles. Four of those who collapsed were found dead where they lay; hundreds more died in the days that followed. From the 57th Pioneers alone, nearly 200 men lie buried in the American cemetery at Lambezellec, looking out across the ocean. It was as near to the war as they got.

In total, from 1 September to the Armistice on 11 November, the American Expeditionary Force lost 35,000 men in battle. Starting from the same date, in the six months through April 1919, in Europe and America the US Army lost very nearly the same number of men to flu and pneumonia. As for the Navy, they lost over 4,000 men to the pandemic in the last four months of 1918; nearly twice as many as the Germans managed to kill in the whole year.

One soldier who survived was Private Harry T. Pressley, who later wrote a memoir called *Saving the World for Democracy*. He fell sick in Brest on 11 September, and at first he dismissed it: 'My usual case of grippe, but outside of a little pain in the head, not enough to worry about.' A week later, he was prostrate in a hospital ward listening to an orderly say of him, 'That new fellow will only last about two days. Keep him warm and as comfortable as possible, but that is all we can do.' Though Pressley lived, he was weak for months afterwards.

Some soldiers tried to avoid going to hospital, because 'Buddies who went to hospital were never seen again.' Private Robert J. Wallace fell ill crossing the Atlantic on the *Briton*; with no bunks left for the sick, he had to lie out on deck in the middle of a storm and let the spray wash over him, when he had a temperature of 103°. Orderlies collected the dead off the deck every morning; after a few days, Wallace was at last taken down to lie on the carpeted floor of one of the ship's saloons. A nurse appeared and got him a drink; she asked him, 'How would it be if I washed your feet?'

She loosened his leggings and peeled off socks stuck to his skin where salt water and fever sweat had dried. When she asked him how long it had been since he'd put on those socks he told her, 'Twelve days, I guess.'

She murmured, 'Oh, you poor lad.'

Wallace told his story half a century later to historian Alfred Crosby, who included it in *America's Forgotten Pandemic*, the best account of these events in a bafflingly small body of literature. Wallace told Crosby he still remembered that nurse as a kind of miracle: 'That gentle washing of my feet with her soft soapy hands engraved a memory in my mind I shall record in Heaven when I get there.'

The man on the floor next to Wallace died; when Wallace stumbled off the *Briton* on to Liverpool docks and formed up in line, another man beside him collapsed and fell to the ground. An officer came to look and said simply, 'He's dead.' Wallace had no mess kit, no cap or puttees; they'd blown away in the storm when he'd been lying out on deck. In driving rain, he marched to camp; ravaged by the disease, all his hair fell out, and he got an infection in his ear. Opportunistic, sometimes fatal infections were a common side-effect of the 1918 flu; Private John Dos Passos cured his with a bottle of rum he got from an English pimp, but Robert Wallace needed more help than that.

He avoided the hospital; instead he went to huddle by a cookhouse stove, where a chef fed him a mess of stewed apricots. When the worst of the fever passed, he went back to his unit; he'd been AWOL for three days, but his unit was so disabled by disease that no one had even noticed.

While Wallace recovered, the virus that had laid him so low was racing all around the world – through Europe and the Americas, through Asia and Africa and the Pacific. General Pershing, commanding American forces in Europe, cabled urgently to Washington for nurses and hospital units; in October alone he had over 45,000 men hospitalized through illness, and over one in ten of them died.

It was plague on top of slaughter. Surgeon George Crile wrote in his diary, 'Everything is overflowing with patients. Our divisions are being shot up; the wards are full of machine-gun wounds. There is rain, mud, flu and pneumonia. At one hospital unit he visited, he described hundreds of pneumonia cases packed in together, dying by the score, with no one to look after them but an ophthalmologist.

The official history of the US Medical Corps states that while the pandemic couldn't stop military operations, 'It slowed them perceptibly.' Troop numbers were depleted, transport and evacuation systems were disrupted, and hospitals were swamped; General Pershing himself fell sick with it, as did Lloyd George in London, and Woodrow Wilson during the Versailles Peace Conference the following spring.

At the peak of the pandemic in the United States,

conditions in the immigrant-packed slums of the country's burgeoning cities came to resemble the worst images of the Black Death of the Middle Ages. In Philadelphia, 7,500 people died in two weeks. The supply of coffins ran out; tramcars were used as hearses; there were too many bodies, and not enough men fit to bury them. Thousands of children were orphaned; thousands of young people lost the partner they'd just married.

Nurses came on plague houses in which whole families lay sick or dead – and the disease did not discriminate. It took whom it pleased – rich or poor, noted or humble, hungry or well-nourished, healthy or infirm. In the words of the official British report, 'The disease simply had its way. It came like a thief in the night and stole treasure.' George Newman, the Chief Medical Officer of the day, wrote that the world had endured 'one of the great historic scourges of our time, a pestilence . . . carrying off upwards of 150,000 persons in England and Wales alone'.

If it comes again – if a new strain of influenza emerges with the same order of virulence that wrought such catastrophe in 1918 – then given today's population the death toll in proportionate terms, in the course of a year or less, would be something exceeding 100 million people. That's one in sixty of all the people on this earth.

For a host of reasons, it is impossible to be precise about the numbers who died in 1918. When the pandemic began, influenza wasn't a notifiable disease anywhere in the world, with the exception of Scandinavia. It rapidly became so in many Western nations, but even when it did, it's certain that many flu deaths weren't reported as such.

For a start, no one knew what caused the disease. The human influenza virus wouldn't be isolated for another fifteen years, and in 1918 the culprit was widely held to be the bacterium called Pfeiffer's bacillus. This had been discovered in 1892 at the tail-end of a previous pandemic, and was quaintly described in one Calcutta newspaper as having 'the form of a minute and perfectly transparent sausage'.

The disease also spawned many other conditions in its victims, principally pneumonia, as bacterial infections battened on organs and immune systems already damaged by the flu. Thus the illness could vary widely from one case to the next. One person would die within twenty-four hours – there are reports of people literally falling dead in the street – but another patient might linger for weeks. Even in the most advanced nations, therefore, an understandable ignorance (compounded by horror, and the debilitating stress endured by physicians trying to treat hundreds of patients every day) means that any figures the authorities arrived at are at best inexact.

The United States is reckoned to have lost somewhere from half a million to 650,000 people – more souls than that nation has lost in every war it's fought this century put together. We'll never know for sure, however, because in 1918 the United States had no nationwide network for collating data, and because the healthcare system in the country's remoter regions could in any case be pretty rudimentary. The Commissioner of Health in the state of Washington, for example, frankly admitted that his department was inefficient because his staff weren't paid much, 'And their policy is to do as much as the pay justifies.'

Epidemiological work in the twenties would settle on a final toll of twenty-one million fatalities worldwide, a figure that continues to be widely used today. Scientists tend to be conservative about numbers, however, unwilling to overstate a case on uncertain evidence, and that figure is all but guaranteed to be sizeably short of the mark. How many died in Africa, in China or Latin America? How many died in Russia, as that country collapsed into revolution and civil war?

The answer, as on so many questions concerning flu, is that we simply don't know. We do know, however, that in India the impact of the disease was absolutely calamitous. It arrived on troopships in Bombay at the end of May; moving along the railways with soldiers, postal workers, railmen, and many other people simply fleeing in helpless panic, it spread throughout the sub-continent by August.

In one week in mid-July, nearly 1,500 people died in Bombay. In Madras, tram services stopped running as one-third of the company's staff fell ill. Mail deliveries were suspended in Calcutta; the legal system ground to a halt, the courts standing idle and deserted while crowds laid siege to surgeries and pharmacies. College examinations were postponed, because so many candidates were too sick to sit them. Production in the city's jute and cotton mills collapsed, as over 60 per cent of the workers fell ill.

The disease peaked in Bombay in October, in the centre and north of the country in November, and in Bengal in December. Supplies of firewood to cremate the dead ran out, and rivers became clogged with bodies. In *Invasion by Virus* Charles Graves writes:

The hospitals were so choked that it was impossible to move the dead quickly enough to make room for the dying. The streets and lanes of the cities were littered with corpses. The postal and telegraph systems were completely disorganized. The train service continued, but at all principal stations the dead and dying were removed from the trains . . . the Medical Service, itself severely stricken with the epidemic, was incapable of dealing with more than a tiny fraction of the cases. Almost every household was lamenting a death. Terror and confusion reigned everywhere.

The situation was made worse by famine. In several parts of the country the monsoon hadn't come that year, so crops were failing already. With over half the population falling sick (and with the most severely affected people being those from twenty to forty years old), the harvesting of what crops there were was drastically affected. Production of food crops declined by nearly 20 per cent compared to 1917; as a result food prices doubled, and the malnourished rural poor spilled into the disease-torn cities enfeebled and destitute.

While the 1918 influenza didn't pay any attention to whether its victims were hungry or not, pneumonia on the other hand will always take a greater toll among the poorly fed. This combination of circumstances in India led to an appalling death rate, estimated by different historians at anything from seven to over seventeen million people. Rajendra Kumar Sen, the company doctor on the Hurmutty Tea Estate in Assam, estimated in his 1923 report on the disaster that 'one crore and fifty lakhs of Indian people' had perished – that is, fifteen million. Kumar Sen wrote simply, 'Men died like flies.'

On that basis, one is obliged to conclude that fatalities

worldwide must have been nearer forty than twenty million. That would be four times as many people dying as were killed in the Great War then coming to its end – and most of them died in less than a year.

Just as we do not know the exact numbers of fatalities, so too we don't know where the 1918 pandemic came from. The standard account describes three waves of disease; a mild but widespread outbreak in the spring of 1918, a devastating onslaught in the autumn, and then a third assault – a kind of aftershock – in the spring of 1919. This third wave was worse than the first, but not so bad as the second.

That picture is broadly accurate; less likely to be true is the citation of Camp Funston in Kansas as the initial locus of infection in the first, generally mild, spring wave. Alfred Crosby starts with Funston, and others have followed him – but Funston probably gets this attention because the US army medical team of Drs Opie, Blake, Small and Rivers started work there on a detailed report titled *Epidemic Respiratory Disease*, published by Yale in 1920.

In fact, it is probable that precursors of the 1918 virus had been smouldering away around the world for at least two years before the final mutation clicked into place and set the killer loose. Most virologists believe that when a virus jumps species, it's not going to be too deadly at first – that (as probably happened in Hong Kong) it'll need some period of time to shuffle its genes about before the molecular deck finally deals out a human adaptation that is readily transmissible. There is, moreover, plenty of evidence to support the idea that something was on the move well before the pandemic got properly under way.

In 1920, as the virus began to attenuate and the disaster to recede, the British Ministry of Health published a compendious report on every aspect of what had happened. With appendices, it runs to 577 pages, and it begins with a historical survey citing outbreaks of flu going back through nearly 1,000 years. Symptoms of what they called 'the epidemical catarrhal fever' in the seventeenth century were described as aches and weariness in the head, back and limbs, coughs, vomiting and haemoptysis – the spitting and coughing up of blood and blood-stained mucus. In the eighteenth century, prominent features of the disease were high fevers, racking pains in the head, delirium, incessant coughing, upset stomachs, anorexia, languor and rheumatic pains.

In the 100 years before 1918, there'd been pandemic eruptions with similar symptoms in 1830–33, and then in 1847, when 7,000 deaths were reported in London in six weeks. A minor epidemic took hold in 1855, but after that the disease seemed in steady decline – until, after nearly half a century of quiescence, there was 'a great pandemic' in 1889–90.

Estimated to have killed 250,000 people in Europe alone, the 'Russian flu' was said by Rajenda Kumar Sen to have emerged in Bokhara in Turkistan during the summer of 1889. Six months later, in Stoke Newington in East London, on the evening of Sunday, 19 January 1890, it prompted the Reverend Daniel Bell Hankin to deliver a memorable sermon from the pulpit of St Jude's Church in Mildmay Park. Hankin took his text from the prophet Amos: 'Shall a trumpet be blown in the city, and the people not be afraid? Shall there be evil in a city, and the Lord hath not done it?'

Solemnly Hankin told his congregation that the words

49

of the prophet suited their situation well. 'A strange mysterious sickness has laid low tens of thousands of the people, and in some cities – notably Paris – the mortality has been alarmingly high. In that gay city, into whose lap but lately the nations of the world poured their treasures, there has been little more than lamentation, mourning and woe.'

In London too there had been 'a vast amount of suffering and distress'. Hankin readily accepted scientific explanations for the outbreak – an army of microbes, 'a malignant type of malaria' – but who made the microbes? It was the work of the Lord, aghast at the vice and overmightiness of modern man; in the title of the sermon this new influenza was 'a visitation from God'.

Less catarrhal than previous outbreaks, the principal features were extreme prostration, weakness and nervous depression, with headaches and pains in the eyes and muscles. This outbreak, says the Ministry of Health's report, marked 'a partial victory of the germ . . . a fairly constant infective power has been secured, and much infection is produced throughout the world'.

The Ministry of Health thought there was a direct road from 1889 to 1918. In 1918, the report claimed, the disease then entered a new phase, 'the phase of complete victory in which infective power is maintained, even enhanced, and to this is added a toxicity surpassed by few epidemiological competitors'.

In fact, modern work in the arcane science of sero-archaeology suggests that the 1889 strain was an H2, and that it was replaced in a new outbreak ten years later by a strain of H3. While the report's authors in 1920 knew nothing of haemagglutinin, however, they were closer to events, and they could only record what they'd lived through – noting that there'd been marked upswings in flu activity in 1895, 1900, 1908 and 1915.

This last may well have been the initial incursion of what would become, three years later, the worst strain ever. The doctors of the day couldn't tell what caused it, although the notion of a virus as the causative agent was certainly coming into play. Experiments by various scientists had already produced the working hypothesis of an organism so small that it could pass through any filter then available and still cause flu, so there was a growing inclination to discount Pfeiffer's bacillus as the villain of the case; that bacterium was found in some victims, certainly, but in very far from all of them.

If flu was caused by a filter-passing virus, scientists didn't have the technology to prove it. What they could state, however, was that, 'The characters of the disease which proved most fatal and which we must assume would be attributable to such a new and enhanced virus had already manifested themselves sporadically and even epidemically in England, France, and America in the years immediately preceding.'

In 1915, there were outbreaks of infectious pneumonia in German military camps and prisons. That same year, there was a lot of flu about in the United States, while more people died of it in England than in any previous year of the century; for three years from 1915 in England and Wales, there was 'a continuous smouldering of influenza'. In both 1916 and 1917, there were 'obscure but extensive febrile pneumonic outbreaks' on both the Western and Eastern Fronts, and also at the English military bases in Aldershot.

Pneumonia accounted for 16.8 per cent of US Army mortality in 1916; in 1917, that figure rocketed to 61.7 per cent. The disease was unusually severe; the doctors called it 'purulent bronchitis'.

Something similar broke out among soldiers in France during the winter of 1917–18; disturbingly, given what we now know about inter-species transmission, from 1917 a lot of horses started falling ill as well. The numbers of army horses dying of broncho-pneumonia and similar ailments soared high above previous years. Another disease of horses that the French call *gourme*, an inflammation of the respiratory tract, increased dramatically in 1918; whereas normally a veterinary hospital might see only one or two cases in a year, the vets at Ravenel near Mirecourt found themselves dealing with over 400 between April and October.

Some villages reported every horse sick and coughing, and the disease was worse than usual too; the animals fell victim to fevers, nasal infections and pulmonary complications. There were also reports of moose going down with a flu-like disease in Canada, and of monkeys and baboons falling ill in South Africa and Madagascar.

There were, in short, all manner of alarm bells ringing in the run-up to 1918, long before any soldier fell sick at Camp Funston. Intriguingly, given what the disease would come to be called, there was an outbreak of grippe at San Sebastian on the north coast of Spain in February, a month before the flu took hold in Kansas. Eleven miles from the French border, San Sebastian was, ironically, a health resort – and there were allegations that the municipal authorities tried to play down the outbreak so their summer season wouldn't be affected.

By May, the disease in San Sebastian was epidemic. The Spanish strongly maintained that the malady had come over from France, just as the French argued equally strongly that it had started in Spain. Either way, it might be that in San Sebastian the 1918 virus was emerging in its penultimate, pre-lethal form; on the other hand, there are reports from early 1918 suggesting an epidemic spread of flu in Central Europe as well. It's more probable, however, that the precursor of the 1918 virus first emerged in China.

The notion of southern China as an influenza epicentre has been argued by Ken Shortridge and others for a while. Large numbers of people, pigs and poultry living in close proximity to one another offer the virus a rich opportunity to juggle its genes between the three host groups, and the results of Shortridge's sampling in the region bear out the idea that it's doing just that.

Specifically, Shortridge points to the system of raising domesticated ducks in conjunction with rice crops. The Chinese first started raising ducks along river banks over 4,000 years ago; in the countryside today, you can still see duck herdsmen bringing the birds out of their sheds to the river for the day, and taking them back again in the evening. In the early part of the Ching Dynasty, moreover, from about the middle of the seventeenth century, farmers also started raising ducks on their flooded rice paddies.

Ecologically, it's a beautifully balanced system. The ducks control rice pests and when the paddies are drained, they can fatten on any fallen grain not used by people. When the Chinese first domesticated the duck, however, Shortridge argues that they were unwittingly bringing the birds' viral parasites to human beings as well. Flu had probably lived happily in the guts of the birds for millions of years; now, at some point in the last few thousand years, it was introduced to a new host.

It would have tried to set up home in human intestines first. When that didn't work, it had a go at our respiratory tracts, thereby discovering a new site for regular infection, from which occasional pandemics caused by new mutations could break out to bring untold misery worldwide. The virus does this because it isn't properly adapted to us yet; it's the effort to sustain itself that results in our illness. In essence, from our point of view, flu in people is a mistake; from the viral point of view, it's an opportunity. Either way, flu is very far from the only virus to have made that mistake (or seized that opening) when it's come into contact with a new host in the form of people.

In Rotterdam, Ab Osterhaus suggests that measles may have originated from rinderpest in cattle; HIV coming over to us from monkeys is another example. Once the mistake has been made, however, and the species barrier has been vaulted, there's no going back – and the relevant point for 1918 is that during the First World War, thousands upon thousands of Chinese labourers were heading for Europe to work for the armies of the Western Front. So maybe they introduced the new strain of virus there, or into America while in transit across that continent, or both.

An alternative theory points to migrating wildfowl as the source. Geese and ducks shed the virus in their droppings, and Rob Webster has found substantial quantities of it in birds spending summer on the Canadian lakes; he reckons around 30 per cent of birds heading south out of Canada before winter would be carrying flu. Alternatively, in May, he could take you to Delaware Bay and show you the ruddy turnstones (small shorebirds, related to plovers and sand-pipers) stopping off on their way north from Latin America to feed on horseshoe-crab eggs. Again, 30 per cent of their droppings on the beach will have virus in it.

So the new strain might literally have fallen from the sky. Maybe a bird flew over a pig farm, shed virus in its droppings, and a pig rootled round and picked it up. In the pig's throat and lungs, the viral genes started dancing their deadly quadrille – and maybe in this way the beginnings of the pandemic were invisibly set in motion.

Certainly, we know that in 1918 a new strain of swine flu emerged. It wrecked the Cedar Rapids Swine Show in Iowa at the beginning of October; across America, millions of pigs went down with temperatures, coughs and dripping noses, thousands of them died, and pig farmers were laid low with it too. J. S. Koen, an inspector in the Division of Hog Cholera Control at the Bureau of Animal Industry, stated firmly, 'It looked like flu, it presented the identical symptoms of flu, it terminated like flu, and until proved it was not flu, I shall stand by that diagnosis.'

A series of experiments in the late twenties by an Iowan called Richard E. Shope would eventually result in the first ever isolation of an influenza virus, when a swine flu strain was identified at the Rockefeller Institute in 1930. Four years later, adult Londoners who'd been through the 1918 pandemic were found to have high levels of antibodies to Shope's swine virus, whereas children under ten, born after the pandemic had faded away, turned out to have no such antibodies.

Another study in 1953 found that no one under twenty-nine had the swine virus antibodies; high levels of them, by contrast, were found in people born during the last years of the First World War. All diseases leave these traces in their wake – Crosby calls them 'footprints in our serum' – and this evidence obviously suggests a link between the 1918 pandemic in people and the virus that struck pigs at the same time.

Which way that link goes, however, we cannot say; it is just as possible that we gave the virus to pigs as it is that they gave it to us. Ultimately, we can never truly know the answer without the virus itself in front of us. As Crosby wrote twenty years ago, 'It has been the dream of scientists working on influenza for over half a century to somehow obtain specimens of the virus ... but only something as unlikely as a time capsule could provide them.'

We therefore remain unable to say for sure either where the flu started, or how; whether it began as a bird flu, a pig flu, or a mixture of the two. If it came from Chinese ducks, however, the 1918 pandemic would not go down in history as an Asian flu. Though it may have come to us through American pigs, we would never call it Kansas or Iowa flu either. Instead, because King Alfonso XIII was one of over 200,000 people to fall ill in Madrid during the summer of 1918, one of the worst diseases in history would come to be known as the 'Spanish flu'.

In the spring and summer of 1918, as the first phase of the disease ran round the world, it was understandable that no one really paid it much attention. On the Western Front, thousands of men were dying every week. Under the revolutionary regime in Moscow, the Russians had withdrawn from the war; freed up in the east, the Germans were moving division upon division westwards, and French President Georges Clemenceau pleaded to Woodrow Wilson in the White House for aid. 'A terrible blow is imminent,' he said, 'tell your Americans to come quickly.'

The United States was accelerating into the largest mobilization in its history: the army was growing more than tenfold to over two million men; 84,000 doughboys crossed the Atlantic in March, and 118,000 in April; newly enlisted men were gathering in training camps all across America. It was the race to the endgame; on 21 March the Germans broke through French lines, and from a distance of seventy-five miles Big Bertha began shelling Paris, a bombardment that would last 140 days. In the circumstances, who'd pay much mind if a cough and a cold were going round?

At Camp Funston, the soldiers began falling ill on 4 March. Flu had been prevalent in the camp since its establishment six months earlier, but this was something different. The men were knocked out flat; they ran high temperatures, and had head and back aches so bad it felt like they'd been beaten with a baseball bat. While some died of pneumonia, however (there were no antibiotics yet, so these deaths would not have seemed exceptional), most victims otherwise were back up and about in a few days. Before long the disease was dubbed 'the three-day fever', or 'knock-me-down fever' – but whatever you called it, in crowded military bases it was hard to avoid.

That spring, soldiers fell ill in camps all over the United States; in some units, up to 90 per cent of the men were affected. It moved into the civilian population; in Detroit at one point, Henry Ford had over 1,000 workers absent with the flu. One in four of the 1,900 inmates at San Quentin Prison in California fell ill, and three of them died.

For the great majority who lived, there was still no doubt that you'd been hit by something packing a considerable punch. First you'd get a cough. You'd get pain in your ears and behind your eyes, and in the base of your back. A dulled stupor would set in, as your temperature shot up to 104°. Your pulse would get rocky, your tongue would fur up, and you'd have trouble getting food down. You'd be laid up for several days, and you could be weakened for weeks afterwards; it was later said of the Spanish flu, 'The grippe is a sickness you don't get over until a month after you've done with it.'

By the summer of 1918 this could be happening to you anywhere, from Lisbon to Lima, from Berlin to Bombay. By June it was in China, New Zealand and the Philippines; in Manila, the docks ground to a standstill as three-quarters of the city's longshoremen fell sick. In Europe, it raced through the armies on both sides of No Man's Land. It was so pervasive that during two weeks of May the British Grand Fleet had over 10,000 cases and couldn't put out to sea. The Germans called it '*Blitzkatarrh*', and Haig's Tommies called it 'Flanders Grippe'; in Persia they called it 'the disease of the wind', and colonial wits in Hong Kong christened it 'the too muchee hot inside sickness'. Later, when it entered the worst phase, people would simply call it 'the purple death'.

Even before it got that bad, German commander Erich von Ludendorff reported, 'It was a grievous business having to listen every morning to the Chief of Staffs' recital of the number of influenza cases, and their complaints about the weakness of their troops.' He blamed the failure of his summer offensive (which came close to winning the war for Germany) on the low morale and debilitated condition of his forces, and he specified flu as a contributory cause of that.

Across the Channel, in three weeks of July in London, 1,175 people died of flu and pneumonia; one of them was Robert Graves's mother. Doctors guessed it was a new outbreak of the 'Russian flu' that had swept the world thirty years earlier – but wartime censorship kept a lid on it as a story, and anyway the war was, obviously, a bigger story altogether.

In neutral Spain, there was no such censorship. Some eight million Spaniards got three-day fever that summer; one in three of the citizens of Madrid fell ill, offices and businesses closed, trams stopped running, and among those afflicted were the king and several members of his cabinet. The Agencia Fabra cabled Reuters in London, 'A Strange Form Of Disease Of Epidemic Character Has Appeared In Madrid. The Epidemic Is Of A Mild Nature, No Deaths Having Been Reported.'

Thus did it become the Spanish flu. If this was unfair on Spain, since it's unlikely that the disease really originated there, the fact is that by then everyone was trying to blame it on somebody else; the Spanish themselves called it 'the Naples Soldier'. Wherever it had come from, however, it was spreading round a world in turmoil and dissolution, at a time when unprecedented numbers of men were moving in crowded trains and troopships from country to country, continent to continent. Given these conditions, the official history of the US Army Medical Corps states, 'It is difficult to imagine a greater opportunity for enhancement of virulence by rapid passage from man to man of the organisms causing influenza, and those producing secondary infections.'

Today, of course, we have air travel.

Just north of Padua, in a makeshift hospital in a schoolhouse in the little town of Cittadella, Second Lieutenant Giuseppe Agostini tried to relieve the congestion in the dying men by withdrawing blood into a syringe. Starved of oxygen, the blood was dark and viscous, clogging the syringe before it was even half-full. The men's faces turned grey, their lips and ears purple. Helplessly Agostini watched them drown in their beds, their lungs flooding with foam, blood and mucus.

It was a sight that would be seen all around the world; it was the hallmark of the worst phase of the 1918 flu, and it started in the second half of August. It emerged more or less simultaneously in Boston, Massachusetts, in Brest on the Atlantic coast of France, and in Freetown, the capital of the West African country of Sierra Leone. The first cases appeared in Freetown after the arrival of HMS *Mantua* from England on 15 August; by the end of September, the colonial authorities estimated that two-thirds of the population had been ill, and that three out of every 100 people had died.

In Brest, the new disease appeared on 22 August; it surfaced in Boston five days later. In the latter port, it began with a couple of sailors on Commonwealth Pier reporting sick with flu; the next day eight men fell ill, the day after that fifty-eight, on the fourth day eighty-one, and on the fifth day 106. Medical facilities were overrun, as men collapsed into fever-laden immobility in just one or two hours – and of those who fell ill, nearly one in ten developed massive pneumonia.

At Boston City Hospital, the first civilian case was recorded on 3 September. The disease appeared across the river at Harvard the following day; on that same day, 1,400 new Massachusetts recruits arrived at Camp Devens, thirty miles west of Boston. Four days later, on 8 September, the disease started tearing through Camp Devens as well.

Devens was typical of US Army camps at the time: 45,000 men crowded into a place designed for 10,000 fewer, with 5,000 of them living under canvas. In these flu-friendly confines, the first man to fall ill was a soldier of Company B, 42nd Infantry; the onset of the disease was so abrupt that he was initially diagnosed as having meningitis. The following day, a dozen men in his unit were sick; hospital admissions, which on a normal day might be thirty or so, rose to 142 on 10 September, and continued to climb.

On 23 September William Henry Welch, one of the most distinguished physicians of the day, arrived bringing with him a team of America's leading medical experts. By that time, in the two weeks since it started, 12,604 men had fallen ill; sixty-three died on the day Welch arrived. Some took ten days to die; others were gone inside forty-eight hours. Hospital wards overflowed on to the porches and into commandeered barrack huts, and the bed linen was stained everywhere with blood and phlegm. The number of new flu cases were starting to fall off, but pneumonia was on the increase; as their lungs failed and their bodies were starved of oxygen, men turned blue, or purple, or grey-black. Bodies lay stacked like logs in the corridors to the mortuary; Welch had to step around them to get into the autopsy room.

Catching Cold

Your lungs are the lightest part of your body; 750 million tiny air sacs as light and gauzy as soap bubbles, with a combined surface area over twenty-five times larger than the area of your skin. Put them in water, and they float. Welch found that the lungs of these flu victims, however, were heavy and sodden like pieces of liver; they were clogged with pink fluid. Put them in water, and they'd sink like a brick. There was so much fluid in them that sometimes, as the men died and rigor mortis set in, it would froth out from their noses and soak the sheets.

Welch said grimly, 'This must be some new kind of infection, or plague' – and he didn't use the word 'plague' lightly. Spanish flu was so bad, some doctors thought at first it might be a new kind of Black Death come back among us. It struck so many people that by September, when a quarter of a million Americans were crossing the Atlantic each month, the soldiers were as likely to die of flu on their way to the Front as they were to die in the fighting when they got there.

In the harbours of the eastern seaboard, the Surgeon General tried to institute pre-departure quarantines to ensure that no ship sailed with the disease on board; he tried to suspend all but the most urgent ship movements, and to get the number of men carried on each transport halved. With the war at its climax, the military couldn't accept this; the Chief of Staff told President Wilson that the shipment of troops should not be slowed or stopped for any reason, and that every soldier who perished on the voyage 'has just as surely played his part as his comrade who died in France'. In other words, the soldiers as they boarded were handed over to a viral lottery; six in every 100 men who fell ill aboard ship would die.

How else could they describe it but as some new kind of plague? It is therefore wholly bizarre that in the public mind, the events of 1918 have all but fallen off the historical map. Yet they did so with extraordinary rapidity; only five years later, when Rajendra Kumar Sen sought a publisher in London for his report, he had no luck. The pandemic, he was told, was already 'over and forgotten'.

Today, Arno Karlen writes in *Man and Microbes*, 'Many Americans know more about mediaeval plague than about the greatest mass death in their grandparents' lives.' As a consequence, outside of a tiny and inadequately funded community of scientists, we simply fail to regard influenza with the degree of seriousness it deserves; we shrug, we confuse it with the common cold, and we talk about 'a flu bug going round' as if it were no more than the viral equivalent of an itch or a scratch. Yet just eighty years ago, it killed maybe 2 per cent of all the people in the world.

Even a lesser pandemic is still an event of enormous scale. In both 1957 and 1968, flu killed hundreds of thousands of people; these were major public health disasters. Reporting to a conference on pandemic preparedness in Maryland in 1995, the CDC's Nancy Cox and Peter A. Patriarca of the US Food and Drug Administration described the two out-breaks as involving 'high rates of morbidity and social dis-ruption, and combined economic losses (in 1995 dollars) of $32 billion'.

An influenza pandemic, they said, brings death, disease and social dislocation 'on a scale similar to or even greater than that caused by other natural disasters, but on a much wider geographic scale'.

The Spanish flu killed more people in one year than

have so far been infected with HIV in the best part of two decades – and to say this is not to belittle AIDS for one second. AIDS is a massive global tragedy, made particularly awful by the fact that infection remains ultimately a death sentence. On the other hand, given luck and caution, AIDS isn't easy to catch – whereas when the next flu pandemic comes, you can't stop breathing, can you?

3 ON THE EDGE OF LIFE

Influenza and HIV have several traits in common, the most important being their ability constantly to mutate and evolve. This capacity to renew themselves in an all but infinite sequence of variations on a theme has led to their sometimes being described as 'quasi-species'. More bluntly, while other scientists deploy the analogy with terrorism, Ken Shortridge (in a gleeful burst of political incorrectness) compares flu to a sensuous woman: 'Just when you think you've scored, she changes.'

Another thing shared by flu and HIV is that we know more about them than any other viruses; certainly, until HIV came along and sparked the research effort of the past fifteen years, no other virus had been studied as much as flu. Any scientist in either field, however, will tell you that all the knowledge we possess is still desperately incomplete.

The name influenza comes from the Italian word for 'influence'; it was given to the disease by astronomers in Italy in the sixteenth century. Noting that it seemed to run on a seasonal timetable, they ascribed its sporadic appearance to the influence of conjunctions of the planets and stars – and while that may seem outlandish today, it's not a notion that's entirely gone away.

Sir Fred Hoyle, the British astrophysicist, has put more than a few scientific noses out of joint down the years with his unorthodoxies on a number of issues – most notably, his theory that life on earth began with comet-borne spores from outer space. In 1990, Hoyle suggested that flu outbreaks were linked to sunspot activity.

A similar idea had been proposed twelve years earlier by Dr Edgar Hope-Simpson, then working at the Epidemiological Research Unit in Cirencester. Hope-Simpson hypothesized that the influenza virus might lie dormant in people, in some latent or hibernating form; not in itself an implausible idea, as Japanese scientists have since found residual material of the measles virus lurking in the brains of cadavers many years after those people would have actually had the disease. Hope-Simpson went on to argue that perhaps these latent viral entities could be reactivated by variations in solar radiation.

We shouldn't write these ideas off as quickly as you might think. From a strategic point of view, pursuing survival – the replication of its genes – what's better for a virus? Should it spread rapidly through the population like flu? Or should it just pop into a nerve cell and wait there, like herpes does? On the face of it the herpes route is probably better, because it can always pass on to the host's child, whereas an individual flu strain will always (apparently) die out sooner rather than later.

Given the mystery of flu's seasonal cycle, therefore, people have often wondered whether flu also has some mechanism for lying low – for the viral equivalent of loitering with intent. Hope-Simpson came up with his theory of solar radiation to explain this, after noting that the Hong Kong flu of 1968 seemed to emerge in Australia and England at exactly the same time (just as the 1918 killer showed up in Boston, Brest and Freetown within a matter of days). Now it's very hard actually to prove that these emergences were simultaneous, but no less an authority than Dr Brian Mahy, the Director of CDC's Division of Viral and Rickettsial Diseases in Atlanta, says we shouldn't dismiss the idea out of hand.

The occupant of a corner office somewhat grander than those of his minions, in keeping with his position as the man overseeing the work of some 450 virologists, Mahy is a thoughtful, donnish Englishman who began working on flu at Cambridge in the sixties, and who came to CDC in 1989. He says of Hope-Simpson's work, 'Of course he's not a molecular person; he's never understood quite what might or might not be involved in that. But he's been knocking away at this idea that maybe there are dormant flu genomes, and that when we see a new virus they've somehow been reactivated. I personally don't think there's much credence in it – but these people do need to be considered.'

Others have more straightforward explanations. Ken Shortridge suggests stress; maybe at certain times of year we're just more susceptible to attack. In Western countries, for example, as we start getting cold and miserable when autumn sets in, maybe flu takes advantage of that.

Alternatively, considering what happened in the autumn of 1918, Rob Webster suggests a straight molecular explanation. If, for the sake of argument, the virus that was already in circulation needed twenty mutations to change from merely unpleasant to downright murderous, what if around the world there were viruses that had managed nineteen of those changes? Statistically, you're dealing with many billions of viruses – so why shouldn't three of them click randomly into their final deadly shape at more or less the same time in different places, whatever the weather or season?

Ultimately, it's all speculation. What happened in 1918, why flu is seasonal, whether it has some means of hanging around undetected – we don't know any of this. What we do know, however, is that there will be another pandemic. We don't know when, we don't know what virus will cause it because it hasn't evolved yet, and we don't know how bad it will be – but we do know there exists what thrillers like to call a clear and present danger. You'd think, therefore, that we'd be more urgently on the case – but as a society in general, we're not.

Reporting to Brian Mahy, Nancy Cox runs a team of around thirty people in the CDC's Influenza Branch. As a graduate student, she started working on flu with Mahy at Cambridge in 1970; she moved to Atlanta five years later, and she's headed the flu section since 1991. A neat, precise woman, well aware of the sensitive politics of her business, she chooses her words carefully, which gives her warning all the more weight.

She says, 'I think in most countries, over the past ten or fifteen years, it's been difficult to survive working in certain areas – and influenza, while it is still viewed as a public health problem, doesn't have the same profile as some other diseases like HIV do. I'm not saying the resources that have gone into HIV shouldn't have, they were very much needed – but there's been sort of a dry period for influenza researchers. I'd say things have gone on at a minimal level, and there hasn't been as much research as there should have been on drug development, on new vaccine development, on basic research. We understand a lot about this virus – but we haven't been able to figure out a way to stop it.'

I said, she would say that, wouldn't she? Cox replied, 'Yes. But when you see the toll it takes, you realize that we do need better tools. We need better ways to control this disease, particularly because the global population is ageing. A lot of people get hospitalized with flu, and it's very expensive.'

She's speaking here of normal flu, the strains that go around every year – running up an annual medical bill, depending on how serious those prevalent strains are, of between five and ten billion dollars. As scientists, the CDC's people naturally incline to the lower, more provable numbers, but Brian Mahy says influenza in the United States can kill 10–15,000 people in a non-epidemic year, and in a bad year, up to 40,000. And yet, he sighs, 'These events are not considered significant.'

In 1997, says Mahy, 'We had two deaths from rabies, and each one made national headlines. But you can say that forty thousand people quietly passed away in one year with flu – and we're just to take that as part of normal social activity?'

On the top of Bittacy Hill in a leafy, well-heeled suburb of North London, Great Britain's National Institute of Medical Research is housed in a giant, gaunt brick building with a stained green copper roof. Built in the 1930s, it looks like a prison or a poorhouse, but in fact it contains a vital link in the world-wide chain of humanity's defence against flu.

The Institute looks out over farmland towards Harrow School; it was at the Institute's farm just down the hill that the human flu virus was first discovered in 1933. People had been searching for the causative agent behind 1918 ever since it happened – but when Mill Hill succeeded, it was in part one of those lucky breaks that litter the annals of science. During a project mostly funded by huntsmen wanting a vaccine for canine distemper so they could chase foxes with healthier dogs, the Institute's research work span off down a variety of viral sidelines; flu was isolated from ferrets when it was found by chance (because a researcher sneezed on one) that they react to it much as humans do.

Now, in an office the size of a broom cupboard, Alan Hay rummages through mountains of files and pencil-scrawled paperwork for a photograph of the Institute's farm at that time; it tickles him that the picture shows the farmworkers wearing suits, and he wants me to see it, but he can't find it. I can't say I'm surprised; every square inch of desk, wall and filing cabinet in the room is cluttered to overflowing with stacks of notes, graphs and diagrams, and it's not the only item he fails to find during the course of our afternoon's conversation.

Hay is a soft-spoken Scot who first studied at Aberdeen; after a couple of years in South Carolina, he came to the National Institute in the early seventies. He'll not reveal how old he is – 'old enough', is all he'll say – but I'd put him in his mid-fifties and he is, in his looks and manner, the very archetype of the batty British scientist.

Eyebrows as thick as hedges jut from his forehead, a nervous tic in his right eye makes it seem that he's sporadically winking at you, he drinks randomly from a cup of cold coffee, and his efforts at document location suggest he long ago left any such practical matters to his postgrad students. If his style is otherworldly, however, his speech is considered, concise and very much to the point. As the British counterpart to Nancy Cox in Atlanta, running one of the World Health Organization's four centres for world-wide flu research and surveillance, the point he arrives at isn't hugely reassuring, either.

On the paucity of funding, Hay shrugs and says, 'You deal with what you've got. In general, the politicians aren't going to change their position – and if they do, it'll more likely be to decrease resources than to increase them. I can think of countries where very useful labs have been closed – following Western concepts of value for money, no doubt. We'd certainly like to have more people monitoring the virus in Russia, for example – the old Soviet Union was very much better at it, and Russia's a problem now. Or in India, we have places dotted around, but there are great big holes in a huge population there. So you just have to hope that you don't have a significant initiation of something in an area like that, where it reaches critical mass before you notice it.'

On the other hand, even if the next pandemic should begin in full view of the surveillance system, Hay says, 'It's likely to spread pretty widely. You've got a virus that's ultimately going to spread to every part of the globe, and everyone's going to catch it at some stage.'

He'd recently been quoted saying, 'People are getting concerned. There's a feeling that another pandemic is due.' Now he told me, with his customary precision, 'I don't like the term *due*. It's a question of chance as to whether it'll happen tomorrow or next year or in ten years' time. We just don't know when another one might crop up.'

Recently in Morocco, in an isolated group of hamlets encompassing some 200 people, there'd been an outbreak of something that killed about twenty of those people; it decimated those villages. Hay spoke to colleagues at the Pasteur Institute who'd managed to get there late in the day, and to get a small number of samples from the later cases, but they didn't know what it was. It was, he said, much more serious than the new Hong Kong virus – but was it flu? Was it viral, bacterial, a parasite? They didn't know.

He said, 'You have these pockets of outbreaks in isolated places, where the effects locally can be dramatic – but because it's not affecting a significant number of people, it passes, and you have a limited amount that you can do. You're interested in understanding any and all of these, obviously – but you focus on what's closer to home. In Europe, for example, you've got a significant amount of flu in pigs. One of these types is an H3N2 that came from people, and it still has a coat like the original human virus, but the internal genes are now all avian. Now, you don't know if that has the ability to get back into people and cause havoc. You just don't know. You know the chance of it happening is low, that we're talking about infrequent events – but they're infrequent events that *can happen*.'

So there will be another pandemic?

'Yes.'

And what can we do about it?

'No more than we could fifty years ago, basically.'

For healthy people, the best defence against a regular strain of flu is to get it – to get sick, maybe, and to get immune while you're at it. For people more likely to be badly affected by a respiratory disease – the elderly, people with heart complaints, with asthma or diabetes – we vaccinate.

The composition of the vaccine changes every year,

keeping track of changes in the virus itself. Every spring, half a dozen scientists (Hay and Cox among them) meet at the WHO in Geneva to discuss their global road map of flu – what the disease has been doing, and where they see it going next. They decide what strains the next batch of vaccine should be designed to counter; through the next six months, drug companies grow the new vaccine in eggs, and in the autumn those who need it get vaccinated. To date, Hay and his colleagues have got it pretty much right – though just recently a new strain cropped up in Sydney, throwing that year's vaccine somewhat out of kilter with the virus that was around by the time people had their shots.

There's always the danger that genetic evolution in the virus can lessen the effectiveness of any given year's vaccine to some degree. By definition, however, when you get something dramatic like a reassortment event, the resulting new pandemic strain threatens all of us, and not just the vulnerable subgroups. It's true that today we can get any new strain genetically sequenced inside a week of its appearance – but knowing what it is won't necessarily help us too much.

In its essentials, the vaccine production system has stayed the same for decades – so if it takes six months to produce a normal batch in a normal year, how long does it take to produce six billion batches? Economically, practically, any way you look at it, you *can't* produce six billion batches. Besides, if the next pandemic should prove to be an H5, all of the above is irrelevant anyway. You can't grow an H5 vaccine in chicken eggs, because it kills them.

Apart from the vaccine, there are two antiviral drugs available, amantadine and rimantadine, with a couple more in clinical trials. But again, there's no practical or economic possibility of producing enough of these drugs for six billion people; they will almost certainly be reserved for those working in the emergency services.

At least we have antibiotics now; we can tackle the opportunistic pneumonias that seize on people weakened by flu, and on that front we can stop it being as bad as 1918. Even there, however, we have to recognize that many bacteria are now developing resistance to antibiotics, and some of the bacteria which cause pneumonia are among them.

In short, says Hay, when you add it all up, 'There's not a lot you can do for a lot of the people. In Britain, and some other countries, we can limit the damage – but you're not going to get that in the middle of Africa, are you?'

In the face of this, there are two questions the scientists would badly like to answer. Firstly, they want to find a better way of making vaccine – and, specifically, of making a vaccine that can beat an H5.

Secondly, they want to know what the 1918 virus was like, and why it was so deadly. Nineteen-eighteen happened fifteen years before the first human isolate was obtained; scientists can guess from antibodies what that killer strain might have been like, but they'd dearly like to know what gave it its particular properties. We still don't know, at this point, which specific genetic traits give a flu strain that extra order of virulence – and understanding the 1918 virus could tell us a lot about that.

Viruses are microscopically tiny parasites. For a rough idea of scale, if you're reading this book in your living room, imagine that a bacterium is the size of that room. Now hold up a squash ball – and that's how big a virus is.

The core particle is a packet of nucleic acid – either DNA or RNA – surrounded by a protein coat called the capsid. The virus reproduces by getting hold of a host cell (in the case of flu, that's the job of the haemagglutinin spikes) and then inserting its genetic material. Once inside, this dismembers the host, and uses the material from it to make new viruses; these are released as the host disintegrates, and head off to attack more cells in their turn.

In essence, it's a destructive form of molecular burglary; flu gets into the building, cracks the safe, takes what it wants, and wrecks the place on its way out. Moreover, the chemical intricacy of the process by which it breaks in is dazzlingly ingenious. It has to be because the genome, the heart of the virus, is extremely vulnerable; left out on its own, this genetic material would fall prey to marauding enzymes and be chopped to bits in no time. The genome is therefore secured inside a lipid, spherical envelope, on whose surface the haemagglutinin stands ready to tie up with the victim.

In concert with another protein called the M2, the haemagglutinin effects entry for the flu's RNA by fusing the membranes of cell and virus in a process called invagination. The core of the virus then folds itself through the merged membranes to get inside the cell. If you think of it as picking a lock, haemagglutinin is the key – except that while the genome is being infiltrated into the strongbox, it's still inside one of its own. This is where the M2 comes in; it channels an increased acidity from the cell back into the viral interior, so that the genetic core is destabilized and set free to go to work on the host cell's material.

Whether the ability to do all this makes the virus a fully paid-up life form is a question that's been widely debated.

Although viruses replicate and evolve, they can't do it on their own, and the host cells they need to help them do it are, obviously, quite different and much larger entities altogether. How viruses evolved in the first place isn't clear either; it's thought they either descended from more complex parasites that got into a dependence routine on their host cells, or else they're breakaway groups of host genes that got a quasi-life of their own.

Either way, it's hard not to stand in awe and mystery before them – but seeking definitions of exactly what they are can take you down a road without end. Brian Mahy came up with one of the best; asked if the flu virus was a living thing he said, 'If I give a popular lecture, I usually call it "Smaller Than Life", after a BBC programme from the fifties. It's on the edge of life, between living organism and pure chemical – but it seems alive to me.'

Mahy's 'edge of life' is a canny median position – and there are as many opinions about this as there are virologists, most of whom tend to baulk at entering the more abstract realms of thought. As Nancy Cox puts it, 'I prefer to avoid philosophy. But you look at it and you can't help thinking, well – who cooked *that* up?'

Jan de Jong in Rotterdam is more stern. He says, 'The term "life" when you're talking about molecules has no meaning. A molecule is never alive. Flu does something, yes, but so does water vapour when it condenses and turns into rain. These are processes. Of course, flu is very ingenious in the process by which it multiplies, but dead things can multiply. When a fire burns, it multiplies – more crudely than flu, OK – but you cannot apply the term "life" to this.'

I said that flu instructs a cell to make copies of itself,

and to the layman this was surely a determinant activity. De Jong laughed and said, 'Philosophy is not science, and I'm not a well-known philosopher. So you can talk about these things in philosophical terms, but it has nothing to do with reality. These are models, creations of the mind, and it's fascinating to do that – but it's not scientific. The virus doesn't have *intentions*. It's purely biochemical, and there's no need to introduce a life principle. I have difficulties explaining what a man or an animal does; you need more than biochemistry to explain that. But not with a virus.'

Take a short walk down the corridor to Eric Claas's laboratory, and you'll come on a different opinion altogether. When I asked Claas if flu was a life form he said immediately, 'It's alive, oh yes. Obviously it can't live by itself – but it's able to maintain itself over such a long period of time that you can call it a life form. It's just a little bit of protein and nucleic acid . . .'

Yet it killed forty million.

'It's an amazing molecule. But then, we're amazing molecules. The whole basis of a human being is just four letters of nucleic acid. There are 13,000 letters on the flu virus genome, and we have several billion. So we're *much* more amazing – and yet we can't stop flu. We've gone to the moon, yet we can't stop flu – and I wonder if we ever will be able to stop it. We know more about it than any other virus except HIV – and yet we hardly know anything.'

Whether viruses are life forms or not, they surely go back in time to the beginnings of life; they're built out of the most elemental materials of organic life. The nucleic acid comprising the genetic material in most of them, and in all larger cellular organisms, is DNA, deoxyribonucleic acid – the chemical substance responsible for the genetic transmission of characteristics from parent to offspring. The genetic material of some viruses, however, is based on ribonucleic acid – RNA. This is a simpler beast, used in higher life forms for protein synthesis and assorted messenger duties. What matters here is that flu is an RNA-based virus – and as such, being simpler, it lacks one key ability of a DNA-based creature.

In essence, DNA has got a proof-reading mechanism; when it is transmitting genetic instructions, it can check whether it has made any spelling mistakes. RNA can't do that – so when a virus like flu makes a reproductive mistake, that mistake keeps on going. Flu has what the scientists call 'enormous genetic plasticity'; in other words, the chances of mutation are high, and that's why new strains crop up all the time.

Most mutations lead to strains that don't work; you don't see the result, because they die. So in any host population, there's a soup of shape-shifting virus busy selecting out those new variants most likely to prosper – most able, in other words, to cause infection and reproduce. It is survival of the fittest at a molecular level; it is about the ability of a new strain of virus to out-compete the previous resident, against whom the host has developed antibodies.

We understand certain properties that the virus requires to do this, but we don't understand the full complement of characteristics it needs to be successful; much of the relationship between virus and host remains obscure. Meanwhile, even as we study it, it's changing under our noses all the time. The surface changes, the gene segments change, they all encode for different components, and those components all work together in ways we don't fully appreciate.

What we do know is that the engine of the virus is a loose bundle of eight gene segments carrying ten genes, all of which can be reconfigured into a near-endless variety of new combinations. The changes come in two forms, called drift and shift. Drift can be characterized as an ongoing process of evolutionary adaptation; shift is more startling, when something wholly new appears, sometimes (but not always) in a reassortment event. That new virus can then move rapidly round a world that's never met it before, and is all but entirely without immunity.

That's what they feared in Hong Kong – that the avian H5N1 would reassort with a human strain. Rob Webster, however, now believes it was a reassortant already. He argues that the haemagglutinin gene was remarkably stable; that it had been around in chickens for some time. The other genes, by contrast, were evolving at maximum rate – so it looked to him as though the haemagglutinin had picked up a whole new package of the other seven gene segments, all of which were then engaged in a hectic, random hunt for a new structure that would work.

It was like a man in a gigantic clothes store trying on every suit in the place very, very quickly, and without looking at any of them before he puts them on. Is he going to find a suit that fits before someone shuts up the shop? Luckily, as far as adaptation to people is concerned, it seems they killed all the chickens before the virus found a new suit it liked.

While it didn't find new raiment allowing airborne transmission among people, however, the haemagglutinin on the Hong Kong H5 already had another mutation in place. Normally, flu can only attack the cells of the respiratory tract; to grab hold of those cells, the haemagglutinin spikes have to break in two at what's called 'the cleavage site'. What distinguished the Hong Kong H5 was an extra batch of amino-acids tacked on to this crucial piece of the spike – and the effect of this extra molecular muscle was to enable the virus to spread out from the throat through the victim birds' bloodstream, and to infect different cells all round the body.

That's how fowl plague turns into the system-wide onslaught previously seen in Pennsylvania and elsewhere. Whether the Hong Kong virus had the same impact on its human victims, however, is harder to gauge. It certainly wrought damage in the first victim's blood – but overall, those who died didn't exhibit widespread general haemorrhaging (except, in some cases, in their lungs). The picture is further muddied by the fact that once patients are on a respirator, some of the factors leading to their death might not be flu-related at all; any organ failure may instead be caused by the stresses involved in keeping someone mechanically alive.

Having said that, there were still many troubling signs that Hong Kong's H5 went to work further afield than just the respiratory tract. Kidneys and livers failed, there were bone marrow malfunctions, six patients had stomach pains with vomiting and diarrhoea, and one went into septic shock. Members of the Hong Kong medical profession concluded in *The Lancet* that H5N1 patients 'are at risk of major complications'.

Definitely and extensively in birds, therefore, and at least possibly in human beings as well, the mutation at the

H5N1 cleavage site allowed it to infect more cells than flu normally can – and scientists badly wanted to know whether the 1918 virus had that capability too.

On 9 August 1918, the US Navy Bureau of Medicine and Surgery in Washington put out a warning that flu was prevalent in Europe, Hawaii and many other places around the world. A week later, the Surgeon General ordered medical officers in ports all round the country to hold any ship with flu victims on board, pending notification of the local health authorities.

More than that they couldn't do – they couldn't quarantine people with a mild disease just because the disease was widespread, and they couldn't strictly quarantine the ports anyway because of the war. Colonel S. M. Kennedy, chief surgeon in the port of New York, acknowledged that flu cases had been coming ashore for a couple of months, but he said, 'We can't stop this war on account of Spanish or any other kind of influenza.'

In late August, the disease turned from mild to vicious. In the second week of September, forty-six people died in Boston; the death rate climbed to 265 the next week, 775 the week after, and 1,214 in the first week of October. While they started dying in Massachusetts, the first cases were reported in Rhode Island, Connecticut, Pennsylvania, Virginia, South Carolina, Florida and Illinois. At the same time, even as Boston pleaded desperately to the Red Cross for nurses, millions of young men all round the country were crowding together in schools, post offices and town halls to register for military service – and to breathe, cough and sneeze on each other while they did so.

The time was as fevered with patriotism as it was with flu. While politicians on the stump railed that their opponents took money from the Germans, brewers with Teutonic names took out ads proclaiming their loyalty; so did the Bayer drug company, feeling obliged to announce that 'every officer and director of the company is an American'. Wild charges were put about that German spies had landed off U-boats to spread the flu germ in cinemas and theatres. At the end of September, General Pershing launched the biggest American military operation since the Civil War against German lines on the Meuse; on the same day that offensive began, 156 people died of flu and pneumonia in Boston.

Calvin Coolidge, Acting Governor of Massachusetts, wired urgent appeals for doctors and nurses to Washington, to the Governors of neighbouring states, and to the Mayor of Toronto. Massachusetts now had some 50,000 people sick, and the state's medical staff were 'worked to the limit . . . many cases receive no attention whatsoever'.

But the disease was now everywhere; everyone else needed doctors and nurses too. In four weeks, it had reached as far afield as New Orleans, Seattle and San Francisco; 2,800 Americans died of flu and pneumonia in August, but in September that figure climbed to 12,000, and – because an area of the country covering one-fifth of the population didn't report mortality figures to the Census Bureau – the true number was probably even worse.

Spanish flu was now as important as the war; although Pershing in France wanted more men, draft calls for 142,000 soldiers in October were cancelled, and military camps went into quarantine. Battling to help the civilian population, doctors came out of retirement to work twenty-hour days.

Massachusetts Senator John Weeks told the Senate Appropriations Committee that he and five other members of his family had been ill, that their maid was desperately sick but no nurse or hospital bed could be found for her, and that his doctor had told him, 'If he had twice as much time he could not have performed his duty.'

To tackle the flu, Weeks wanted Congress to approve $1,000,000 for the United States Public Health Service – more than one-third of that service's annual budget at the time. Officers of the service told the Appropriations Committee that when flu took hold in industry, 'It is certain that all war projects . . . will be knocked out fifty per cent.' The money was passed in two hours, without a single vote against.

On the other hand, what the health authorities could do with the money was limited. They could buy beds and recruit nurses, but the only treatment was rest and hope. Struggling to contain the outbreak, towns and cities all round the country ordered schools, cinemas, theatres, churches, pool halls and dance halls to close; in some places they even set limits on the number of people permitted to attend a funeral. Any check this might have placed on the spread of the disease, however, was nullified by all the parades then taking place to raise war funds from the citizenry in the form of Liberty Bonds.

In essence, Spanish flu was unstoppable; unless you shut down society altogether, any airborne disease always will be. The result, in street after street, city after city, was tragedy upon tragedy. When Johnny B., a pneumonia patient fourteen years old, was discharged from Boston City Hospital, a social worker went home with him to check that they could take him back. She found the boy's father and two out of six children sick; two others had already died. The youngest, a baby, lay on the kitchen table; with the father too sick to work, those still alive had no money and no food.

All across the country – all across the world – bodies were lying untended for days. Undertaking firms ('coffin ghouls') doubled or trebled their prices; cemetery officials made the bereaved dig graves for their own dead. In Philadelphia, hit harder than any other city, there was only one morgue. Its capacity was thirty-six bodies – this for a city where, on a single day in mid-October, 711 people died. They had to stack the corpses three or four deep in every room and along the corridors, unembalmed, covered in filthy, sometimes blood-stained sheets. As the bodies began to rot they had to throw the doors open, so everyone passing could see.

In Montreal, a family accustomed to eating in their front room took to drawing the curtains at mealtimes; that way, they didn't have to watch the endless funerals going by. At Camp Grant in Illinois, meanwhile, Colonel Charles B. Hagadom shot himself in the head in despair over the ravages of the pandemic.

All round, it's hard to conceive of the fear and confusion Spanish flu must have brought in its train. In a climate already hysterical with war fever ('Prick a German, You Find a Beast') the disease would have seemed as terrible and mysterious as any mediaeval plague. Alfred Crosby reports nurses in the slums drawing crowds of desperate supplicants, or alternatively, being shunned like vampires for what their gowns and gauze masks might betoken.

Ignorance, optimism and exploitation merged in newspaper advertisements promoting syrup of figs as a remedy, or eucalyptus salves that would 'relieve you of disgusting snuffles, hawking, spitting and offensive breath in a week'. The Chas. A. Smith Drug Co. of Peachtree Street in Atlanta recommended keeping your nose and mouth clean with 'a reliable antiseptic spray' called Dobell's Solution – made of sodium borate – to be applied with a De Vilbiss Atomizer.

Kolynos Dental Cream jumped on the bandwagon, promoting 'cleanliness of the teeth' because 'pernicious microbes do not readily flourish in a sanitary environment'. So did Grove's Tasteless Chill Tonic, with an ad proposing that since 'Spanish Influenza is an exaggerated form of Grip', the tonic 'should be taken in larger doses than if prescribed for ordinary Grip. A good plan is not to wait until you are sick, but PREVENT IT by taking GROVE'S TASTELESS CHILL TONIC in time'.

Some cities ordered the universal wearing of masks, and instituted stringent fines for 'slackers' who failed to do so. In Atlanta, a Mrs Hunnicutt said women should wear heavy silk veils instead, as these would be 'much more becoming'. Police forces were instructed 'to keep vigilant watch over persons who expectorate in the streets', public expectoration being 'a matter of common, everyday and promiscuous occurrence'. In a crusade against spitting in New York, 500 people were arrested.

In Pittsburg, a doctor reported success against the flu when he injected his patients with iodine and creosote; another doctor in Georgia told people to ward off the disease by putting sulphur in their shoes. Also in Georgia, a railway employee, sleeping fully clothed in the hallway of his boarding house 'as a precautionary measure against flu', was robbed of $46 for his pains.

In Washington, DC on 17 October, ninety-one people died; the judges of the Supreme Court decided not to return from their recess. Many lesser courts around the country stopped hearing their cases, because the jurors didn't want to be locked in a room together. Congress, having already voted $1,000,000 to tackle the emergency, was now presented with a bill by an Illinois senator for ten times that amount. New York was so short of nursing staff that the city appealed for professional and business men to work hospital night shifts; apart from nurses, the city ran out of gravediggers too, and was using a steam shovel to dig trenches for mass graves.

It was a time of delirium, and not just in the flu's victims. One David Hoffman of Philadelphia, arrested for being drunk, told the court he'd heard that whisky was good for flu, so he'd 'proceeded to stave off the dreadful disease with a vengeance'. For his trouble, Hoffman 'was allowed to contribute $6 to the city'.

It was also a time of obstinate denial. One list of instructions on how to avoid the disease concluded, 'Buck up. Be cheerful. We'll get over the grip trouble just as we will get over every other obstacle on our road to Berlin.'

And that, of course, is one of the main reasons why Spanish flu fell off history's map in the way that it did. Terrible as it was, it wasn't as terrible as the Western Front. Fund-raising advertisements for Liberty Bonds make plain the tenor of the times: 'The enemy is malignant and merciless beyond our power to believe . . . we have got to win this war and never let the Hun get to America to crucify our old men on their doors.'

Another showed an American soldier at the front saying,

'WHEN I COME HOME, I will point my finger of scorn toward Liberty Bond slackers with such vengeance that it will make the Kaiser, with his blood-stained hands, look like an angel in comparison. Are you going to desert me in my hour of triumph over such scoundrels whose crimes, whose moral turpitude and inherent vileness has made them the mental and moral lepers of all the ages and the willing murderers of millions of men, women, and children? MAY GOD FORBID!'

In the second week of October, British losses – in one single week – were 7,489 officers and men killed, with 28,221 missing or wounded. Spanish flu happened at the climax of the most appalling war yet seen in history. At any other time, it would have been everywhere acknowledged, instantly and in horror, as a global disaster. At that time, however, it was just another layer atop the deepest pile of nightmares.

A sense of perspective is one thing; the degree of wilful complacency shown by the authorities in the city of Atlanta was another thing altogether. While other cities reacted with varying degrees of urgency and competence, many of the worthies of Atlanta persisted in a stubborn refusal to acknowledge the severity of what was happening. It came down to commerce; always a city of boosters, they were due to host the great South-Eastern Fair, and they weren't going to let flu stop them.

Atlanta started out as 'a forest in search of a city'; Stephen Harriman Long, an engineer for the Western & Atlantic Railroad, said in 1837 that the terminus there 'will be a good location for one tavern, a blacksmith shop, a grocery store, and nothing else'. He was wrong. Determined, unlike most of the rest of the South, to face forward after the Civil War – which had so painfully emphasized its importance as a railroad hub – Atlanta blossomed into a major commercial centre, with the first skyscrapers going up in the early years of this century. By then the population had topped 100,000 and was climbing fast.

In the autumn of 1918, the war dominated the headlines. First word of the new disease appeared quietly in the *Atlanta Constitution* on 11 September, in two paragraphs from Boston on page sixteen: 'Naval officials said today that 1,109 cases of grippe had been reported among the men of the first naval district since August 28th. Thirty-six of these cases developed into pneumonia and twenty men died.'

Amidst the news from the Front, the Senate and local elections, the horrors of the Bolsheviki, the pursuit of slackers and the calls to enlistment – 30,000 men aged from eighteen to forty-six were due to register for the draft the next day – the grippe was a footnote.

Three days later, it was reported to be spreading; there was news of illness in Philadelphia, New York, New Orleans, at Fort Morgan near Mobile, and of Lloyd George in London having a chill and a temperature. The Surgeon General made a telegraphic survey to determine the extent of the flu's spread, and recommended that sufferers should go home, go to bed, and take quinine and aspirin. Dr William Brady's 'Health Talks' column on the editorial page, however, made no mention of it, preferring instead to discuss dandruff, rheumatism and the virtues of bran.

Outside Atlanta at Camp Gordon, a quarantine was announced on 18 September; the flu was reported to be epidemic at military bases in New York, Virginia, and at

Camp Devens in Massachusetts. There were seventy deaths in twenty-four hours in Boston, and every hospital bed in the harbour's forts was full, but the authorities were 'confident they had the situation in hand'. Notwithstanding that confidence, the American Red Cross issued a mobilization call for nurses.

The pandemic became front-page news three days later, with four paragraphs at the bottom of the page: SPANISH GRIPPE RAGES IN NINE ARMY CAMPS. The following day, however, it retreated to the inside pages, because Atlanta was safe: NO DANGER OF EPIDEMIC OF 'SPANISH FLU' HERE. The quarantine at Camp Gordon would contain the disease; besides, 'According to the United States health authorities, the Spanish influenza is nothing but an exaggerated form of the old-fashioned grip, and is not particularly dangerous unless complications arise.' People were advised to avoid crowds, and to sneeze into their handkerchiefs.

Reports continued of many deaths at army camps and in New England, of schools closing and hospitals filled to overflowing, but still the newspaper repeated official mantras – the disease was in decline, and the situation was much improved. This improvement included outbreaks of flu spreading through the Carolinas, Kentucky, Pennsylvania, Maryland, Kansas and Texas, and the number of cases in army camps mounting daily. Finally, on 25 September, Dr Brady's 'Health Talks' took note, stating bluntly that 'Spanish influenza is ordinary influenza ... tomorrow we will tell how to get along with influenza and how to get along without it. You reads your paper and takes your choice.'

While reports the following day spoke of the disease

racing rapidly far and wide, of north-eastern cities sending out calls for help, and 'considering drastic steps to curb its spread, including the prevention of public gatherings', Dr Brady asked, ARE YOU COMING DOWN SOON?

He was comfortably sanguine: 'The Spanish influenza has arrived on this side of the big pond. It proves to be ordinary Russian or American influenza, the same old influenza that swept over this country in 1889–90, if you can recall an ancient event like that. If you plan to come down with it soon, this is the most satisfactory way to get along with it.'

His advice was to go to bed and stay there, to avoid quack cures, to get fresh air and sunlight, to take 'one bottle of Solution of the Citrate of Magnesium', and to make sure not to give the disease to anyone else. You'd do that by covering your nose and mouth when sneezing, by wearing a mask made from two or three layers of cheesecloth or gauze, and by burning or disinfecting any discharge in whatever cloth you'd used to contain it.

To avoid catching flu in the first place, you were to keep a minimum of five feet away from everyone else. You should 'refuse to work or sit alongside of anybody who apparently has a fresh cold, or a sore throat, or a nice new bottle of dope labelled cough medicine'. Finally, you should take regular walks: 'Two miles of oxygen three times a day on the hoof puts the fear of the phagocytes into the bacillus for influenza.'

The following day the draft call for October was cancelled; one in four men at Camp Devens were reported sick, with one in ten contracting pneumonia. By the end of the month, there were 85,000 cases in Massachusetts, with the death list growing hourly; the situation at Camp Gordon outside Atlanta was worsening too. The women of the city clubbed together to gather 40,000 gifts for the quarantined men; Georgia's State Health Commissioner wired the Surgeon General in Washington with 'a crying need for nurses and doctors, especially nurses'. His message added, 'The situation in a given city often changes from "not alarming" to "swamped" in 48 hours.'

Atlanta's nurses were called to serve in Camp Gordon: 'If you have a nurse's certificate, you can begin drawing a salary from the government at once.' At another Georgia camp, two cases were reported one day, and 716 the next; the army around the country now had 88,000 men ill. 'Every available medical officer is on duty . . . wherever possible, civilian medical personnel is being recruited to assist the army doctors.'

At the beginning of October, flexitime was introduced in Washington to stop streetcars getting crowded at rush hour; the capital's schools, churches, cinemas, theatres and children's playgrounds all closed, Liberty Bond parades and other public gatherings were banned there, and the Surgeon General said they should be banned nationwide. Shipyard workforces were down 10 per cent; the disease was prevalent in forty-three states. The Camp Gordon surgeon asked Atlanta's chapter of the Red Cross to make 100,000 flu masks; the whole base was now wearing them. Violence broke out; 115 men tried to break out of quarantine and visit the city, stones were thrown in their clash with the camp guards, and twenty-five soldiers were arrested.

From the newspaper, however, you'd never have known the disease was abroad in Atlanta itself; Dr Brady's Health

Notes continued soothingly calm, writing only that 'Spanish is the latest variety of influenza . . . much the same thing, but more so.'

Then, on 8 October, the city council closed all public gathering places for two months, to stop the spread of the flu which was finally admitted to be 'now raging here'. Anyone staying open faced a $200 fine or imprisonment. All public vehicles carrying passengers were ordered to run with their windows open, unless it was pouring with rain. It was reported that, 'The increase in the spread of the malady is causing uneasiness to health authorities and practising physicians, but it is hoped that no more drastic action will have to be taken.'

Atlanta's Health Officer, Dr J. P. Kennedy, declared the situation to be extremely serious; doctors were reporting to him that they had hundreds of cases, far more than they could cope with. Kennedy said, 'Conditions that now obtain are such that I can see no chance of controlling it unless we resort to the closing of these places. It looks like we are going to have a serious epidemic.' If it got any worse, he went on, 'The situation would be grave indeed.'

The South-Eastern Fair, however, was still to go ahead, as was the Liberty Pageant and Parade, this decision justified by the fact that these events were in the open air. This rather contradicted the state board of health's advice to avoid all public gatherings – but evidently Atlanta meant to have its fair and parade no matter what. One of the pageant's organizers, a Mrs Linton Hopkins, declared, 'I have two children who are far more precious to me than a thousand pageants, and they are most certainly going to take part . . . I really do not fear for their safety at all.'

More accurate accounts of the disease were to be found in advertisements for a 'powerful reconstructive tonic' called Taniac. Obviously, they had their commercial imperatives – but *pace* Mrs Hopkins, Taniac's manufacturers correctly described Spanish flu as 'a great and terrifying menace to the public health', disrupting war work and claiming victims by the thousand. The army had now listed 167,000 men falling sick in three weeks, with 4,910 deaths; in Washington, the situation was so bad that 'hundreds of persons suffering . . . are without care of any kind'. Camp Gordon's entire complement of men, meanwhile, were now sleeping in the open, still wearing their masks.

Yet in Atlanta, the worthies backpedalled. The two-month closure of public places would be rescinded, said the council, if they got flu beaten in a week or ten days. H. G. Hastings, President of the South-Eastern Fair, said the closures were 'not because there is any semblance of an epidemic in Atlanta, but is purely a precautionary measure'. The newspaper's lengthening deaths column told a different story – but then, the city authorities had no true idea how many were dying, not least because physicians were too overworked (or too sick themselves) to report it.

Still there was, said the council, 'no reason for alarm'; Health Officer Kennedy, reversing his previous position, professed himself 'optimistic'. The makers of Taniac thought otherwise: INFLUENZA CLAIMS MORE VICTIMS THAN GERMAN BULLETS.

On 10 October, 342 people died in New York, and 514 in Philadelphia. At the same time, Atlanta was reporting that it had only had eight deaths in a week – even while the newspaper's deaths column showed more than that passing

away daily. Certainly, the city's beautiful people thought
the situation more serious than the council was claiming;
the society pages noted a steady stream of cancellations of
rummage sales, receptions, dances and concerts.

The Liberty Parade took place on 12 October; the deaths
column that day noted nine people dying in their twenties,
and three in their thirties. Occasionally, flu or pneumonia
was mentioned; more often the phrase used was simply,
'after a short illness'. The South-Eastern Fair was due to
open the next day; the *Constitution*'s editorial sang out
blithely, 'Go to the fair! Go early and often! Go, not only
for the entertainment . . . but also for the benefit of the fresh
air and sunshine – the two most effective preventatives of
the Spanish influenza.'

In other words, somewhat incredibly, they were saying
that joining in with a big crowd could be good for you. Still,
things weren't so bad in Atlanta, were they? Health Officer
Kennedy said, 'I feel that we are very fortunate here . . . of
course, we have our hands full handling the present situation,
but efforts at prevention seem to have been very successful.'
Not so successful, however, that he could spare any nurses
when other towns and cities called for help.

The day the Fair opened, Sunday, 13 October, the deaths
column included two babies, a child of eleven, a teenager, a
young married man, two people in their thirties including a
doctor 'after a short illness with pneumonia', and two people
in their forties. The saddest story was that of Mrs C. M.
Ames of Waycross. Her husband had died several days
before; now she passed away herself at the age of twenty-
four, leaving behind two children who themselves were
seriously ill.

Health Officer Kennedy said, 'There are no indications that the Spanish influenza situation in Atlanta will develop into an epidemic.'

A tour by the Paris Symphony Orchestra was postponed on account of the flu; coal production in some southern and eastern states was down by as much as 50 per cent. A quarter of a million people were sick in Louisiana. On 14 October, the *Constitution* recorded the deaths from Spanish flu of Myrtle Hunt, seventeen; Mrs A. H. Wilson, thirty-two; W. W. Mince, thirty-eight; George Humphries, eighteen; C. O. Holbrooks, forty; and a leading young businessman named Paul W. Marrell.

Dr T. F. Abercrombie, Secretary of the Georgia Board of Health, said everyone going to the Fair had to wear a mask. Understandably, the city's theatre and cinema owners protested that it was unfair to close their businesses when the Fair stayed open; they claimed that many of the Fair's amusements had worse ventilation than their own premises. Still the death toll mounted; a girl of six, three teenage girls, two soldiers aged twenty and twenty-four, a father of two aged thirty-nine.

LOW DEATH RATE FROM FLU HERE, said the *Constitution*. Dr Kennedy said the ban on public gatherings would be necessary for another week; the Fair stayed open. The mask edict wasn't rigidly enforced; Red Cross workers were drafted in to get sewing, so patrons could be given masks for free.

The Colombian consul died in New Orleans; the President of the Southern Coal & Coke Company died in Knoxville. Army deaths climbed above 10,000. A Georgia boy died of flu and pneumonia in the Charleston navy yards, and

another at the naval station on Hampton Roads. Mrs LeRoy
Smith, a prominent Atlanta woman, died two days after her
husband. The city's officials continued to proclaim that they
had 'no decided epidemic'. Deaths listed on 16 October
included more souls in their twenties and thirties, among
them William Mike Melton, who died of the flu while away
in the army. Melton came 'of one of the oldest and best
families of the state, and was a very bright young man'.

Drs Abercrombie and Kennedy visited the Fair, and
declared it to be fine. It was the only fair still open in all
the South. City officials said the situation in Atlanta was
'satisfactory'.

In Richmond, Virginia, a man aged forty-six went into
the room where his wife lay dead, and shot himself. In
St Louis, Congressman Jacob E. Meeker died of flu, after
marrying his secretary at midnight. Army deaths passed
12,000. In Atlanta, eighty switchboard operators were off
sick, and the newspaper pleaded with the public to refrain
from 'idle, social, frivolous or unnecessary' telephone calls.
A woman of thirty died, leaving a husband and three children;
a woman of forty left a husband and nine children. There
were a boy of five, three soldiers in their twenties, a judge
in Cairo, a baby girl; there was Mrs E. V. Cunningham, 'a
lovely young woman of twenty-six', leaving her husband
and son.

18 October was Confederate Veterans' Day at the Fair;
there were war and automobile exhibits, roller-coasters and
carousels, concerts, circus acts, fireworks, and a convalescent
soldiers' parade. That day the death was reported of Dr
Albert Wilson, aged forty-six, leaving a wife and child. Dr
John Hale passed away, fifty-two years old, leaving his wife,

three sons and a daughter. Virgil G. Craig was taken at the age of nineteen, Miss Marie Judd at the age of thirty-two, and Eugenia Beck at the age of twelve. James Crosland Yates, thirty-nine years old, left his wife and two children; William H. Templeman, fifty-seven, left his wife, five sons and five daughters. First Lieutenant Ben Stone died in New York, *en route* to France, leaving a wife and child; Edward Churchill, eighteen years old, died at Camp Meade in Maryland.

Ever sanguine, Dr Kennedy stated, 'Notwithstanding that 209 cases were reported to this office today, this cannot be taken as an indication that the malady is on the increase.' He professed himself 'much encouraged over the fact that the influenza has gotten no greater hold upon the city, and that he does not expect . . . that it will spread further'.

Half the 600 staff at the Covington cotton mills were sick. The county courts shut down, and all work on the roads was suspended. There were reports of many deaths in Buenos Aires and Santiago; in New York, the city's Public Health Officer described the situation as 'serious beyond description'. The Georgia Federation of Women's Clubs called off their annual meeting.

On the last day of the Fair, meanwhile, there were parades of soldiers and livestock, and a concert by Johnny G. Jones at Larkland. Adaien Ehmilaire wasn't there to enjoy it; a French midget forty inches tall who'd come to Atlanta with the Fair, he'd died of flu the day before.

A policeman in Macon lost a son and a daughter in the space of ten days. On Savannah Street, Roy Rowan and his little sister Dorothy, just seven months old, both died on the same day. Lewis M. Coleman, a friend of the President and a former US district attorney, died of pneumonia. Mrs Bettie

Weinstock, twenty-four years old, left her husband and a young child. L. M. Landrum Jnr left his wife and four small children; Mrs S. T. Dodson, thirty-eight, left her husband, two sons and five daughters.

The South-Eastern Fair was proclaimed a great success; George L. Susong, 'one of the best-known livestock men of Tennessee', who'd had a big exhibit at the Fair, caught flu there and died of it at the age of twenty-nine. Dr Kennedy said the disease was 'well under control'. On the same day he said this, there were 3,435 new cases in Georgia, and an editorial in the *Constitution* cried out, 'The world needs nurses today as never before.'

At a meeting of the city council, Alderman Steve R. Johnston moved that churches be allowed to reopen: 'If people want to meet and pray for an end to flu, let's allow them to do it.'

The death column stayed long, a litany of bereavement. It was a unique feature of Spanish flu that it took so many men and women in the prime of their lives, leaving children orphaned, young husbands and wives torn from their partners. In Albany, south of Atlanta, a farmer called Mark Williams died, as did his wife and two children; only a four-year-old boy survived.

The worst was over by the end of the month; cinemas and theatres reopened on 26 October, and Dr Kennedy declared Atlanta past the danger point three days later. In truth, the city had not suffered as badly as some others; given their refusal to close the Fair, they were lucky.

Today, Atlanta is a lively and engaging city of three million – and, with the CDC in town, one would expect it to respond to the next pandemic more wisely. No institution knows better what influenza can do, after all; at least one of the staff there knows personally what it can do.

Helen Regnery is a public health scientist working for Nancy Cox in the Influenza Branch. In 1918, her husband's grandfather was in his thirties, a successful businessman with a growing young family. Then the flu took him, and one of the children with him; they were buried together and, says Regnery, 'My husband's grandmother was left with the other young children to raise. Fortunately he'd made money and she was able to do it, which wasn't the case for a lot of people – but I don't know how she coped. She never remarried – and from the family history, I don't think she was ever really happy again.'

What did this? When the 1918 virus clicked into lethality among young soldiers crammed together by the war – whether in the trenches themselves, or in camps and transports travelling to and from them – it certainly found itself in an environment ripe for rapid transmission. Some have speculated, furthermore, that if it was evolving in that great body of young men, this might explain why it settled on an adaptation so peculiarly lethal for people aged from twenty to forty.

Others have suggested that the unusual age pattern in the victims may have been due, precisely and paradoxically, to the good health of those victims. One of the body's prime reactions to infection is inflammation; confronted with this singularly virulent disease, fit young people may have produced a more massive inflammatory response than the very young or the very old, and effectively killed themselves with it, drowning in their own erupted lungs.

At the time, there was a natural inclination to blame the war. As mystified as any mediaeval astronomer, people wondered if the world's air had been poisoned; if the fantastical quantities of ordnance being exploded in France, and more especially all the chlorine gas, were somehow polluting the planet, girdling the globe in germ-friendly toxins.

Today, we're more inclined to look for the molecular explanation – to ask whether, for example, the 1918 virus had that mutation at the haemagglutinin cleavage site which would let it spread beyond the lungs and through the body. Without the virus in front of us, however, to answer that question you have to turn to the pathology.

It certainly looks as though it spread body-wide. The British Ministry of Health's report describes the progress of the disease thus: 'The pulmonary involvement was an acute infective inflammation; sometimes progressing as a bronchopneumonia, at other times it swept through the body like a virulent toxaemia or septicaemia.'

The deadliest symptom was 'heliotrope cyanosis'. Starved of oxygen, the victim's lips and ears would turn purple or blue, while the rest of his skin first flushed, then turned pale white or grey, the colour of wet ashes. This would herald widespread haemorrhages, with blood-soaked swellings in the intercellular tissue, and the coughing and spitting up of 'enormous quantities of purulent sputum'. When heliotrope cyanosis appeared, your chances of survival became vanishingly small.

Writing on this and other features of the pandemic's pathology, Dr Herbert French states that he cannot recall how many flu cases he saw; all he can say is 'many thousands'. He treated patients in civilian hospitals in London, in military hospitals in Aldershot, at two Canadian camps, and among American troops on ships or in hospitals in Liverpool, Portsmouth and Winchester. He also performed or attended over 100 autopsies – and his account of the experience is both dramatic and appalling.

'The patient would be seized rapidly, or almost suddenly, with a sense of such prostration as to be utterly unable to carry on with what he might be doing; from sheer lassitude he would be obliged to lie down where he was, or crawl with difficulty back to bed.'

Hospitals filled within a day or two as temperatures rocketed to 103° or 104°, tongues coated, faces flushed, eyelids drooped, and voices became hoarse, interrupted with hawking coughs. People ached all over and grew so sore that they couldn't swallow or speak; frothy liquids welled up in their throat. Nosebleeds were incredibly common – sometimes just enough to stain a handkerchief, in other cases a flood so heavy it would soak the sheets. Most did at least sleep well, and just wanted to be left alone with a cold drink; after three days or so, many then got better fairly fast.

Others developed pneumonia; among these came the heliotrope cyanosis, 'the dreaded blueness'. It appeared in under half of the pulmonary cases, but when it did, French estimates that 95 per cent of the time it was a death sentence. On the other hand, he said, any and every case could be fatal anyway. A patient might be mildly ill for a day or two, and seem to be improving – then his condition would abruptly alter for the worse, and in twenty-four hours he'd be dead.

French also makes the point that the pneumonia he saw was no ordinary pneumonia. 'Totally different to anything ordinarily seen in the post-mortem room', it involved a whole battery of impacts; the victims' lungs were soaked, collapsed and pulped. Some sections would be so shattered that they were barely recognizable as lung tissue; others, where the air sacs had disintegrated, looked like bloody Gruyère. The victims would complain before they died that they were 'all raw inside there'; they'd cough up bloody froth, or eight or ten ounces of pus in a day, and their breath rate would soar to forty, fifty, even sixty breaths a minute. They died, said French, like victims of gassing.

Some fell into delirium or coma; some had spasms, with jerking legs and arms, twitching faces and shoulders. Others would be heliotrope-blue, panting like dogs, yet fully conscious and rational to within half an hour of their death.

More pertinent to the issue of whether the virus could spread right through the body, French avers that in every one of over 100 autopsies, the victims' kidneys were swollen, inflamed and oozing blood. The swelling was generalized, and sufficient that he worried about survivors having kidney problems later in their lives. Some patients' livers were swollen too, with 'acute degenerative changes'.

In others, some of the stomach muscles were ruptured, or found 'in a haemorrhagic necrotic state such as precedes rupture . . . the affected muscle has much the appearance of the breast of a bird that has been badly shot at close quarters, the muscle being soft, pulpy, and infiltrated with dark extravasated blood'.

French feared that the disease affected people's hearts as well. Though post-mortems didn't turn up any endocarditis (inflammation of the heart valves) he found in the months after the pandemic that he was 'constantly meeting with cases of the chronic type of infective endocarditis, whose origin was obscure'. Normally, it would have been rare in all his years at Guy's Hospital to have more than one such case at a time; in 1919, by contrast, he'd have five at a time, and he saw over seventy in all.

A better-known aftermath of 1918, thanks to Oliver Sacks's work and the subsequent film of his book *Awakenings*, is the massive number of cases around the world of encephalitis lethargica. Through a period of fifteen years, millions succumbed to this sleeping sickness, left as much on the edge of human life as a virus is on the edge of life itself. One of them, Philip Leather, was diagnosed with the disease by by W. H. Auden's father, and admitted to a Birmingham hospital at the age of twelve; he remains in the care of the National Health Service sixty-seven years later, and is said by John Oxford to be the longest-surviving patient of that institution.

A link between Spanish flu and the condition that struck down Philip Leather, and many millions like him, has never been proven – but did the 1918 virus get into the brain or the central nervous system, or both, and spawn this second, chilling pandemic of unconsciousness as a lingering aftershock of its first assault?

Overall, certainly, the evidence is compelling that in many cases the 1918 virus attacked more than just the respiratory tract. Without the actual virus in front of us, however, we can never know for sure how it did that – and that's why, eighty years after it came among us, an expedition was mounted to try to dig the thing up.

4 THE FROZEN COAST

The tent weighed half a ton. It was a ribbed white bubble with a rectangular base and semicircular blue ends. Measured along the outside of its walls, which were themselves half a yard thick, it was eight yards long by six and a half yards wide. The logo on one side said HYGECO, and on the other, HYGECOBEL. It had been hired from a French company; normally you might find it in use as a field surgery in a war zone, or as a mortuary at the site of a plane crash.

Now, in August 1998, it stood 100 yards above a single-track grit road, incongruously bright on the barren, mist-wreathed flank of a glacial valley 800 miles from the North Pole. A fence of yellow plastic webbing stood looped around it, to keep out the prying eyes and lenses of the media. On the roadside beneath it there was a pale blue wooden portakabin, and two red freight containers marked NOR-CARGO. A stony trail led up the hill; a new path of blue plastic matting had been laid beside it, to protect the fragile ground surface, and a trolley-load of plywood boards was being slowly, painfully winched up the slope. Other members of the team struggled up and down on the soft, boulder-pocked tundra, toting tools and gas cylinders, breathing clouds of vapour into the dank, chilly air.

We were outside the Norwegian settlement of Longyear-byen – a name which might look impenetrably Scandinavian to an English reader, but which in fact just means 'Longyear

Town'. Home to some 1,500 souls, it was founded to mine Arctic coal by an American capitalist called John Munroe Longyear in the early years of this century. It's the biggest settlement on Spitsbergen, itself the largest island in the Svalbard archipelago, Svalbard being a Norse word that means simply 'Frozen Coast'. Given that two-thirds of these islands are permanently covered in ice, it's an apt enough name.

High above the tent on the granite scree, under giant crags and parapets of veined and shattered rock, wooden scaffolds and pylons from the early coal workings ran across the mountainside. Beneath it, a shallow river of glacial meltwater ran in many channels along a wide bed of grey dirt and stones. All day, every day, there came from the riverbed the whine and grumble of a digger's engine, its scoop clanging through rock and gravel as it strove to keep the river in its course.

The river flowed from two glaciers at the head of the valley, the Lars and the Longyear, and ran out through town into the matt green waters of the Adventfjord. Under sodden skies of low, unbroken cloud, when you walked beside it you could hear it ceaselessly, restlessly rolling and clacking the stones against each other as it flowed, a forlorn sound-track for a treeless, windswept and unforgiving place. In its way, the valley had much beauty about it – a spartan monumentalism – but it was not a beauty made to any human scale, and the functional little town seemed grafted on, unnatural, misplaced. It was certainly no kind of place to die.

Not many people do die there. Most of Longyearbyen's citizens are on short-term postings, doing highly prized tours of duty on cut-rate taxes with the coal company, in government service or scientific research. One young man told me he loved it there, he didn't want to go 'back down', but it was an unnatural society. What idea of society would a child get growing up there, he asked, when there were only a couple of senior citizens in all the place? Outside of war, mining accidents or unfortunate encounters with polar bears, people hadn't often died in Longyearbyen; when they had done, usually their bodies had gone home. As a result, Pastor Jan Hoifodt wasn't often called upon to do funerals; the cemetery outside town was pretty small.

In October 1918, however, seven young men died in Longyearbyen in the course of one week. They'd arrived on the *Forsete* on 24 September, after three days' sailing from Tromso; fishermen and farmers, they'd come to work a winter season in the mines, and among sixty-nine passengers and crew they'd brought the Spanish flu with them.

The first, milder wave of the disease had already passed through Svalbard in the summer; about 100 miners worked there at the time, and at least half of them fell ill. One man died on 8 August; he wrote a telegram home saying, 'A little sick. Hoping for the best', and two days later he was gone. Three other men died on 20 August, one from the coal company and two from prospectors' camps elsewhere around the fjord; like the first man's, their bodies were all returned to Norway. The *Forsete*, however, was the last boat of the year before the ice set in. This final ship's complement, arriving with the deadliest wave of the virus, had now to live or die on Svalbard – and if they died, they'd have to rest there.

The disease had broken out on the voyage. The sick

were brought straight from the ship to the hospital; it didn't have enough beds, and barrack houses were commandeered around the town. While the victims lay in their fever, the *Forsete* left for Tromso on 29 September; Ole Kristoffersen died two days later, on 1 October. He was twenty-two years old.

Magnus Gabrielsen died the next day; he was twenty-eight. On 3 October, he was followed by Hans Hansen and Tormod Albrigtsen, twenty-seven and nineteen years old respectively. Johan Bjerk was twenty-six, William Henry Richardsen twenty-five; they both died the day after. Kristian Hansen lasted three days longer; he was twenty-eight years old. In a week, one in ten of the *Forsete*'s people were gone.

Twenty days passed before they were buried. Kjell Mork, the local schoolmaster who doubles as Chairman of the Svalbard Museum, believes that the delay most likely came about because so many people were sick that they simply couldn't dig the graves. At least it was an unusually cold autumn that year, so storing the bodies wouldn't have been a problem; even in a normal year, average temperatures on Svalbard only nudge above zero four months out of twelve, and October isn't one of them.

The seven miners were buried side by side in a single grave on 27 October; the site was marked with six white crosses and one headstone, and for eighty years these men were left to lie there. Then, in August 1998, a team of scientists from Canada, Norway, Great Britain and the United States erected their big white tent over the young miners' resting place, and began exhuming the bodies to see if they could learn what had killed them.

It was a difficult task, and a sensitive one – which was

why, on the morning of Saturday, 22 August, the project's leader brought a wreath to the graveyard. She was Canadian, and her name was Kirsty Duncan; she was thirty-one years old, a medical geographer from the Toronto borough of Etobicoke, and the exhumation in Longyearbyen had been the goal of her life for five years.

In the last months of 1918, Canada suffered at the hands of the Spanish flu just as all the world did. In the state of Ontario 300,000 people got sick, and 8,700 of them died. In the state of Quebec, more than half a million fell ill, and 14,000 were lost; in Montreal, they couldn't keep up with the demand for hearses, and had to resort to streetcars taking ten coffins at a time.

There are few stories sadder or more eerie than that of Arthur Lapointe. Recorded both in Eileen Pettigrew's account of the Spanish flu in Canada, *The Silent Enemy*, and in Richard Collier's earlier, anecdotal history of the disease all around the world, *The Plague of the Spanish Lady*, this is the tragedy of a young Canadian soldier who crossed the Atlantic to fight in the trenches in 1916.

Two years later, on 30 June 1918 in the front lines at Agny, Lapointe described what happened to himself and some of his fellows as he was climbing from a dug-out. 'As I reach the top my head swims with sudden nausea, everything around me whirls, I totter, then fainting fall headlong to the ground . . . for more than an hour, limp as rags, we drag ourselves through a communication trench under the boiling afternoon sun. One man can no longer stand erect, and crawls on hands and knees. We leave him behind, with a comrade looking after him . . .'

Like most people, Lapointe survived the first wave; like many others who did, he seems not to have been struck down by the second, lethal outbreak in the autumn, the first having presumably conferred some degree of immunity. By then he was training in England, during which time he got a letter to tell him that his brothers were very sick back home in Quebec.

One night soon afterwards, his youngest sister Martine appeared to him in a dream. She was dressed in mourning; she led him to a row of graves on which were marked the names of his brothers and sisters. She told him, 'I too am dead. But God in his mercy has allowed me to spend this day with you.'

When Lapointe finally got home, he found his father's hair had turned white. In the space of nine days, two sisters and three brothers had died. 'Dear God,' Lapointe cried out, 'if it was only for this that I came home, why did I not fall in action out there?'

Eileen Pettigrew reports that all over Canada there was 'fear so thick that even a child could feel it'. People spoke of being 'inured to sorrow', of how 'every day there was someone we knew in the obituary columns', of how 'we got so we didn't even mourn'. An Algonquin woman named Marguerite Brascoupe Budge recalled, 'It was sad and lonesome, in the mist, with never any sun. We could hear people crying, and children coughing, and the funeral processions passed by with the people wearing black veils over their faces.'

In Toronto, if a child died, you put a white sash on your door. If an adult died the sash was grey, and if the victim was a senior citizen it was purple. Arthur E. Parks, then seven years old, remembered, 'It was as if a black, sombre cloud fell over all. People closed their doors and stayed within to keep their lives . . . when we heard the church bells ring at St Alban's, we knew another one had died.'

One evening, two young women attended a lecture together, then went back to their room at the YWCA. The next morning Claire Hunter told her friend, 'Vera, I'm going downstairs to breakfast.' Vera said nothing, so Claire went to eat; when she came back she said something again and still there came no reply, so she went to her friend's bed, and found she'd died in the night.

At Rivière Qui Barre in Alberta, Benjamin McKilvington was headed home from a dance one night in his horse-drawn buggy, when he felt a giant hand suddenly clasp his chest tight. By the morning, he was too weak to lift his head from the pillow. He was sick in bed for three weeks, dreaming at one point that he fell into the grave; it was three more weeks before he was strong enough to dress himself, and three more after that before he could go outside. His weight fell in those nine weeks from 137 pounds to eighty-four – and that second weight included two sets of underwear, three pairs of socks, two shirts, a sweater, an overcoat, a pair of gloves and a fur cap.

At least he lived. In Montreal, on the single day of 21 October, there were 201 deaths. Priests gave the last rites in the streets, carrying the Sacred Host through the city to take Mass to the people. In the countryside, in the rural settlement of Bartibogue, a man brought the bodies out on a portage sled before the roads iced over – but water splashed up on them, the bodies froze together, and to bury them he had to hack them apart with an axe.

Few suffered anywhere in the world, however, as they suffered in the Inuit settlements of Canada and Alaska. In the east coast province of Labrador in mid-October, the mail boat went from village to village dropping off fuel, food, post and newspapers. The papers carried the first word these remote communities had heard of the Spanish flu, but they knew about it at first hand soon enough; the disease was on the boat right along with the papers.

Many of these places were served by the Grenfell Mission, which had been started by a doctor from the Royal London Hospital. Grenfell had first gone with a hospital ship to the fishing banks, where there'd be anything from 10,000 to 20,000 men working for months, their only release the grog boats sailing alongside them. Then he went to work in Labrador – and the mission records of what happened there are chilling.

On the last day of October, the Reverend Henry Gordon arrived at the settlement of Cartwright. He found 'not a soul to be seen anywhere, and a strange, unusual silence. Going along the path to the parsonage, we met one of the Hudson's Bay Company men staggering about like a drunk man, and from him learnt that the whole settlement was prostrated with sickness. It has struck the place like a cyclone, two days after the mail boat left. After dinner I went on a tour of inspection among the houses, and was simply appalled at what I found. Whole households lay inanimate all over their kitchen floors, unable to even feed themselves or look after the fire . . . I think there were just four persons in the place who were sound.'

Ninety-six out of 100 people were sick. The nearest doctor was 200 miles away; in Labrador in October 1918, he might as well have been on the moon. The people had no firewood; on 1 November, the day after he'd got there, Reverend Gordon started sawing and splitting logs for all he was worth. His head, he noted in his diary, was beginning to feel heavy.

The next day he was 'feeling rotten, head like a bladder full of wind'. He heard news of a death, but digging graves in Cartwright was 'labour out of the ordinary. About one foot of soil lies over the ground, then comes a layer of tightly compressed blackish gravel . . . beneath this are huge boulders almost cemented in with the pressure.' In freezing weather, the very idea of digging was a nightmare.

Three days later, Gordon was too ill to move, never mind dig graves. He managed to note later, 'I know Mr Parsons [the Hudson's Bay agent] came to ask me about burying somebody or other. I thought it was myself at the time.'

The Hudson's Bay clerk, a boy fourteen years old, recovered enough to start making coffins. He could barely keep up; someone was now dying almost every day. When Gordon got better, he took to doing the rounds with Mrs Parsons, who by chance was a nurse, but all they had was aspirin, liniment and poultices. 'It was very upsetting,' wrote Gordon, 'people crying, children dying everywhere.'

By the end of November, twenty-six out of 100 people had died. Gordon started going out to check on other settlements, travelling by boat through the new-forming winter's ice. At North River he found ten out of twenty-six people dead, all still in their beds because no one was strong enough to bury them. With four other men he'd brought with him, Gordon dug a mass grave and buried the dead still in their bedclothes. One of the survivors, a woman of seventy-two, had lived alone for nine days with the rest of her family dead about her, no fire, and the food running out. For water she'd chipped chunks of ice out of frozen buckets and thawed them in a mug under her arms, 'while outside the starving dogs tore at the door'.

At Mountaineer Cove, Gordon found three out of four families entirely wiped out. In the fourth family five children remained, huddled with the bodies of the four people who'd died. At Okak, only fifty-nine out of 266 people still lived; one mass grave, thirty-two feet long, ten feet wide, eight feet deep, took 114 bodies, but not before it had taken two weeks to dig it. At Hebron, where seventy survived from a community of 220, they took a more expedient route; they dropped the bodies into the sea through holes in the ice with rocks in their pockets.

One of the worst stories came from Okak, where a man, his wife and two of their children had died, leaving only a girl of eight to survive alone, in temperatures touching −30°C, for five weeks. As she kept herself alive by melting snow for water with the last of the Christmas candles, Reverend Walter Perret of the Moravian Mission reported, 'The huskies now began to eat the dead bodies, and the child was a spectator of this horrible incident.'

By coincidence, one of the virologists on the team that went to Svalbard eighty years later knew a fair bit about these events in Labrador – because, like Grenfell before him, Professor John Oxford works today at the Royal London Hospital. In their quest for frozen bodies that might still contain at least fragments of the genetic material of the 1918 virus, there were a number of reasons why Oxford and the others went to Svalbard, rather than Labrador or Alaska – but one of those reasons, Oxford told me, was the huskies. A husky is nine parts wolf to one part dog; it's not an animal you take lightly, and certainly not when it's starving because its masters are all sick or dead.

'Lots of those people are buried in permafrost,' said Oxford, 'but many of them were eaten by the huskies after they died. Or,' he said, '*before* they died . . .'

When the pandemic first erupted in New England, the news spread ahead of the virus all across North America. From the doctors of the east coast came this stark message: 'Hunt up your wood-workers and cabinet-makers and set them to making coffins. Then take your street labourers and set them to digging graves. If you do this, you will not have your dead accumulating faster than you can dispose of them.'

What it was like waiting for the flu to arrive is hard to imagine. In Toronto on 19 September, the *Star* ran extracts from a letter from Germany (they called it 'Hunland') sent to a soldier at the Front, and found on his body. The letter said, 'The new sickness is raging in our part of the country; about 300 men of the mine are laid up with it. The least bit of a cold seems to affect everybody, being underfed, and makes them entirely unfit for work.' In Germany they had no sugar, no potatoes, and were rationed to one and a half loaves of bread per fortnight; the letter said drily, 'I think fat bellies are out of season now.'

As Toronto would soon find, however, you didn't have to be hungry to fall victim to Spanish flu. On 23 September, the disease was reported to be raging at a camp of Polish soldiers by Niagara, ninety miles away; five men had died there. Seeking presumably to maintain some spirit of levity in the face of the looming disaster, the *Star* ran a single sentence of somewhat unjust editorial comment: 'Is this Spanish influenza the only contribution Spain has to make to world effort at such a time as this?'

The flu was blamed variously on nakedness, on fish contaminated by the Germans, on dust, on unclean pyjamas, on open windows, on closed windows, on old books, and on our old friend 'cosmic influence'. Toronto's Medical Officer, one Dr Hastings, published the following tips on how to avoid it: You should steer clear of crowds, smother coughs and sneezes, and breathe through your nose. You should keep your mouth, skin and clothes clean, and your windows open. You should 'keep cool when you walk, and warm when you ride and sleep'. You should wash your hands before eating, chew your food well, and 'don't let the waste products of digestion accumulate; drink a glass or two of water on getting up'. You shouldn't use towels, napkins or cutlery that had been used by others; you should avoid tight clothes, shoes or gloves. Finally, 'When the air is pure, breathe all of it you can.'

As in Atlanta, some Ontario authorities tried to play down the disease. Dr J. W. S. McCullough, the provincial health officer, declared there was 'altogether too much made of the seriousness of this Spanish influenza'.

Two days later, on 26 September, the disease was reported to be firmly established in Canada. From Boston came news that 720 people had died there, that there were new cases hourly, and that all places of public entertainment were closed; along with this news came Calvin Coolidge's appeal to Toronto's Mayor for nurses.

115

Flu arrived in the city in the next few days: OVER 200 CASES OF FLU AND ONE DEATH HERE, said a headline in the *Star* on 30 September. The first victim was thought to be a twelve-year-old girl from Wilmington, Delaware; she'd had a slight cold when she'd left home on Wednesday; on Thursday on the train to Toronto she became delirious; on arrival she went straight to hospital with pneumonia, and on Saturday she died.

RAF camps were quarantined, all leave to the United States was stopped, and patients in civilian hospitals were isolated. Dr George Ross of Jarvis Street said grimly, 'The disease is certain to spread. I believe twenty to forty per cent of the population will be attacked.' Statistics from England suggested at this point that six in every 1,000 people would die. Still Dr McCullough remained sanguine, stating that the seriousness of the disease 'was altogether over-rated', and blaming Toronto's large number of 'colds' on the unseasonably damp weather.

Dr Hastings echoed his lack of concern. 'There is absolutely no necessity for anxiety. Just tell the people to keep as fit as possible . . . and not to worry any more about it. One good suggestion would be to walk more.'

The next day, 2 October, the *Star* reported the city's second death, and an admission from Hastings that the disease had arrived. The victim was James Hamilton of McGee Street, who'd been sick for just a short time, and then died at home at the age of thirty-two. Five other cases were reported – a mother and all four of her children – and her husband fell sick the next day. There were now 500 cases at the military hospital, with 'beds in the corridors, and wherever they can be located'.

'It is apparently the Spanish flu all right,' conceded Dr Hastings. 'If it is the same type Boston has been fighting, there is no doubt that the situation here may also be serious.'

From the United States came an unofficial estimate, on 4 October, of one death for every twenty-seven cases. Toronto now had nearly 600 people known to be ill with flu in hospital; in one family Edna Wills died, just ten years old, and her brothers Albert and William, twenty-eight and thirty respectively.

While Hastings claimed helplessly that a bout of good weather would see the city through it ('there is no necessity for hysterics'), reports spilled in from all around the country of the disease remorselessly advancing. Hospitals were crowded, factories were 'more or less crippled', and the most appositely named Dr Risk, of the local health board, suggested closing all places of amusement. 'I do not think,' he said, 'that there is any use in any longer saying that the thing is harmless.'

The Mayor fulminated, 'The trouble is that the health officials seem all to have gone asleep.' Dr Hastings, in fact, had gone altogether, shooting off to New York and Washington to see how bad it was there – but he might as well have stayed at home and waited, because Toronto in the next few weeks would lose well over 1,000 souls.

It's one of the extraordinary things about the Spanish flu that when Kirsty Duncan was at school in that city, she never heard a single word about it in her history lessons. In 1998, Duncan was living with her parents in the house where she'd grown up. The house stood on a pleasant, unremarkable suburban street in Etobicoke, an area a few miles west of downtown Toronto that had, until recently, been one of that city's six independent boroughs. To the dismay of their largely liberal and cosmopolitan inhabitants, however, those boroughs had just been merged into one megacity.

A neo-conservative Ontario state government, led by a former golf pro from Thunder Bay called Mike Harris, was conducting its 'Common Sense Revolution'. The politics of Thatcher and Reagan may have fallen from fashion and favour elsewhere, but in Ontario they were alive and kicking at the welfare, health, education, taxation and local government structures of the state. As a result, crime and homelessness were rising, and public services creaking – but even so, relative to the cities of the United States, Toronto remained a safe and tranquil city, very pleasant to live in.

Certainly, Kirsty Duncan was proud of it. If it had changed out of all recognition in the thirty-one years of her life, much of that change was for the better; once a byword for dullness, Toronto today is a vibrant and sophisticated place. Downtown has a striking, well-ordered skyline; when Duncan was a child, not one piece of that had been built. Asked to define her city now, she said without hesitation, 'It's multicultural, it's the lake, and it's the Maple Leafs.'

The Maple Leafs are the Manchester City of Canadian ice hockey; they haven't won the Stanley Cup since 1967, and Duncan says she still rebukes her father for not taking her to a game that season. 'I know I was only a baby,' she tells him, 'but you could have taken me and shaken me in the air or something. At least I'd have been there.'

If she was proud of her city, however, she was also proud of another strand in her identity. Her father's family was Scottish, originally from Aberdeen; the bagpipes were played in their house, and Duncan had started learning Scottish dance from the age of four. She still danced now, and taught dance as well; she'd also been a gymnast. A short woman with angular, prominent features, it was no surprise that she had a trimly fit figure; in a photograph she showed me of her doing a reel in her tartan, knees out and toes together in mid-air, her calf muscles were strikingly pronounced.

But then, so was everything else about her. She had an emphatic mode of address, and was hectically busy. She said she did 1,000 sit-ups a day, she only took a day off work every six weeks or so, she worked eighteen- to twenty-hour days, whenever she came home she'd have eighty faxes waiting for her on the Svalbard project, she had files full of this and binders full of that, she taught at the University of Windsor, commuting 500 miles each way every week to do it, she taught part-time back home in Toronto, she jogged, she lifted weights, she had her dancing – all round she was, she told me readily, even eagerly, a workaholic.

Well, if you're looking for a virus that came and went eighty years ago, and if the only place you're going to find it is in frozen bodies buried hundreds of miles from anywhere in the Arctic permafrost, you'd need a bit of energy about you.

As an undergraduate, Duncan studied geography, anthropology and psychology in Toronto; then she went to Scotland, and got a PhD in geography at Edinburgh. When she terms herself a medical geographer, she means by this that her interest lies in climatic change and all the ways in which such change might impact on health. How do shifts in temperature or humidity affect disease? What might global warming mean for the spread of malaria?

She found out about the Spanish flu in Edinburgh, when she was twenty-six. Helping her boyfriend prepare for his final medical exams, she came on Alfred Crosby's book; like most of us, she'd had no idea that the pandemic had happened, and she found herself both horrified and fascinated. Being the character she is, she decided she was going to do something about it, too. At the age of twenty-six, in July 1993, 'I said to my family, I'm going to find out what caused this.'

She told me the story of her search nearly five years later, in April 1998, over the dining table of her parents' front room. She said, 'I figured if I could find bodies of people who'd died of the flu and they were preserved in ice, that could be a way to tackle the problem. I phoned CDC and asked if 1918 samples existed, and they said they didn't – so maybe this would be an alternative way of looking at it.'

Duncan knew from Crosby that a previous expedition had been mounted to try to do just this. In 1951, Albert McKee, Jack Layton and Johan Hultin – a professor of virology, a pathologist and a young Swedish student from the State University of Iowa – had flown to Alaska to meet up with a palaeontologist called Otto Geist in Fairbanks. At Teller Mission on the Seward Peninsula they'd opened a mass grave, and excised samples of lung, kidney, spleen and brain tissue from the 1918 victims they found there. Although the bodies had been buried for thirty-three years, when they got these samples back to Iowa they found they could still revive pneumococci bacteria and Pfeiffer's bacillus – but no flu virus.

More shadowy, there was also word of an American military expedition at the same time – apparently codenamed Project George – trying to do the same thing, but they had not managed to isolate any virus either.

Nearly half a century later, however, the technology for tracing the genetic footprint of the virus, for skimming the molecular material of its RNA out of tissue samples, had advanced beyond all imagination. The likelihood of the virus surviving intact and infective was vanishingly small; depending on which virologist you speak to, they maintain live virus in their labs at temperatures from −20°C, going as low as −70°C, and no body anywhere was going to have been that cold consistently for eighty years. But if a body or, better, a group of bodies, had at least stayed below zero, then the RNA should still be there. It might be in bits and pieces by now, but it would still be there. So the objective was to find some frozen bodies – and, said Duncan, 'It was a long search.'

To begin with, when she called people about it they said sure, good idea, go to it – if you find anything, call us. So for the first two years, she was on her own. She started with Alaska; knowing the indigenous population had been savaged by the disease, she ordered 2,000 death certificates and when she went through them, 'It was just flu death after flu death. But I couldn't get a very detailed map of continuous permafrost; I couldn't match the cemeteries to continuous permafrost. So it couldn't be done. I thought of Iceland – but geo-thermal energy doesn't allow the preservation of biological material. Then I thought of Russia, and I contacted people there, but I never had any response to my queries. Then a friend I'd been at school with in Edinburgh came back from Longyearbyen; he'd led an expedition across a glacier there. He mentioned the permafrost, and I got *excited*.

'It was guesswork, but I knew people had been up to mine coal in Spitsbergen in the early part of the century, and I knew flu had been in Norway, so possibly people could have gone there bringing the disease with them. So I contacted the Norwegian authorities. They said, This is fascinating, but you have a very difficult task ahead of you. Essentially, there're no government records because Svalbard didn't become part of Norway until 1925. There's no church record, because the first minister didn't go there until 1920. There's no hospital record, because the hospital was destroyed. But there were these diaries kept by the mining company. I called them and they said, No, we no longer have the diaries.

'This is two years now. I asked, does anyone have them? Yes, the local schoolteacher does. So I called him, and he was good enough to translate them – and sure enough, they record the deaths of seven young men, and they're buried in the cemetery at Longyearbyen. Well – this is only the start. I know they're buried there, but does the cemetery still exist? Are the graves marked? I wrote to the local minister, and I found out that it does exist, the graves are marked, and they haven't been disturbed.

'So then I needed to know, what were the burial customs of the time? If there were cremations, of course it ended there. I contacted funeral directors in Norway, the Lutheran Church, historians, the Norwegian authorities – and I found out that at that time, people were buried in simple wood coffins, and there was no embalming fluid. That was important to the project, because formaldehyde can alter the structure of the virus. So this was exciting. Of course Svalbard was No Man's Land, there was no law, we don't know what was done – but it was a matter next of determining how deeply they were buried, and what the ground temperatures were at that time, and was it worth going ahead?'

Duncan was reaching the limits of her expertise. After two years' work in her own time, and at a cost to her own purse that she estimated at Canadian $40,000, she'd found named flu victims, in marked and undisturbed graves, in a cold place. Permafrost, however, wasn't a subject she knew much about. It was time to start building a team.

Duncan had already been talking about her project with a pathologist named Charles Smith at Toronto's Hospital for Sick Children. Forty-eight years old, a lean, trim, gently spoken man with a wit as sharp as his manner was mild, Smith was a committed Christian who'd trained at the hospital and been on the medical staff there for nearly twenty years.

He worked mainly in forensic and paediatric pathology; he and his boss had convinced the Solicitor General seven years earlier to set up a unit specializing in the investigation of the sudden or suspicious deaths of young people. If a coroner ordered an autopsy on a child, it'd likely be Smith's unit that took it on; he was used to exhumations, and to doing them in less congenial places than Toronto, too. In 1997, he'd exhumed a child for autopsy outside Chandigarh, on the edge of the southern Himalayas, though the remains on Svalbard, it was hoped, would be in somewhat better condition than what he found in India.

Smith had been discussing another idea with Duncan; they'd wanted to study what environmental factors might contribute to Sudden Infant Death Syndrome, or cot death. They knew there were environmental triggers – high winds, sudden falls in temperature, a higher incidence in winter than in summer – and they'd wanted to look into whether there was a difference in urban as against rural distributions. Like the great majority of research ideas, it never got off the ground, but meanwhile, Duncan told Smith about Svalbard.

They talked about the autopsies that had been done on three sailors from the Franklin expedition of 1845. A doomed effort to find a North-West passage, the expedition had foundered in the ice, and 140 marooned sailors had died of starvation and lead poisoning (the tins for the first canned food at that time were soldered with lead, the lead leached into the food, and the expedition had a lot of canned food). Three sailors who died early in the course of the disaster were buried in wooden coffins, and were later found to be incredibly well preserved. But more generally, said Smith, given the knowledge of his trade, he was able to give Duncan some feel for the things they might be able to do with the miners' bodies in Svalbard.

They had first to establish, however, that it was worth digging down for them at all – so in 1995, Duncan approached Alan Heginbottom at the Geological Survey of Canada, part of the Department of Energy, Mines and Resources in Ottawa. Heginbottom has since retired from that office, but he stayed with Duncan's project; three years after she first approached him, he directed the dig in the Longyearbyen cemetery.

Over a cup of tea in the portakabin at the foot of the

slope, Heginbottom said, 'Kirsty came to me for information on permafrost conditions here, and the likelihood that these bodies would be preserved or not. I thought, well, gee, this is a *neat* project. She knew the people had died of Spanish flu here, and she knew there was discontinuous mountain permafrost on Svalbard. So she needed to know whether there was permafrost at this site, and how deep the active layer was. She more or less knew from the Norwegians how deep the bodies were likely to be buried – so what was the ground temperature history? What was the temperature regime that was likely to have occurred here in the last eighty years?'

Heginbottom hadn't been to Svalbard, but he had colleagues, both Canadian and Norwegian, who'd visited and worked there on various site engineering issues, so they knew what the conditions were like – not specifically at the site of the cemetery, but at the site of the hospital a kilometre down the valley. There were enough data available, Duncan later told me in Toronto, 'to work out the ground temperature chronology at an assumed depth of a metre to a metre and a half over the last eighty years. And what we figure is, the temperatures would have ranged from −10°C to 1°C. A standard morgue is 4°C. So at an assumed depth of one to one and a half metres, temperatures are much colder than a morgue.'

Heginbottom said, 'I was able to say with reasonable confidence that the probability that they had not thawed was very high. That the active layer – that is, the surface layer of the ground above the permafrost which thaws out each summer and refreezes each winter – was very probably no more than a metre deep.'

The next question was how deep the bodies would be buried. When it came to working that one out, said Duncan, 'The answer is that no one knew, but from historians, there was good evidence to suggest they'd be buried rather deeply.'

One gruesome piece of supporting evidence for that supposition was the fact that the bodies hadn't come to the surface. If you bury people in the active layer, the melting and refreezing mean the coffins move in the ground, and, as has happened elsewhere with the bodies of trappers in Svalbard, in Greenland, and all across the North American Arctic, they literally float to the surface.

It's called frost-jacking, and since it hadn't happened in this case, said Duncan, 'that would suggest they were below the active layer. That was one piece of evidence. A second piece of evidence was the fact that the time of year they died, early October, would be the time of the greatest melting of the permafrost. It's like water – you get the warmest air temperatures at the summer solstice, but the warmest water temperatures are August and September, because it takes time to work through. It's the same with permafrost. The warmest temperatures are in the fall, which means that when they died it was easy to dig, so they could have dug deeper. And then, we're guessing that they knew what this disease was by that time – and if you knew what it was, you'd want to bury it as deeply as you can. And the last thing is, they were miners. If anyone knew how to dig through this, they did.'

Heginbottom said, 'The standard depth of burial in Norway is about two metres at the bottom of the coffin. If a coffin's about forty-five centimetres deep, then we're at least half a metre below the active layer. If that is the case, the probability that the bodies have been below zero Celsius throughout that time is very high.'

Duncan had learnt everything she could without actually going to Svalbard, so in May 1996 she flew there. She said, 'It's an incredible place. That first time I went, it was white. But I wanted to go, in order to assure the people of Longyearbyen that this would be done properly, with the greatest respect and dignity. I should tell you, personally, I find the project very difficult. It was against everything I believe in, to disturb a cemetery – I find it really hard. I try to think of the potential for good that could come out of it, but going to the cemetery was one of the hardest things I've ever done.

'When I went to Longyearbyen it was exciting, because I got to meet many people who'd helped me along the way, and it was my turn to say thank you to them. It was really exciting to meet these wonderful people, who'd been so good to me – here I am, an outsider, wanting to do something potentially very hurtful – but I have never been so welcomed in my life. So on the second day, I took all my courage to go to the church and see the minister, and I introduced myself and I said, "I hope I have in no way offended you or your church." And he gave me a big hug and said, "No, this is exciting work, this *has* to be done."

'Well, I can't describe my sense of relief. This man was so wonderful. He asked if I'd been to the cemetery and I said, "No, I didn't feel I had any right to go until I had your permission." He said, "You go." It's quite a distance from the church to the cemetery, and it was completely white, the snow was quite thick, the glaciers were coming down the end of the valley – and I can honestly say it was the longest, hardest walk I've ever taken. I got to the cemetery, it's on quite an incline, and I knew the seven graves I was interested in were in the last row, so it was quite high up.

'So I walk up there, and it's completely white – white crosses on a white background – and I get to the graves and I read the names, and of course I'd seen them in print, but this is different. They were roughly the same age as me, and here I am looking at their grave markers, and there they lie. Really hard. It's a beautiful resting place. They look out at the fjord . . . I just find it very difficult.'

It had been difficult all along. She was young, she was a woman, and – worst of all, in the eyes of some more exalted scientists – she was a geographer. What sort of discipline was that? 'Don't get her talking about flu,' said one lofty colleague, 'she's a geographer. When she talks about flu, she's *deadly*.'

Duncan knew what was said about her behind her back. She said, 'I keep to my goal. I want an answer, and I'm not interested in the politics, if they're out there. I don't want to be. I do my business.'

By the time they started digging in August 1998, that business had occupied her life for five years. Working alone to begin with, then assembling a team, whose composition changed as time passed, members joining and leaving after assorted spats and disagreements, she had driven past every obstacle to find frozen bodies that might hold the clue to what happened in 1918. Along the way, her marriage had broken up – hence her living back at home – and when I met her in April, four months before the spades first bit into the tundra, she told me, 'It's been a hard road. It has. It's been emotionally draining from beginning to end.

I'm tired. I'm thirty-one, and I'm really tired. That's all I can say.'

Duncan found some of the team; others came to her. Charles Smith and Alan Heginbottom, fellow Canadians, were two of her early calls; Rob Webster was on the project from the early stages too. As Smith tells it, Duncan called him one day and said, 'I just had the most incredible call with some guy in Memphis. He phones me up with this New Zealand accent and he says, "Hello. I'm Rob Webster. I'm one of the world's experts on influenza. I'm good. You need me."'

As it turned out, they did; Webster would secure a good part of their funding from the National Institutes of Health in Maryland. Long before it came to raising money, however, the team had to establish how they were going to go about the project in the first place. Beginning with the Governor of Svalbard in November 1995, Duncan was already seeking permission from the relevant Norwegian authorities – but permission to do what, exactly?

Their first meeting, at the University of Windsor in Ontario, was in the autumn of 1996. A whole raft of different disciplines was involved (geography, geology, geophysics, pathology, microbiology, virology) and among those present were people from CDC. Later they'd bale out, for reasons we'll come to, but Duncan's concern at that time was that all these people, speaking their different scientific languages, should help each other to see where they were coming from.

Heginbottom explained what permafrost was, and what digging in it would involve; Smith took them through what working on the bodies would mean. 'Doing the work in a safe way,' he told me, 'keeping the world of 1918 from contaminating our world, and keeping our world from contaminating the specimens – that was the major challenge. But most of the others had a pretty limited view of what pathology was. They hadn't seen autopsies; they really didn't have a feel for some of the issues about handling these bodies. They wanted them up out of the ground, they wanted them in a mortuary at the local hospital – and I die when I think of the risks associated with that.'

The work on the bodies would have to be done right there, in the hole in the ground. They weren't going to do full autopsies; they were there to take specimens of tissue from a range of different organs, and Smith laid down the principles of how a sampling team could do that. It would be like a rudimentary operating room, with a four-person team: the pathologist, the pathologist's assistant, the technical support person, and a fourth member to communicate between the people inside and outside the tent. These four were the equivalent of a surgeon, a scrub nurse in sterile garments, a circulating nurse fetching tools and equipment, and someone on the desk taking phone calls.

But what tools and equipment do you use to get material from corpses that have been frozen for eighty years? 'The kind of situation we're going into,' said Smith, 'we do not want to thaw out the tissues to any degree. But if you're attempting to work on a frozen body, that's a dangerous exercise. If you take a pound of ground beef out of your freezer, then try to cut it with a knife, you'll slip. You're more likely to cut yourself. Now, the tissues may not be frozen like a block of ice – if you take bacon out of the freezer, for instance, or anything with a high fat content, it's still somewhat pliable. Fat doesn't freeze like water does, so if these men had much subcutaneous fat, the surface won't be absolutely rock solid. It'll be like stiff cookie dough that's been in the fridge.'

Smith went to the Windsor meeting with a tree corer. It's a forestry tool – a long steel cylinder, narrow-walled, with a sharp cutting edge. It's threaded on the outside, with maybe four turns of a spiral thread over the first inch of the cylinder's exterior. The one he took to Windsor had an outer diameter of a quarter of an inch, an inner diameter of three-eighths of an inch – and tools like that, he said, in a variety of sizes, were the way to get the material they wanted from these bodies. They created as neat an excision as you could manage; the tissue came out undamaged, and because you dug in with them slowly, using hand power only, you were less likely to slip and shred up either the tissue or yourself. In the darker realms of fear – that tiny outside chance that the 1918 virus might still be intact down there – with these tools you wouldn't create an aerosol either, spraying up microdroplets with the killer flu on board that someone might then breathe in.

Smith told the team how the sampling would work, and he told them something else. He told them the first rule of exhumation: You don't know what you've got until you look.

They met again in April 1997 in Atlanta; they agreed that the project should proceed in two phases. First, they'd survey the site using Ground-Penetrating Radar (GPR). This was a non-invasive procedure that, all being well, should tell them whether digging was worth it; using radio waves, GPR can detect buried objects in the ground from depths of just a few yards to many tens of yards, depending on soil conditions. So if the results were good, they'd go ahead and dig.

CDC pulled out; the NIH in Maryland agreed to fund the radar survey, and in October 1997 a team flew to Longyearbyen. The survey was conducted by Alan Heginbottom and Les Davis, from a Canadian company called Sensors & Software Inc. Duncan and Smith also went, along with John Oxford from the Royal London Hospital, another virologist called Rod Daniels from the British Flu Centre in Mill Hill, two Norwegian scientists, and a professional exhumation specialist from a company somewhat spookily called Necropolis. They were on Svalbard for four days, meeting twice with the Governor's Office, giving a lecture at the University, speaking to the church congregation after the Sunday service, and to various other local institutions. While this was both necessary business and good PR, however, the main object was the radar scan.

Founded in 1988, Sensors & Software are based in Mississauga, just south-west along the lakeshore from Toronto; their pulse EKKO equipment is used in a wide range of fields. It can detect underground pipes, tanks and barrels, or unexploded ordnance; it's used in mining, archaeology, groundwater location and nuclear waste disposal. In a publicity brochure, a colour drawing demonstrated another use for GPR; captioned 'find unmarked graves', it shows a cross-section of soil, and a radio wave bouncing back from one piece of kit to another via a coffin underground. Police in Canada, England, India and the United States had all used it to locate bodies in unmarked graves.

On Svalbard, of course, the graves were marked; the team knew exactly where they were looking, and when the results came in they were promising. Where the grave markers stood, the data showed a substantial pocket of ground disturbed to a depth of six feet, with the active layer half that deep, or less. There was no clear indication of where the coffins lay within that pocket, but for the ground to be disarranged to that depth accorded with what they knew of Norwegian burial practice. Back at NIH, the data were reviewed towards the end of 1997, and funding was agreed for the dig to proceed.

The team confirmed in a subsequent press release, 'GPR showed the most probable location of the graves of the influenza victims. The radar also showed that the graves are well below the active layer. This suggests that the bodies of the young victims should be well preserved.'

Meanwhile, even before the survey was conducted, Duncan had applied to the Governor of Svalbard to renew her permission for the project. On 13 September 1997 she wrote, 'I appreciate that I am applying early for the permission [i.e. before the Phase 1 analyses], however I believe that this is necessary in order to continue the Project by planning properly ahead. I want to assure you, however, that the team will not proceed to Phase 2 if there is little evidence to suggest that the bodies of the seven young miners are not well preserved.'

From the GPR, they had their evidence. The following summer, when the topsoil was soft, Duncan's team started digging for the 1918 virus.

5 STRESSED TO THE MAX

It takes four and a half hours to fly from Oslo to Longyear-byen, with a forty-minute stop at Tromso *en route*. The approach into Tromso was remarkable, the plane dropping from the clouds to skim over jagged, snow-streaked grey peaks, then banking between the fjord walls to find the runway.

Equally striking in its way, when we deplaned, was the sight of a lean, bearded man wandering round the airport hallway clutching a *papier mâché* model of the influenza virus as big as a beach ball. Bright yellow, with black spikes for the proteins on the outer skin, and a cutaway section revealing wiggly strands of red telephone cord to represent the genome within, this was the battered, much-travelled possession of Professor John Oxford.

An amenable, engagingly eccentric character, Oxford had used his model to explain the intricacies of the virus in many lectures and TV shows; he was a useful performer before the camera, with a lucid, accessible, quietly passionate manner. When we'd met at the Royal London Hospital two months earlier, the first words recorded on my tape, before I'd even got a question out of my mouth, were, 'Scientists don't sit back. Science doesn't sit back. Science is like an express train. It's on the rails. It's going.'

Now Oxford was going to Svalbard, in company with his wife and a colleague, Noël Roberts, from the pharmaceuticals giant Roche. Through the agency of Oxford and others, Roche had put up half the funding for Duncan's project; she'd approached Oxford a couple of years before, and although CDC in Atlanta had since backed off, the concept still greatly enthused him. Fifty-six years old, he'd spent 75 per cent of his working life studying flu; in the words of a colleague, he'd recently been looking for 1918 samples 'in a voracious manner'.

Originally from Dorset, he'd trained in the sixties in Sheffield. There's an indication of the otherworldly element in his nature when he tells how driving up the A1 to start his studies was the first time he'd ever been north of London – and how, as they approached Sheffield, the night sky filled with an amazing glow. Oxford thought, my God, this must be a fire, until the hitch-hiker he'd picked up told him, 'Don't be stupid. That's the steel industry.'

He trained with Sir Charles Stuart-Harris, who'd been on the team that first isolated the human flu virus at Mill Hill in 1933. Flu, says Oxford, 'is probably the most important virus we know about. Certainly, 1918 leaves HIV looking like a bit of a picnic. That's not to say HIV isn't serious – but the fact that flu spreads by aerosol means you can't restrain it. HIV, you can be careful. Polio, you can clean up the water supply. CJD, you can slaughter the cows. But a respiratory virus – no, that's scary.'

Regular flu gets Oxford exercised, never mind pandemic strains. It is, he says, 'the continuous, grinding impact on the community, and the impact on the extremes of ages. I was always interested in this attitude, which is still a little bit about, that flu and pneumonia are the old man's friend. There's a wonderful Blake drawing called "Death's Door";

it's this really old chap, he's opened the door and he's tottering in – and there's been this prevalent idea that elderly people *want* to exit, and that flu and pneumonia are convenient ways to go. Well, it's a completely mixed-up, old-fashioned idea, and it should be squashed. Because most elderly people who contract flu and get seriously ill don't die – they end up in an old people's home. And you can't tell me that's being *anyone*'s friend. You can't tell me elderly people want the exit, they want to *stay*. They want to enjoy themselves, they want to enjoy their grandchildren, and they don't want to end up entombed in a box.'

Yet for all the threat flu poses, there hadn't been the funding for Oxford to stay with it all the time. He'd worked on HIV, scrapie, measles, because in science, he said, 'You have to go with the wind. You'll find very few virologists who've managed to stay with flu exclusively all their lives. I suppose Webster's the example – but when I came to the Royal London ten years ago, flu wasn't one of their priorities. Their priority'd be everything *but* influenza. Then, as the years roll by and HIV appears to be a bit less of a problem, suddenly they all wake up and realize there could be a new flu pandemic, so it takes on a new urgency, and you can work on it again.'

A good thing too, because the flu community, he said, 'are like vulcanologists. We're all sitting round the volcano wondering when it's going to blow. We don't know when – but we do know it will.'

Flu, Oxford said, 'is a living, vibrant, changeable, *amazing* concoction of nucleic acid and protein. It's never static. You look at this model; in the real thing, all these little particles are whizzing round, thousands of revolutions a second – so it's not an inert bit of nothingness. And you have to look at it and say to yourself, how does *this* cause *this*?'

He pulled out a copy of the Ministry of Health's 1920 report, with its watercolour illustrations of Spanish flu patients lying pale on their pillows, their lips blue and purple. And, he then asked, 'Did it cause *that* as well?'

He pulled out another textbook, on encephalitis lethargica. The caption beneath the photograph read, 'Post-encephalitic Parkinsonism with marked catatonia in a young woman. Note the immobile, expressionless face . . . the arms were placed passively in this position with no request to hold them there. This patient also has marked disorder of the blinking reflex.'

Known in the twenties as the 'sleepy sickness', encephalitis lethargica is one of the great medical mysteries of all time. It's also sometimes called Von Economo's Disease, Von Economo being a professor of psychiatry and neurology in Vienna who noticed, towards the end of the First World War, that patients on his wards were beginning to exhibit strange neurological symptoms. They came in with headaches, double vision, and a peculiar eye effect called oculo-gyric crisis – they'd throw their heads back, and their eyes would roll. Above all, they came in tremendously sleepy – they'd fall asleep even as you were talking to them – and by 1922, this was happening worldwide. Peaking in the mid-twenties, encephalitis lethargica affected about fifteen million people; a third of them died, a third recovered, and the remaining third went on to develop Parkinsonism.

So the question was, said Oxford, 'Has that got anything to do with Spanish flu? Is that an aftermath? Given the fact that half a billion people *at least* got infected by flu, isn't it conceivable that a low proportion of them developed a neurological disease later on, as a complication of that? Two CDC guys published a paper in the early eighties, giving ten reasons suggesting that it is – but it's a total mystery, and it's been forgotten. And until very recently, so was 1918.'

It's no surprise, then, that when Duncan broached her idea to him, John Oxford became excited. They could look for the 1918 flu, they could look for the co-infecting bacteria; they could, as he put it, 'get a greater understanding of a virus that killed forty million, with a view to developing new drugs and vaccines to prevent it ever happening again'.

Helping to secure money from Roche, Oxford became one of six people on the project's controlling Scientific Advisory Group, the others being Duncan, Heginbottom, Webster, Sir John Skehel from Mill Hill, and Tom Bergan, a microbiologist at the University of Oslo who served as the project's Norwegian co-ordinator.

On this group, Oxford chaired the health and safety committee; the team were taking extensive containment precautions to deal with the remote possibility that the virus in the permafrost might still be intact and infective. He said, 'We've done a risk assessment, and we think the biggest risk is someone slipping on the ice and breaking their leg. Nevertheless, this is a virus that killed millions, and we'd all look pretty silly if we didn't take precautions, then found we had live virus. There's a very, very low chance – it's pretty fragile, it's been sitting there eighty years, the temperature's been up and down – but who knows? So you behave as if the bodies are infectious. Now, even if they are, how do you catch flu from a frozen corpse? It's not going to come running towards you, is it? Unless there's a terrible accident, unless a sample somehow falls open and you sniff it – well, it's very difficult to envisage how you'd catch it. But you take precautions all the same.'

They did so partly because of the stature of the individuals and institutions now involved. Roche, the National Institutes of Health – these bodies could only back the project if it was run to the highest standards in terms of both safety and ethics.

From small beginnings, Duncan's project had grown into a sizeable undertaking. To start with, said Oxford, 'Kirsty did all the work. She put a small Canadian team together, but they didn't have the oomph, the prestige, I suppose, or the scientific punch to get very far.' So the thing grew, as he told it, pretty much by chance. 'You sort of stumble on each other – but the virological community's a small one. You call each other, and then you get the problems that being a big international team brings. You start off with a cosy little national team under your thumb, as it were, then suddenly you've got a big team that's not under your thumb. It gets more unwieldy.'

It also gets more attention, leading, in some quarters, to stories along the lines of 'Mad Boffins Dig Up Killer Bug'. To deal with this, the Advisory Group had taken on a PR company, Hill & Knowlton, to be paid for by Roche, who to all intents and purposes were putting in their part of the money as a gift. Oxford said, 'They're not likely to get much from it. But what they don't want is a load of negative publicity.'

He went on, 'I think, in a way, the problem has been portraying it as a single person's project – as Kirsty's. And she's a geographer, her knowledge of infectious diseases isn't high, so I guess you could rubbish her quite easily, which some people have done. But now, we're going to change the whole perception of the project, because you've got some internationally high-powered scientists on it. John Skehel, Rob Webster – these are Fellows of the Royal Society, these aren't mad boffins. So we've kept quiet in the team, and perhaps that's been our mistake, because we need assistance. We can't have Kirsty just answering the telephone when she feels like it.'

There were hints of annoyance here, a suggestion that the project hadn't always been handled as he'd have liked. Oxford demurred; he said, 'Not annoyance. But from now on, I do want it to be much more professionally organized.'

By the time we got to Tromso airport, whatever improvements he'd hoped for plainly hadn't materialized. A tediously prolix press pack didn't appear at the cemetery until a good number of the news journalists had already been and gone; much of it appeared to have been written by Duncan anyway, containing as it did verbatim chunks of earlier press releases. Otherwise, there was no sign of Hill & Knowlton on Svalbard at all. One of the other scientists said later, 'There's been a certain amount of resistance to appointing anyone, because Kirsty thought she could handle it herself, and I think that's been a problem. Because she clearly cannot.'

At first, Oxford had been greatly charmed by the young Canadian; as his daughter put it later, he'd described her as 'exotic', they'd swapped torrents of phone calls and faxes, Duncan had wept down the phone to him when her marriage broke up, and when she came to London in February 1998, in a macabre image of scientific bonding, he'd taken her to see the skeleton of the Elephant Man. By the evening of Friday, 21 August, however, as we waited to reboard our plane for the last leg into the Arctic, any charm she might at first have exerted had very plainly faded. Duncan was, he said grimly, 'a megalomaniac. A control freak.'

He said the Mill Hill people were getting near their limit with her – but that wasn't new. One of them had told me as early as February, 'She's not the easiest person in the world to get along with.' Oxford muttered that he was a mild-mannered man, 'But I'm finding it hard to take myself.'

It had been plain from early on that some of the relationships between these strong-minded individuals were far from rosy. The following morning, as the team lugged equipment up the bleak, fog-shrouded hillside to the cemetery, one of them grumbled to me about a dispute they'd had before departure over leadership, and Duncan's efforts to keep control of the project. 'If that's the way she wants it,' he said wearily, 'fine. We'll send her a bill for a quarter of a million quid, and she can analyse the samples.'

As for having to listen to her frequent perorations on treating the dead with the greatest respect and dignity, another said, 'It's like it comes off a typescript. It makes me feel sick.'

By that Saturday morning they'd been working for three days, and they'd winched or carried twelve tons of equipment to the gravesite. Helping to steady seventeen big plywood boards on a trolley as one of the gravediggers worked the winch, Rod Daniels, a virologist from Mill Hill, puffed and panted and grinned, 'Lessons to be learnt from this project? Don't do it again.'

Daniels came from the Somerset village of Puriton and had a ripe West Country accent; forty-three years old, heavily built with silver hair and a short beard, he looked and spoke more like a scrumpy farmer than a molecule man. In keeping with his manner, he was a practical type, good with his hands – after seeing his lab in London, Charles Smith had had no hesitation in wanting Daniels to be the third member of his sampling team – and he'd been responsible for putting together all the medical equipment, then shipping it to Svalbard.

On the other hand, the distractions of a life spent wrapping your mind around infinitesimal fragments of bio-chemical matter could get to him as much as the rest of the team. When I'd first met him at Mill Hill six weeks before the dig, the two cargo containers had left Hull for the North Atlantic the day before. We'd not been speaking long when the phone rang; after he'd taken the call Daniels grinned and said, 'I've shipped £10,000's worth of gear out of here, and I haven't insured it.'

I laughed and said, 'You're a scientist, right?'

'Yup. We're all mad.'

He was a techniques man; part of his game was rescuing RNA from the kind of tissues they hoped to find here. Like John Oxford, Mill Hill had been looking for 1918 samples for some years, and through Oxford they'd turned some up in the Royal London's pathology archive – formalin-fixed lung and brain tissues from 1918. They'd screened about forty of these specimens and come up blank; it was, shrugged Daniels, the luck of the draw. Then, again through Oxford,

Mill Hill got together with Duncan, and Rod Daniels first met her in February 1997.

He was at the meeting in Atlanta a couple of months later, because her project, he said, 'opened up a much greater chance of getting something back. The survey we did last year very much says, yes, the bodies go down deep enough, they should have been in a good frozen state, they're well below the active layer – and we hope for very good tissue preservation.'

The tools to extract that tissue, the human equivalent of Smith's tree corers, had been engineered at Mill Hill; enough sharp-edged cylinders, all being well, to get a couple of hundred samples. The engineers had come up with a little memento for Daniels, too – one of the drill bits passing through a miniature coffin lid with the legend in Norwegian, 'Just Passing Through'.

Though the tools were good, Daniels worried that organ shrinkage might make some of the sampling difficult; the Arctic's dry environment, a polar desert, and some degree of desiccation might well have occurred. The brain, consisting almost entirely of water, can shrink to a little bit of nothing, but overall, he was optimistic. The one thing he really would have liked, on the other hand – though he never kicked up a fuss about it – was to have been able to go about his work without cameras in his face all the time.

On the hillside that Saturday morning there were news crews from Norway, Iceland and Germany, along with three other crews – one from the *New York Times*' TV company, making a programme for The Learning Channel, one from a Franco-German documentary co-production, and (by some margin the best organized) a joint British–Canadian–

Norwegian team, making a major film about 1918 and these efforts to find out what had caused it. Another guy from Canadian TV was somewhere about; Daniels said good-naturedly, 'They've shot some yardage, I'll tell you. And I'd like to see it, 'cause I'd like to know which one of these bright sparks pulled the cable on us.'

They were working in the tent when suddenly the power went off, and half a ton of plastic and canvas started deflating all around them. One of the cameramen would later charge that, no, it had been one of the scientists who'd pulled the plug – but to be fair, relationships at this point between journalists and scientists were largely cordial. This was no baying press pack; they kept out of the way as best they could, the scientists appreciated that they had their job to do, and also that there would be, as a result, a documentary record of what they achieved.

In short, they liked the attention – after all, they didn't often get much. Daniels, one of the more level-headed among them, smiled contentedly as someone filmed him working the winch and said, 'That's another thirty seconds of fame. What is it you get, fifteen minutes? So I'll have used all mine up this week.'

There were strict rules about filming and photography in the tent itself. Only one crew was allowed inside it – inside the perimeter, even – and that was the big co-production involving, among others, NRK, the Norwegian public network. The deal arrived at between them, the team and the Svalbard Governor's Office over the preceding months was that they should pool a few minutes of whatever footage they got with all the others every day; in this way, the Norwegian authorities were happy that everyone who wanted to be could be informed as to what was happening, while the team weren't pestered with a swarm of cameras as they toiled with their shovels. One Norwegian press photographer was also allowed in – again, one only, on the understanding that he too would pool his material.

Bearing in mind the ethical concerns, the moment the coffins were exposed, the tent would be off limits altogether. All round, it seemed a straightforward arrangement, but even so, the scientists remained wary. Every night one of them, or one of the Necropolis workers, stayed up all night in the portakabin at the entrance to the site, in case someone tried to sneak in and get pictures. It's Necropolis policy to maintain strict security at the site of an exhumation anyway, but it was the media the scientists were worried about.

'All it takes,' said one of them, 'is a guy to fly in with a camera and a Stanley knife, get in there, be gone the next morning, then someone at Roche or NIH wakes up the next day and there's pictures of the bodies in the paper. And then the whole project's down the tubes, isn't it?'

Seeds of mistrust, in other words, were there from the beginning. Before the dig, some of the scientists had tried hard to persuade me not to go to Svalbard at all; Rob Webster had been particularly brusque on that point. John Oxford had been more understanding; he'd seen why I might want to go, but he said, 'There's no reason to have a load of TV people there, 'cause there's not much to film. A load of scientists running round in anoraks, and a big tent they can't get into? There's not even going to be any snow.'

Others fretted with a kind of nervous fascination – a mix of alarm and vanity, I'd say – that Longyearbyen's few hotels were getting booked up; one talked wildly about 300 journalists spilling into Svalbard. And the team's hotel, the Svalbard Polar, was indeed booked solid – it was hosting the annual four-day conference of the Lady Amateur Radio Operators of the World. The media, in short, weren't really that interested at all; the news crews only came in for a day or two each, only three newspaper journalists came from anywhere other than Norway, and one of those was Oxford's daughter.

After all, as he'd said, if it was pictures or an instant story you wanted, there wasn't a great deal to look at. Though he had access to the tent, Elliott Halpern, a charming and well-informed Canadian who was directing the big documentary, sighed and said, 'A shoot like this, you can get desperate for something. Look! They're hauling some plywood up the hill! Shoot it!'

I wandered around the containers, peering aimlessly at stepladders, jackhammers, plastic trays, cardboard boxes and lighting equipment. On top of one of the containers stood a big water tank, 'because the English need their tea'. Oxford turned up, fell into conversation with Daniels and Heginbottom, and they were immediately fenced in with a thicket of three cameras and two sound booms.

I went to talk to the Necropolis guys, the professional gravediggers. One was a cheerful South London wide boy in a pale blue fleece; the other four were straight out of Dickens. They had Cockney accents and woolly hats, they smoked roll-ups, and one of them, sporting a gold earring and silver sideburns, was covered all over in tattoos, with an image under his left armpit of an ejaculating penis. To complete the surreal impression of their grisly trade, they'd flown in on a Lear jet.

The company had been founded by Private Act of Parliament in 1852; it was empowered to exhume and rebury human remains at sites where new roads, housing or commercial development were planned. They were now part of an outfit called Service Corporation International (SCI), a multinational funeral director established in Houston in 1962. Good company men, the gravediggers had brought with them some bizarre corporate literature about how SCI had carried out half a million funerals worldwide in 1997, and had 'an impressive global track record which demonstrates its ability to grow both organically and through acquisition'.

If they'd brought management-speak PR material about the funeral market worldwide, however, they didn't speak that way themselves; they were friendly, hard-working, and relaxed about their business. Their leader, Roger Webber, a portly type in tinted shades, said that apart from the presence of the TV cameras, the contract wasn't much different to work they'd done in Scotland. The ground was cold and hard there too, and had boulders just like here; the only difference would be the permafrost.

As for handling the bodies, he wasn't bothered. 'Nah,' he said, 'we've handled thousands of 'em. We've dug up bodies buried 250 years ago, and when you take 'em out they're the same as the day they went in. You get a wet day, it seals the coffin, you get a vacuum, and then there's no deterioration at all. They've even still got the colour in their eyes.'

At four o'clock that Saturday afternoon, Pastor Jan Hoifodt came to the graveyard to conduct a brief ceremony. He stood in white and purple robes amidst a litter of planks, blue

matting and black plastic sheets inside the fenced-off perimeter; the scientists stood about him as he spoke and gave
a reading, their hands clasped before them, their heads
bowed. Outside the fencing, cameras swarmed. The pastor
was kindly, practical and unemotional; he said the local
community was glad the team had come, and that they'd
showed sensitivity to the nature of their task. 'Yet still you
feel it is wrong,' he said, 'to disturb the graveyard. But your
work is important, and we hope you will learn from it.'

They filed into the tent for another reading; they said
the Lord's Prayer, and the pastor oversaw the first breaking
of the ground. Afterwards, John Oxford interviewed him;
more comfortable than the others about the workings of the
media, he'd got recording equipment from the BBC, and was
making a half-hour documentary about the project for the
World Service.

The pastor told him, 'It was a very simple ceremony,
and a reading from the Holy Book. All will be dust, that's
only realistic – so we pray they succeed. This is a serious
subject, and of course it is a dilemma – but they have to go
on, because they do it for the better. For the benefit of
mankind, maybe.'

His pragmatism was in keeping with Longyearbyen's
attitude as a whole. In eight days, I met no one there who
seemed remotely bothered about the exhumation; Pastor
Hoifodt, and those overseeing the project at the Governor's
Office, expressed gratitude that it had been approached in
a properly tactful and thorough manner, but otherwise they
couldn't see any need to get worked up about it. Asked by
Oxford whether any of his parishioners were upset, the
pastor said they weren't; even the families of the other people

buried there, he said, 'are understanding of the project'.

Soon afterwards, I found John Oxford sitting on the little deck outside the portakabin. He joked nervously, 'Alan wouldn't let me have a cup of tea. Because I was media.'

To one side, two of the Necropolis workers sipped tea and smoked cigarettes. They were champing at the bit; according to the schedule the hole was meant to be dug by Tuesday, and they wanted to get the topsoil off. One said, 'Can we start digging now?'

The other answered, 'We can now, yeah.'

'What, were we waiting on that for the go-ahead, then?'

The other said firmly and sincerely, 'I wasn't going to start without it.' Then he said, 'I'll tell you what, though. I've been on hundreds of digs with Roger, hundreds. And he's just turned round to me and said, he could feel their presence. He's never said that before. But he said he could feel them.'

It never got dark. Banks of low cloud crept through the looming spurs of rock on the hilltops, smothering the outlines of the wooden pylons from the old mine workings. From the cemetery, the town lay mostly to the left, along the shore of the Adventfjord; the water was a slick, heavy grey-green under the snow-dusted crusts of the mountains beyond. Most of the houses were simple, two-storey blocks, wood-clad, painted a fetching variety of shades of ochre, tan, terracotta, dark red or green; they were all built on stilts, so that in winter they didn't melt the frozen ground beneath them and sink into it.

To the right, the dirt-veined sheets of the Lars and Longyear glaciers lay cupped in their valleys, the gaunt ridge of the Sarcophagus rising high between them. Their faces were a jumbled wreckage of terminal moraine, from which the meltwater streams spilled out frothing, pushing and shovelling, laden with silt and gravel. The moraine was permanently on the move; great holes would open up in the ground, and you could fall and vanish as easily into a crevasse of dirt as one of ice.

It was cold, but not bone-chilling; that first night, the thermometer on the outside of my hotel room's window read a steady 3.5°C through an overcast, grey-lit evening. I walked up towards the head of the valley, to a bar imaginatively named the Huset – 'the House'. It was a substantial place and if its name was dull, nothing else about it was. In the back, an upscale restaurant was eighteen kinds of smart; it claimed to have the largest wine cellar in Norway, and in 1993 had been voted the country's finest eating place. From the quality of the food in the bar, that wasn't hard to imagine.

The quality of the music at the Saturday night disco was patchier, veering through an eclectic mix of genres – 'Sweet Home Alabama', 'Let's Dance', 'Grease' – but if you lived in Longyearbyen, I suspect on a Saturday night you'd probably dance to anything. I had a drink with one of the film crews, and we wondered what might motivate a man to a career in exhumation.

One of the Americans presumed that there had to be a company similar to Necropolis in the United States, but he doubted its name would have such ghoulish undertones. He chuckled and said, 'It's probably called something like Sunshine Productions.'

The sound man mimed digging with a shovel and started singing, 'Let the sun shine in . . .'

Stressed to the Max

On my way out, I paused to read a poster in the doorway giving advice on how to handle polar bears. During the summer the bears should, in theory, be away feeding on the seals off the colder east coast, but that only means that if you meet one around Longyearbyen, it's most likely young, lost, hungry, and you're dinner. In the month before the dig, three had been shot – one by the recently abandoned Russian mining settlement of Pyramiden, and two around a Polish scientific outpost at Hornsund to the south.

Given the risk, you're not allowed to step outside Longyearbyen without a gun. The bears are strictly protected; on the other hand, since any effort to fend off the planet's largest land-going carnivore with your bare hands is likely to finish with a result for the bear, you are allowed to shoot one if needs must. According to the rules, you should then 'find out what sex it is, and take care of the skull and the skin'.

The idea that, having survived a close encounter with 900 pounds of charging white death, you'd then calmly conduct a zoological examination, is eccentric to say the least. On the other hand, compared to the behaviour some of the project team would soon be engaged in, it would come to seem quite rational.

By Sunday morning, they'd made good progress in removing the top layer of summer-softened tundra. This stage of the work was conducted meticulously; the topsoil was taken away in sections sixteen inches square, and laid carefully on boards with an airflow to keep it alive. That way, when the dig was done, it could be relaid exactly the way it had been found. Cutting out the soil like this involved one of their more sophisticated tools: Rod Daniels flicked through his

equipment manifest and pointed out the item in question –
a £10 breadknife.

They took attention to detail as far as placing each
loose rock and stone precisely with the section of earth and
moss from which it came – and for Alan Heginbottom, the
greatest technical challenge wasn't excavation or reburial,
but the restoration of the site to its original condition afterwards. They'd even reserved money for him to come back
in a year or two's time, to oversee any final repair or re-
vegetation that might be necessary; compared to this, relatively speaking, the actual digging was easy.

'It's just sheer effort,' said Heginbottom. 'Shovels for
the soft soil, jackhammers for the permafrost. We're not
permitted to use any wheeled machinery, it'd tear up the
tundra too much; the basic rule in Svalbard is that you don't
take vehicles off roadways anyway. So we do the whole
thing with hand tools.'

That meant shifting somewhere between 120 and 180
cubic feet of boulder-packed soil, about half of which would
be frozen, by hand. The excavation would be six feet wide
and fifteen or eighteen feet long; the sides would be sloped
back, because that was simpler and less effort than putting
in shoring to support vertical sides. The sloped sides would
then be lined with heavy-duty, high-density polystyrene insu-
lation board. 'Not the cheap stuff you pack in cardboard
boxes,' said Heginbottom, 'this is the sort of stuff you could
lay in roadways. Because we want to keep the ground frozen.'

A more ticklish problem concerned identification of the
bodies. The family of one of the seven had refused permission
for his body to be interfered with; the team readily accepted
that, but which body was his? If the coffins had nameplates,

they'd be fine; if they didn't, the Governor's Office said they should assume he was the third one along from the left, since that was where his marker had stood in the row.

As for the risks of contamination, the tent itself wasn't a sealed chamber. They'd realized early on that they couldn't ever fully seal the tent on ground as rough as this was; besides, said Heginbottom, if you were going to get that picky, the ground leaked air anyway. For containment, therefore, the pathology team would all wear specially prepared barrier suits; the tent was more for privacy. It was, he said, 'just the ethically appropriate way to proceed'.

In one of the cargo containers, John Oxford fidgeted nervously; it was hard going, and they were half a day behind schedule. It was Sunday, 23 August; according to the chart on the portakabin wall they were due to hit frozen ground the following day, to be exhuming the bodies by Thursday, and sampling by Friday.

Inevitably, there were other little logistical hiccups; for example, permission hadn't come through yet to import samples into Canada or the States. Rod Daniels' permission to take material into Britain had arrived two days before; to secure that permission, he'd had to construct an elaborate packaging system, and one of the key ingredients in the system was nappies.

When the samples had been taken in the hollow drill bits, they'd be retained in those and packed into aluminium cylinders with padded caps at both ends. The cylinders would be heat-sealed in polythene wrap, then packed into fifty-six-litre steel drums with clip-closed lids. To stop them rattling around, and to provide an absorbent layer, the drums would be filled with nappies, so Daniels expected to be buying a fair slice of Svalbard's supply of these essential items.

The drums themselves would be packed into a thermal control unit, a case with a three-inch-thick polystyrene skin inside which the gap between drum and skin would be filled with bio-ice. Each sample pack would weigh about 200 pounds and keep the tissue frozen for seventy-two hours – a safe margin of error, since all being well they would be able to get their material through Oslo to Heathrow in a day. It had to stay frozen, for the same reason they were there in the first place – if the molecular RNA they were looking for thawed out, it would start to disintegrate.

As for samples going to North America, if the import permits didn't come through in time, they could either store them in a bio-safety freezer at Heathrow – which was expensive – or they could take them to Mill Hill and hold them there. 'In which case,' Daniels groused good-naturedly, 'we'll have to buy another freezer.'

He'd already brought one freezer up to Svalbard in one of the cargo containers; it had cost £319.99, it could store things down to −20°C, and it was, he said, 'a vital piece of kit. That's *got* to work. And if it doesn't . . .' He looked up the valley to the mass of ice in the Longyear glacier, snaking down between the mountains under the murky grey sky, and he grinned. 'Well,' he said, 'presumably you can find a freezer here.'

Apart from freezers, natural or otherwise, another example of Daniels' practical ingenuity was a set of four black plastic foot baths. These would go in a shower unit in the annexe tent, to be used when the pathology team washed off after work; you needed them because the decon-

taminant was biodegradable after forty-eight hours, so you
had to keep it in something until it was ready to pour away.
So what was he using? Cattle foot-rot baths from an animal
husbandry supplier, priced at £566 the set.

Daniels' equipment manifest was a pretty extraordinary
piece of paperwork all round. There were, for example, four
'burnbins' to put 'sharps' in – scalpel blades, broken corers,
anything that might perforate a barrier suit. There was
Araldite and a Mastic gun to seal the specimen containers,
and 'enough polythene tubing to wrap up the world'. There
were:

Four Martindale half-suit respirators, £1,645
Six pairs knee protectors, £34.56
Sixty Tyvex body suits from Du Pont, £247.80
Twenty-four pairs Marigold washing-up gloves, £38.64
Two Metabo drills, £442
100 J-cloths, £9.40
One dustpan, £1.87

In all, the bill for the medical kit – just the medical kit
– came to £9,948.39. It was only a fraction of the total
budget, even so – and as time went by, and the hole slowly
opened up, some of the people who were spending that
money were growing visibly more tense. I bumped into
Kirsty Duncan at the Svalbard Polar that morning; she'd just
returned from the cemetery, after doing an interview there
with Tom Bergan for German TV. The night before, she'd
got to bed at one-thirty in the morning, after writing the
daily update for the project's website; it was, she said, the
earliest she'd managed so far. With it being daylight all night,
she'd then only managed to stay asleep until four. She was,

she admitted, 'tired out of my head. Stressed to the max.'

In April in Toronto, she'd told me she did 1,000 sit-ups a day. Now she said eagerly, her eyes forever wide and beseeching, that her daily sit-up count had doubled to 2,000, with 500 press-ups thrown in for good measure. You could only look at her and wonder at what point diligence and determination tilted over into obsession; at what point healthy exercise became unhealthily manic. Because here she was at the climax of five years' work, with nothing she could do until they found the bodies, and not a lot she could do even then. Would there be virus? Remember the first rule of exhumation: You don't know what you've got until you look . . .

Noël Roberts, whose company had put up half the funding, looked across the yellow fencing round the tent at the jumble of pallets and boards, gas tanks and tools; by now the graveyard looked like a rudimentary construction site. While others fretted, he seemed patient and self-contained; he was a pleasant, mild-mannered Yorkshireman of fifty-four, one of whose goals when he reached retirement was to write a book mapping a new coast-to-coast walking route from north to south Wales.

Now he said, 'If one in ten projects works out, you're doing well – and that's why it's expensive. Because a lot of what you try doesn't work.'

6 RESPECT AND DIGNITY

You know you're a long way from home when you ask at your hotel reception for a stamp to go on a postcard to England, and the receptionist says, 'Is England in Europe?' And you know you're in a small community when the woman at the counter of the local museum also appears in one of the postcards on sale at that counter as 'Norwegian girl wearing the vernacular costume'.

The coldest temperature on record on Svalbard is −46.3°C, in March 1986. The coldest month is February, when the average is 16°C below; with the aid of the Gulf Stream, mean temperatures from June through September do nudge over zero, though 1.8°C in June and 0.4°C in September hardly rate as balmy. For a remote and icy place, however, Svalbard has more history than you'd imagine.

Around 100 flint and slate objects have been found there, of which half are pretty certainly manmade. This has led some archaeologists to argue that people from a Stone Age culture, probably the Russian Pechora people, were present in the archipelago about 5,000 years ago. Since no evidence of any dwelling site has been found, however, the case for this isn't widely accepted.

Norse seamen may have sailed to the islands many centuries ago; Icelandic annals state that 'Svalbard is found' in 1194, but again, the evidence is so thin that few historians are convinced. The Russians claim that the Pomors, hunters from the White Sea, were wintering there at least as early as the fifteenth century, but a definitive record of the islands doesn't appear until 17 June 1596. On that date the Dutch seafarer Willem Barentsz, making his third attempt to find a north-east passage to China, made a detailed entry in his log noting the discovery of land 'high and all covered by snow'. He called it Spitsbergen ('spiky mountains') by which name Svalbard's largest island is still known.

Eleven years later, Henry Hudson sailed by Svalbard; his reports of an abundance of whales spurred competing nations, particularly the Dutch and English, to go whaling there. The Muscovy Company sent the first expedition in 1611, with a team of specialist Basque whalers; the Dutch and Spanish tried to join in the following year, but were driven off by a fleet of seven armed English ships.

Sporadic conflicts over hunting rights and sovereignty flared up through the next century and a half; by the end of the seventeenth century around 200 ships were active in the area, mostly Dutch and German, and the Dutch land station of Smeerenburg ('Blubber Town') probably housed over 100 men. They took the Greenland or Bowhead Right whale for soap, oil, and baleen to go in corsets and umbrellas; forty-five to sixty feet long, weighing from fifty to 100 tons, an average whale could yield 17,500 litres of oil.

In the eighteenth century, the whale population around Svalbard began to fall away drastically, and the trade declined. By that time, the Pomors had been hunting and trapping there for at least 200 years, taking reindeer, seal, walrus, fox and polar bears; they were joined by the Norwegians from about 1780. The first documented survival through a Svalbard winter had been managed by eight marooned English whalers in 1630–31, but fur-trapping Pomors may have stayed there through the long Arctic night a good while before then.

The Pomors lived on rye bread, peas, linseed oil, honey, sour milk, salted meat, cod and halibut; they ate smoked reindeer meat and tongues, as well as seabirds, geese and seals. Apart from furs, walrus were their prize catch; walrus tusks, two feet long or more, were valued higher than ivory because they didn't yellow. In the Svalbard Museum there's a walrus head bigger than a man's torso, with tiny eyes, and a peculiar resemblance to Winston Churchill; there's also a trapper's skeleton in his coffin, still wearing his knee-high wool stockings, from the first half of the seventeenth century.

Scientific exploration began in earnest in the late eighteenth century (on the Phipps expedition in 1773, a fourteen-year-old midshipman named Horatio Nelson fought off a polar bear with the butt of a broken musket) and it developed dramatically in the next 100 years. English, French, Russian, Swedish and Norwegian expeditions either studied Svalbard itself, or used it as a jumping-off point to try to reach the North Pole; some were engaged in science for science's sake, while others prospected for minerals. They found gypsum, phosphorite, anhydrite, silver and marble, but only coal was profitable.

Coal had been taken by sealers and yachting tourists for some time before any attempt at industrial exploitation began. Credit for the first commercial mining is attributed to Soren Zachariassen from Tromso in 1899; in the next few years several companies were formed, mostly by Norwegians, but they were short of capital and soon sold out to larger Russian, Dutch, British and American concerns.

The Svalbard Museum's foyer has a collection of their claim signs, some of them no more than hand-written scrawls on planks. The prospectors came from Bremen and Bergen, Stuttgart and Stavanger; one board quixotically announces, 'This is the property of the Earl of Morton, and the Lord Balfour of Burleigh'.

The Sheffield-based Spitzbergen Coal & Trading Company built Advent City, the first mining settlement, in 1904; John Munroe Longyear formed the Arctic Coal Company two years later, and by 1911, Longyear City was home to 200 men producing 29,000 tons of coal. During the First World War, hungry for a reliable coal supply (imports from England had more than halved), the Norwegian Government pushed the country's five biggest banks into a syndicate to buy out Longyear; the Store Norske Spitsbergen Kulkompani was formed in 1916 to take over this operation.

Meanwhile, the industrial boomlet on Svalbard had drawn the various nations involved into a series of conferences trying to resolve the issue of sovereignty. No settlement had been arrived at when war broke out; by the time of the Versailles Peace Conference, however, Norway's position on the issue had strengthened considerably. Apart from buying out Longyear, the Norwegians had credit in the bank with the Allies because, though Norway was neutral, her merchant fleet had helped them during the conflict. So a commission with representatives from France, Italy, Great Britain and the United States duly granted Norway sovereignty in a treaty signed by the Norwegians in February 1920.

It was a sovereignty hedged with certain restrictions; all signatories to the treaty had equal rights to exploit the archipelago's resources, and in theory they continue to do so today. (If your country is a signatory, for example, you don't need a passport to go there.) However, since the Norwegian Government passed a law in 1925 finally settling on the formulation that 'Svalbard is a part of the Kingdom of Norway', and creating the post of governor, or *sysselmann*, to administer it, the archipelago has been a Norwegian entity.

In the early twenties, with coal prices high, Dutch, British and Swedish mining interests were still active on Svalbard; after the Depression set in, when the Russians joined the treaty arrangement in 1935, only they and the Norwegians remained. A Soviet state trust called Arktikugol ran two mining settlements at Pyramiden and Barentsburg, the latter so called because it was originally Dutch; boat trips to visit these communities from Longyearbyen are now a popular tourist activity, because the contrast between the well-heeled Norwegian town and the straitened Russian settlements is so striking.

The Russians have no money, literally. Arktikugol did try to introduce a company rouble, but the Norwegians wouldn't have it; the miners' wages are therefore paid (if they're paid at all) directly into their bank accounts in Moscow or Kiev, while the settlements are cash-free, self-sufficient operations. They are, in a way, odd little remnant hangovers of the Communist age; Barentsburg has a greenhouse to grow vegetables, it farms its own stock of pigs and cattle, and the company store rations out other essential supplies.

In Barentsburg Lenin still stands on his plinth, and every year there's a Miners' Day, during which the most Stakhanovite toiler at the coalface receives a medal for his productivity. If this sounds bleak, however, it's an indication of how bad things are in Russia now: when Arktikugol started winding down Pyramiden, the Russians who had to leave for home were reported to have wept openly at the prospect.

As for the Norwegians, though the coal mining is hopelessly uneconomic (and is, therefore, somewhat ironically subsidized by the proceeds of North Sea oil), there's no chance they'll ever wind down Longyearbyen. Their presence, estimated by an official at the *sysselmann*'s office to cost the Government around £45,000,000 a year, is as much political as economic; it's a concrete assertion of the sovereignty accorded to the Norwegians in the treaty.

The rich coalfield that Store Norsk wants to work, fifty miles south of Longyearbyen at Sveagruva, isn't easy to get to; the company talks of building a road there, but in the unlikely event that they could get that past the environmentalists, the cost would almost certainly be prohibitive. Whether mining continues or not, however, Longyearbyen certainly will. Tourism is one seam that will be harder worked in the future; already 20,000 people drop in every year from passing cruise liners to buy woolly jumpers and carved glass polar bears, while the 10,000 visitors who now fly in direct are twice the number that went there five years ago.

There are four hotels; the locals run trips into the wilderness by foot, horse, husky or snowmobile, depending on the season. On the day when I climbed the Lars glacier behind the town the weather was bright, it was 11°C, and the Adventfjord glittered between rugged and treeless mountains far beneath us. Our guide Thomas Vold had a Winchester

.308, and a winning manner. He said, 'If you don't work up a sweat in the mountains once in a while, you're not a true Norwegian.'

Putting on the crampons was slightly fiddly, but easy enough; roped up and spike-booted, we crunched across the ice following the serpentine gullies of meltwater streams. Some had carved crevasses too deep for the eye to fathom, in which veins of turquoise ice shone as brilliant as shards of fallen sky.

It was a six-hour hike up the Lars to the crest of the Sarcophagus, then back down the Longyear glacier on the other side. From the top of the ridge, we stared across a chill and barren vastness of ice, scree and tundra, and Thomas fished out a Thermos. That sums up Svalbard; it's as near to the North Pole as you can get and still be comfortable.

Seen from the Sarcophagus, the tent concealing the dig site far below was a tiny fleck of colour in the wastes of white and grey. Besides tourism, science is increasingly Svalbard's other big earner. In the past, from whaling and walrus-hunting onwards, any activity there always had an element of political motivation, people saying, in effect, 'It's ours because we're here.' In economic terms, however, Svalbard's Cultural Heritage Officer Hein Bjerck said, 'They've always been producing for the wider world here, whether it's walrus tusks or weather reports.'

In 1996, there were 146 different scientific projects offi- cially in progress on Svalbard – mostly biology, geology and geophysics – and in an environment like that, given the assent of the families of the 1918 miners, the idea that the local authorities might ever *not* have given permission for Kirsty Duncan's project is pretty much inconceivable. It did help that she'd gone through all the proper channels, and had done so in a proper way, but the authorities didn't just want this thing doing, they wanted everybody to know about it too. Bjerck said, when the team had come to do the GPR survey in 1997, bringing a scattering of the media in tow, 'They wanted to have as little contact with the press as possible. So from this office we've said that they had to have a way to deal with this. It was one of our demands for approving the project that they should give press conferences. So they've done that, and I think it's well handled now.'

Of course, the media can be a pain in the neck. Bjerck said, 'It's very easy to see how something could go wrong. Last week the TV found the daughter of one of the men, and they asked her really personal questions. Had she been to Longyearbyen? Had she known her father? Did she have a picture? Was he a good-looking man? And I was just waiting for them to ask, What kind of person are you that would allow this Canadian lady to dig up your father? I was kind of nervous. They can cause a lot of pain.'

With that in mind, proper management of the media was seen by the *sysselman*'s office as essential – and that included making sure they had adequate access. Elizabeth Aarsaether, the official responsible for Svalbard's PR, said, 'In the first case the scientists didn't want people in the tent at all, and we said that's not acceptable to us. We have to know that the public gets enough information. We're concerned that people all around the world get to know about this project.'

Still, not everyone was happy; the French and the *New York Times* crews groused that they weren't getting enough material from Elliott Halpern's crew in the tent. Halpern's outfit, understandably, retorted that unlike anyone else they had (through the agency of NRK) been speaking to the project team and the *sysselman*'s office for the best part of a year to arrange their access. If the others hadn't done that, it was a bit late in the day to start complaining now, and a bit rich to expect them to share every image they got.

The scientists shuttled back and forth to meetings with Aarsaether, trying to fix these disputes; meanwhile, the Norwegian stills photographer who also had access cleared off. In theory, a guy from Svalbard's local paper was supposed to deputize for him, but when another Norwegian snapper then turned up at the cemetery, the local man wasn't around either.

The Norwegian started working his mobile, and found himself in a surreal Catch 22. The *syssleman*'s office said he could go in the tent if the scientists agreed to that, but all the scientists were in the tent already. So he said, 'How can I go in the tent to ask if I can go in the tent?'

If that was a conundrum, in the next few days things would get much stranger still.

On the Monday afternoon, it was pouring with rain; people said it was the wettest week of the year, maybe the wettest week ever. Charles Smith shrugged and said, 'There's no such thing as bad weather on Svalbard. Just bad clothing.'

He was modelling the barrier suit for the media; his assistant on the sampling team, Barry Blenkinsop from the Coroner's Office in Toronto, was flying in the next day. Rod Daniels would be their back-up technician; one of the Norwegian scientists would be their link man. As for the protective clothing they'd all wear, the first thing to go on was a thermal body suit; in dry runs, Smith had discovered that working in a hole in the tundra in an outfit that had air pumping through it was a pretty chilly experience.

Over the thermals they'd wear a white Tyvex body suit, a 'bunny suit'; Tyvex is wind-, water-, chemical- and tear-resistant, so tough that in Canada it's now wrapped around houses before the outer layer of brick goes on. Wearing one of these, all that's exposed are your hands, feet and face. Over this, they'd wear bright yellow, puncture-resistant plastic trousers with elasticated waists; these had ankle cuffs to snap-seal round their wellington boots. Over their upper bodies, they'd wear the Martindale half-suits; bright yellow again, with a clear cylindrical helmet, they looked like something out of B-movie sci-fi.

Smith worried that in the cold, the plastic got pretty stiff; he said it made it awkward, and they'd have to watch that it didn't crack or puncture. What made it colder was that the suit had a hose running up the back attached to a black, battery-powered pump, like a little electric fanny pack. This filtered air down to 0.2 microns and blew pressure into the suit so that if there was a puncture, air (and any infective material) would go out and not in; it also had the side-effect of turning the wearer into a passable version of the Michelin Man. The more serious downside was that in the cold draught, it wasn't long before your fingers went numb.

They'd wear several pairs of gloves, at least two of them latex, partly for warmth, partly to guard against punctures. Then they had strap-on plastic knee pads, elasticated green sleeve protectors from wrist to elbow for an extra seal over the arms of the suit, and a green plastic apron, also to protect the suit.

For the final touch, they'd gone to see the director of the mine. Smith said, 'We began to play in the environment here, and we thought we could do the exhumations in a more narrow pit, but that creates lighting problems. So we got clip-on miners' lamps that go on the front of your shoulder, like little spotlights.' It was, he said, 'kind of ironic – using a miner's lamp to dig up miners'.

We were talking in one of the cargo containers, away from the dank and sodden weather. Boards and packing cases leaned against the metal sides; the mechanical digger whined and scraped in the glacial riverbed beneath us. John Oxford came in and said the Necropolis team were about a foot down now, and Smith professed himself encouraged. Indeed, he really couldn't wait to get going.

He said, 'Is there viral material present? Are there any other superimposed bacterial infections? Can bacteria survive eighty years in the ground? That's a question the Norwegian Government are particularly interested in; given global warming, is anybody buried in permafrost a potentially infectious object? And this exhumation can answer these questions.

'So we have over two hundred coring devices, and six bodies we're allowed to sample. The most important thing is lung, the upper and lower portions of both lungs. I want to see if we can get trachea. I'd like heart – heart may be the best source of a piece of frozen blood, a little hunk of blood-coloured ice cube. Then you'd have serum from the acute phase of Spanish flu; there's people who'd *love* a crack at that. Then I want liver, for the toxicology; it'd be fascinating to know what kind of drugs were on board these men. Cough suppressants in at least some parts of the world at that time contained opiates; that'd be interesting to look at. Then I want intestine. If I can hit spleen, I will. We want brain . . .'

I asked if he ever wondered what it sounded like, calmly stood there saying he wanted brain, he wanted liver, he wanted lung . . .

He laughed and said, 'It sounds pretty awful, I know. My wife's a medical coroner, so we get involved in cases that are in the news, and then my kids take stories to school from the supper table to gross out the other kids. You know what it's like in the schoolyard.'

Outside, the rain kept drizzling down. The doors of the container stood open, looking down the valley to the fjord; the container was set over a ditch six feet wide by the side of the road, with a silty, pale brown stream flowing fast along the bottom. For easy access to the container, a plywood board had been laid across the ditch in front of the doorway.

It was 4.14 in the afternoon. Suddenly there was a loud crash of heavy boots on the board. I jumped and turned to see one of the gravediggers, Roger Webber's son Keith, flying in through the doorway looking wide-eyed, breathless, and more than a little scared. He barked out, 'Charles, you're wanted. We found a box. I don't know what it is. We were just told to get out that minute.'

Smith headed immediately to the tent; a little while later he and Heginbottom leaped into a car, and careered off to fetch Duncan from the Polar. I wandered round the corner to the portakabin, and found Oxford and Daniels drinking tea, looking nervous and uncomfortable. I said, 'You've found a box then?'

Oxford crossed his arms across his chest in the classic

defensive posture. He said, 'Box? What box? Who said anything about a box?'

Shortly afterwards, I came upon Tattoo Man sitting quietly smoking a roll-up. I asked what was up and he said apologetically, 'Sorry, mate. But we've been told not to speak to anybody.'

They found three coffins that Monday afternoon, and a fourth one at five to nine on Tuesday morning. They'd barely gone a foot down.

They gave a press conference a little later that Tuesday morning, and Duncan read a short statement: 'Yesterday a fifth day of work was completed at the Svalbard Cemetery in Longyearbyen. Late in the afternoon three coffins were located a short distance below the surface of the ground. This morning a fourth coffin was located. The coffins are located in the active layer above the permafrost. Only a small portion of the upper surface of each coffin was uncovered. No attempt was made to open the coffins. The team of workers and scientists are extremely excited by these findings. The work will continue today, with ongoing attention to issues of safety and respect.'

The attendant journalists and film crews scratched their heads. How was this exciting, if the bodies were already turning up a foot deep? Weren't they meant to be frozen?

'I wouldn't want,' said one, 'to be the folks from that radar company right now.'

'Hey, they always said it wasn't necessarily that great about depth.'

'Right. One foot, eight feet, what's the difference?'

In the cemetery, they continued digging round the

coffins. They were now working, said Heginbottom, in 'remoulded late-glacial lateral moraine' – the debris stacked along the edge of the glacier when it formed the valley, which, since the glacier receded, had slid downslope and compacted. It was hard and stony – one of the Necropolis boys said it was like working in a bombsite – but it wasn't frozen, and it wouldn't be for another foot or so.

I wandered down the road to the *sysselmann*'s office, a striking structure of grey metal with an airy, high-ceilinged reception area in pale polished pine. An expanse of floor-to-ceiling glass looked out over the fjord; a stuffed polar bear stood guard in a corner.

Hein Bjerck said, 'It may look bad, you know?' He said the coffins were slanted and tipped, as if there'd been frost movement. He said, 'I kind of feel they're a bit nervous. Because they're too high. They're in the active layer. If all the coffins are that high up . . .'

Elizabeth Aarsaether said, 'If they're not in the perma-frost, the whole project will change.'

Never mind change – the whole project, I suggested, would collapse.

She laughed and said, 'Well, there's nothing to take their samples from if they're not in the permafrost. That's what I've been told, anyway.'

Kirsty Duncan would have no part in such gloomy foreboding. We spoke at the graveyard at about midday; she said, when Smith and Heginbottom first told her they'd found a coffin, 'I realized that it would have been very shallow, but despite that I was extremely excited. It's been five years looking, three years looking at this cemetery, and to find anything was exciting. It was also hard,' she said, and here she dropped her voice to that pitch of breathy, emotion-laden intensity with which followers of her project had by now become familiar, 'because I realized that some-one's grave had been disturbed.'

Well, yes. But from the point of view of the project, there must be an element in your reaction of, Oh my God . . .

'Actually there's not. We've always been prepared for this. From the very beginning Dr Smith told us, you don't know what you have until you do the work. So despite what the GPR said – a strong signal at 1.6 metres, permafrost to 0.8 metres – I personally have always been prepared for this.'

But you'd prefer not to have found anything yet?

'From a personal point of view, from the team's point of view, I'd have liked to have found coffins in the true permafrost. But I am not disappointed, because I am so proud of the way this project has been handled. I know that the work has been undertaken with the highest safety standards, it's been done professionally, and it's been done ethically and humanely. And I'm extremely proud of that.'

The word disappointment did not exist in her lexicon – and at this stage they had, of course, to continue digging, because there might well be other bodies still deeper. In the meantime, Duncan resolutely deflected any query about the possibility of failure with her standard homily about the high standards her team had set, and the very great gift they'd been given by the people of Longyearbyen in their quest to find the secrets of the 1918 virus.

By two o'clock that afternoon, however, the other three coffins had turned up. Half an hour later Rob Webster arrived, coming to the site straight from the Polar after getting off his plane. He'd not been there a few seconds before someone told him they had seven coffins in the active layer; his reaction was characteristically blunt. He said, 'Oh, shit.'

Duncan said she was excited, Webster swore, and it looked like the rest of the team didn't quite know what to say. They'd come looking for seven bodies at a site marked with seven named grave markers, they'd found seven coffins, yet the line now – the somewhat unsteady line – was that maybe these weren't the coffins they were looking for. Maybe there were more coffins underneath. Maybe these seven were some other seven. Maybe more than seven people had died of Spanish flu . . .

Peter Lewin, a paediatrician from Toronto, had arrived on the same flight as Rob Webster. Born in Jerusalem in 1935 of Jewish parents who'd fled Germany the year before, Lewin had grown up in Egypt, studied medicine at St Mary's, Paddington, then gone to Canada on National Service with the British Royal Army Medical Corps. He'd stayed, joining the Hospital for Sick Children in 1964, and he'd pursued a true polymath's range of interests. His surgery in Toronto was densely hung with native American art; on another front, he'd once dug up an Egyptian pharaoh, and proved that the mummy had smallpox.

Duncan had gone to him because of this interest in medical archaeology. He seemed now to be somewhat on the fringes of the team, but if others were leery of the media – particularly now the coffins had appeared – Lewin looked as though he loved nothing better than spouting to a camera.

Elliott Halpern, vexed and baffled at the peculiar obfuscations now emanating from the project as to whether these seven bodies were the right seven bodies or not, therefore set his cameraman on Lewin. He asked, 'Are these the bodies?'

'Oh yes,' said Lewin blithely to the lens, 'these are the bodies.'

'Thank you,' said Halpern, and walked away suppressing a grin. He'd known to ask Lewin because, he said, 'He's such a blab.'

John Oxford had told me earlier that they had seven bodies – not that they were *the* seven, necessarily, just that they had seven in all – and he'd immediately got into trouble with other members of the team for leaking to the press. Paranoia was setting in, more tangible by the hour; Charles Smith said of one member of the attendant media that, being a Christian, he'd always been taught 'to avoid all appearance of evil'.

They'd obliged Oxford to stop making his documentary for the World Service; he'd had to hand his recording kit over to his daughter. Though he'd been instrumental in raising a fair slice of the funds, Oxford like Lewin also seemed to have been marginalized, albeit for different reasons; he stood about on the edge of things, looking tired and bothered and drawn. Whether he was in or out of favour at the court of K. Duncan, however, like all the others he still desperately wanted them not to have failed.

At two o'clock on the Tuesday afternoon he told me, with a kind of glum nervousness, 'We've got seven. Well, for all I know we might have got eight. But at the moment it's seven.'

And they couldn't say these were *the* seven?

'No. One's instinct is, if there are eight, we can relax a

bit. The fact that there are seven, obviously, is ringing a few bells in our heads.'

No one else was admitting to even the faintest sound of bells. I asked, 'What bells?'

'The fact that these might be the seven we're after. Which would be pretty unfortunate, 'cause they're up at the top rather than frozen down there. And the sampling would be . . . well, three or four of them are open. There's only a couple that are sealed. And from a sampling point of view, from a virology point of view . . . well, I hope they're nothing to do with the ones we're after.'

'The coffins have opened naturally?'

'Yes. They've burst open. I don't think there's much left.'

He was determined not to let it get him down. It was a scientific expedition, he said, 'and you can't predict science, otherwise we wouldn't be here. We could just sit at home and work it all out in an armchair. So one is used to this in research, the ups and downs – and this,' he said emphatically, 'is a *slight* downer. But by this time tomorrow, we might be up again. I would say at the moment that I can't see any reason why we should pack it in. I think we should say, well, there's seven at the top – are there another seven down below? And I guess at the moment, the idea would be to press on. We're nowhere near the bottom, we're only just getting down to the permafrost . . .'

He conceded that stopping the dig was an option they should review, but he said that if they did stop, he'd think that a serious mistake. They still didn't know for sure what they had; he was clinging to the hope that they might yet find something deeper. At this point, he said, 'We've got seven coffins, full stop. If those are the seven we're looking for, then that will be very disappointing, obviously. On the other hand, they may not be the seven. They might be seven German soldiers killed in the Second World War. Lots of unfortunate things have happened here; we can't jump to conclusions yet. We have to wait a bit, have a look at them, see if they're men or women, what age they are, all that kind of stuff, and I don't think it'll be too long now before we have all the facts to hand. So I'm fairly relaxed about it.'

With good humour, he made a tense little scrunched-up face as he said this, as if to say, Relaxed? With a quarter of a million pounds turning into skeletons before my eyes? Of *course* I'm relaxed . . .

It was just the nature of research. He said firmly, 'I think you take things as they come. If I'd got myself wound up . . . well, I'd have been dead many years ago. It's like laboratory work – you plan these experiments for months, you come in one day, it's all bloody gone wrong, so you do it again. You don't give up. So I know what the rest of the team are feeling, I know Rod's a bit depressed, but we'll be pressing on. My first thought was, it was a dynamite box, not a coffin at all. Could have been a Mills bomb box, anything. Then my second thought was, well, in the war the village here was destroyed, you had the *Scharnhorst* sitting in the harbour – so still my thoughts now centre round Germany and the Second World War.'

When I asked how he arrived at that idea, he said, 'You could have seven burials from the Second World War on top. I don't think we should knock the scenario, for example, if you've got foreigners here, there's an explosion, something happens, there's seven soldiers dead, you think, my God, it's

October 1944, you look around and someone says, there's a First World War cemetery up there, 1918, it says on it. It wouldn't say influenza, would it? So they say, Ah, Hans, we'll take 'em up there. Dig down, hit the permafrost, ooh, don't fancy that. We'll do our respects now, cover 'em up, and go and tell Mum about it. Then they go to the Eastern Front, never seen again, no one knows about it, and there they are quietly sitting up there. I mean, that's one scenario. You might say it's wishful thinking . . .'

Looking back now, it seems to me something far more than wishful thinking, and something far better too. Oxford's German soldier scenario was more of a full-scale fantasy, developed in fabulous detail, lovingly intricate and inventive. Born of desperation, I'm sorry to have to say that it was also total nonsense.

Rod Daniels went to work in one of the cargo containers, making decontaminant solution for the foot bath. He said grimly, 'I'm not despondent. We'll get something.'

Halpern's camera crew blocked the doorway, filming as he worked, and Daniels did his best to field their questions. Yes, they'd be taking samples now. They had to; with the coffins disturbed and air getting at the remains, 'Things are happening that we don't want.' No, they wouldn't be wearing their protective clothing; there was no risk of infective virus now. And, no, they wouldn't be using the tissue corers either.

He didn't say it in as many words but the bottom line was, there wasn't enough tissue there to be cored; all the equipment they'd so painstakingly prepared had been rendered redundant.

As the questions came in, Daniels tried hard to stay

patient and polite, but his manner was glum and fatigued, all enthusiasm dulled, and his answers were short. The best he could say was, 'If there's anything there, we'll find it.'

Shortly afterwards, at 4.25, Duncan read a short statement. She stood at the foot of the blue plastic pathway to the gravesite surrounded by the rest of her team, facing Halpern's outfit, the French documentary crew, the guy with the handicam from the Canadian *Discovery* channel, and a couple of newspaper journalists.

She said, 'Today is the sixth day of work at the Svalbard Cemetery in Longyearbyen. A total of seven bodies have now been located a short distance from the surface of the ground. We have many reasons to believe that these are the coffins of the seven young men for whom we have been searching. All seven coffins are in the active layer above the permafrost. To date, no attempt has been made to open the coffins. Limited sampling will now begin, and I'm afraid we won't answer any questions as work has to begin now. At nine o'clock tomorrow morning we'll be able to answer any questions. Thank you.'

Then she got into a car and was driven away. The media, unenlightened and restive, hung about in huddled bunches, muttering in her wake. We told each other, if the whole point was to find bodies in permafrost, and now they were sampling bodies that weren't, then they might just as well have dug up someone in Toronto.

One of Halpern's people summed up her statement thus: 'They may fail. But they're damned if they're going to fail in front of us.'

The saddest thing was, nobody wanted them to fail. I've seen some ugly press packs in my time, and this wasn't one of them; this was a handful of people with a genuine interest in what the scientists were doing, and who genuinely wanted their project to succeed. From a selfish point of view, obviously, they'd get better stories if the project succeeded – but if it didn't, they were also people who understood well enough that science was difficult, and more often than not, when you tried things, they didn't work out.

They understood, moreover, all the time, labour and emotion that Duncan had invested in this. She'd spent five years looking for frozen bodies, and they worried, therefore, that to say she was happy and excited when the bodies weren't frozen at all indicated, at best, a somewhat alarming refusal to confront reality. What would it mean to her, after all, when a goal pursued with such determination for so long turned out to be no more than mush and bones?

When Duncan got home, said one troubled observer, 'She is going to hit the ground like a B52 falling out of the sky.'

I had, in fact, already asked her what she'd do when she got home. She'd said, 'I will continue to administer the project.'

At which one could only now wonder, What project?

Over breakfast in the Polar on Wednesday morning, Halpern got word that at nine o'clock the team planned once again to issue a statement but take no questions. He talked to Heginbottom and told him if that were the case, it wouldn't be too good an idea. If you don't disclose, if the media aren't informed, then the media will speculate; you'll get stories going out like, 'Observers are saying that the failed expedition . . .'

Apart from myself and the three TV crews (the *New York Times* had cleared off by now) John Oxford's daughter was doing a feature for the *Independent on Sunday*, and two other journalists had flown in from North America. One was from Duncan's local paper, the *Windsor Star*, and the other was from the *Atlanta Constitution* which, with the CDC in its bailiwick, had good reason to cover this story. Both papers, of course, could syndicate these two writers' stories across Canada and the States, so to continue saying nothing to them really wouldn't be smart. Hill & Knowlton, of course, could have pointed that out – but Hill & Knowlton, it appeared, had been cold-shouldered.

Come nine o'clock at the cemetery, the team went into confab in the portakabin, and emerged ten minutes later. With Smith, Heginbottom, Oxford, Webster, Daniels and one of the Necropolis team standing behind her, Duncan said, 'Good morning, everyone. We'd like to update you on what happened yesterday, and what will be happening today. Yesterday the team completed a seventh successful day at the cemetery in Longyearbyen. Late in the afternoon one of the coffins was opened, and samples were carefully taken. The body was that of an apparently healthy young male. There were no identifying marks. In view of the unique nature of this project, the team will be excavating today down into the permafrost layer. We are now happy to entertain your questions. We are grateful for your interest.'

It made no sense. How was this successful? And if they'd found their seven bodies, why go into the permafrost?

Heginbottom said they had to do that to see what, if anything, was down there. As for the bodies, they were, said Smith, 'Largely skeletonized remains.' From these, we were told, they'd taken samples of bone, and of the tissue surrounding it.

The woman from the *Windsor Star* asked if they'd got any tissue from the lungs or the respiratory tract. Smith said, 'The body was largely skeletonized. Materials from the areas we were interested in were sampled.'

She pressed him further. She said, 'Can I qualify that? There was no tissue remaining from the lung or the respiratory area?'

'There were no identifiable structures apart from the bone.'

As each question was asked, Duncan appointed one of the scientists around her to answer it as appropriate. Her tone was an odd mix of earnest humility and queenly grandeur; she'd say, 'Dr Daniels will answer,' as if she were marshalling a group of students.

They were pressed on how much they'd found, on how they'd gathered it, on whether they had confirmation that these were indeed their seven bodies. The corpses, it transpired, had been wrapped in newspaper, fragments of which still remained; they hoped for clues from that. We went around the issue of the GPR scan for a while, then someone said, 'How would you describe the feelings of the team about this find?'

Duncan said, 'I will address that question. We are delighted. We are extremely excited by what we've found. And we are certainly looking forward to the next few days of work. But we are very, very excited.'

'Are you not disappointed?'

'We are not disappointed at all. We were able to take samples. After five years of work we were able to take samples, we took many samples, and I know the research scientists are looking forward to getting back to the lab and beginning to analyse those samples.'

It beggared belief. For all that one could sympathize with their predicament, the bottom line was that they'd come looking for frozen bodies, and these bodies weren't. Pressed on this point, however, Duncan refused point-blank to concede. She said again, 'This is not disappointing at all. Any information on the 1918 flu would be invaluable. And we've collected good samples, and we are hoping to obtain that information.'

Smith backed her up; he said when Webster was receiving the samples in the tent, 'He looked like a young boy in a candy store.'

Pushing past this somewhat morbid image, Halpern asked bluntly, 'If you'd known the bodies would be found in the active layer, would you have gone forward with the project?'

Webster said of course they would – directly contradicting what Duncan had written to the *sysselmann* when, in September the year before, she'd applied for permission to dig. She'd said then that if there was evidence that the bodies weren't well preserved, they would not proceed.

'How many places in the world,' Webster asked now, 'are you going to find samples from 1918? At least stored in a cool situation . . . ?'

But they weren't meant to be cool, they were meant to be *frozen*. Every interview, every press conference, every statement for years had been permafrost, permafrost, permafrost. Halpern said wrily, 'They're better preserved than they would have been in Memphis . . .'

'OK, thanks,' said Webster, 'I'm going to go and do what I have to do this morning.'

End of press conference – and why they felt the need to act like this I don't know. Reputation was at stake, of course, with some big names signed on the bottom of some fair-sized grant applications, and, certainly, it would have been irresponsible not to take whatever samples they could. All the same, the plain fact was that they'd come for frozen bodies, what they'd got was skeletons, and saying they were happy about it made them look foolish. On top of which – for all that their party line now involved giving nothing away to the media beyond these stiflingly surreal gatherings at the graveyard – this internally fractious project leaked like a sieve anyway.

The tissue on the skeletons, assorted parties learned off the record, was 'soft black goopy material', 'like mushy Granola'. On the record, having enough common sense about him to be reasonably open, and struggling sometimes to veil his exasperation at the way this was being handled, Rod Daniels said, 'The state of the material we've collected yesterday does not fill me with confidence.' As for whether they'd have bothered, if they'd known the bodies were only a foot underground, he said simply, 'We would not have come back to this site.'

So why behave like this? He said wearily, 'Putting a brave face on it. But look, you're a journalist. You can see what's going on.' Then he shrugged and said, 'It's been a great adventure. It'll be sad if we don't get anything out of it – but we'll do what we can to ensure that we do.'

It was a lovely blue day; the sun was shining, and the glaciers sparkled in the distance. I went off and climbed them with Thomas Vold and his Winchester, wondering how many mild summer days like this one had thawed through those bodies in the past eighty years.

Duncan's team started acting like a cult. They'd hold their meetings of an evening at the Polar, then emerge in the morning touting a new line in direct contradiction to that of a day or a week before. I have more quotes than I can count about how the bodies were supposed to be frozen, about how virus won't survive if it's frozen and thawed, frozen and thawed, yet this was now airbrushed from history with a Stalinist ruthlessness.

They should have openly accepted that they'd tried something, that they'd had rotten luck, and that it hadn't come out as they'd have wished. Instead, they sought to prevent any member of the group from speaking freely to the media; they behaved with a secretive paranoia that became doubly comical when Duncan gaily told me, 'People have said to me that they've never seen scientists make themselves so available.'

So what are they like when they clam up? At some point, several boxes stuffed with Hill & Knowlton press packs arrived; when I asked for one, John Oxford felt obliged to tell me unhappily that he didn't think he should let me have it before the others on the team had seen it, in case he got into trouble again. Halpern laughed, and said the diggers had run out of wooden pallets; maybe they could use the press packs to stack things on instead.

Duncan, the high priestess of this increasingly weird sect, was protected by her Canadian acolytes Heginbottom and Smith; the former said nothing, while the latter said all was for the best. Earnestly he told me, 'There are no failures here.' Anyway, he said, 'I don't dwell on the praise of men.'

Meanwhile Webster, their prophet in the wilderness, having smartly recovered from his initial shock ('Oh, shit') now stoutly declaimed that all would be revealed in the laboratory – a pretty good fallback, this one, seeing we could hardly all follow him in there. As for the British, they just shuffled about and looked uncomfortable. All in all, it was no kind of advert for academia.

On the morning of Friday, 28 September, they turned out at the graveyard to dispense more jewels of Duncanist revisionism. As usual, she'd dressed for the press – this morning she wore purple velvet trousers, a smart dark jacket, lipstick and a string of pearls.

She commenced her performance. 'Before we start today,' she told us, 'I would like to remind you of the aims of this project. The aim of this phase of the work is to recover soft tissue samples. If we were lucky enough to recover soft tissue samples, we would move to Phase 3 of the work, the actual analyses in the lab. So the aim of this part is to recover soft-tissue samples.'

She spoke slowly, as if we were a collection of idiots – and this was a canny new formulation, too. Soft tissue, of course, my God – why hadn't we realized that before?

'Yesterday,' she continued, 'five coffins were carefully opened and sampled. Previously a sixth coffin had been opened. We were not allowed to touch the seventh coffin. I want to assure you that this work was undertaken main-taining safety standards, and respect and dignity for the deceased. The six bodies that were found were those of young, healthy males. This further suggested that these were the bodies of the young miners. The team has been discouraged by reports of disappointment because the bodies were not found in the permafrost. Again, it is important to remember that this part of the project was to recover soft tissue. Yesterday,' and here her voice slowed and tremulously lowered, 'I am delighted to tell you, we recovered soft tissues. We achieved our aim. And because of this, we can now move to Phase 3.

'Late yesterday afternoon, there was a very dramatic event. In examining the last samples of the last coffin, one of the team members noted a date on the newspaper. We have been looking for dates. It was 1917. This further suggested that these were the burials of the young miners. Last night back at the hotel, we had a long discussion, and the team decided to continue looking in the permafrost in case there were further possible burials. Finally, I would like to say that we are *so* excited about the findings. We can now move to Phase 3, and we hope that you are equally excited. Thank you. Now the team will entertain your questions.'

The writer from the *Windsor Star* was a pleasant, mild-mannered but bluntly diligent woman called Anne Jarvis. She now asked, 'How much tissue was recovered from the five bodies yesterday?'

Duncan said, 'I'll let Dr Smith and Mr Barry Blenkinsop of the Chief Coroner's Office answer your question.'

Smith said, 'There were a significant number of samples taken from each body. Not necessarily all of the same samples from every body, but a significant number.'

'Can you define significant? You told us maybe a hundred grams from the first body . . .'

'Yesterday, significant was defined for me by the

reaction of the people I was working with. The virologists' reaction to the material was such that I was greatly encouraged by what we found.'

'What parts of the bodies were you able to get tissue from? Did you get respiratory tract, or lung?'

Smith said, 'We were able to identify tissues from more than one body site. But we decided last night that at this point, it would not be best to enumerate in detail all of the organs or all of the tissues that were sampled.'

Jarvis's reaction – as with all of us – was irked and disbelieving. Did they think they were talking state secrets here? Jarvis said simply, 'Why's that?'

'It was a team decision.' Smith's syntax now somewhat deserted him. He said, 'It was felt that at that time, just because they've only been taken and packaged, this was simply the gathering time, this is not the analysis time.'

Jarvis pressed on. What condition were the bodies in? Were they better than the first one? Blenkinsop cut in and said, 'Well, to varying degrees. And, um, to allow sufficient samples for everybody's needs. But I think it's important not to say the type of samples. These are the members of people's families, and I think that this sort of information should be communicated through the scientific community to them. Not at this point.'

With an admirable doggedness Jarvis pointed out, 'It was publicized originally that the team were looking for samples from certain areas. Lung, brain – that was all publicized in the first place. So why not say now?'

Duncan went into sincerity overdrive, her voice dramatically low and husky, breaking with emotion. She said, 'It's different. We now have samples, and it's important to remember that these were seven young men who died tragically. It's important that we remember the very great gift these families have given us, and the people here. Most of us are afforded privacy in death. We would like to at this time maintain their privacy.'

One of the journalists said to me later, 'If she breaks down in tears on me one more time about the tragic deaths of these seven young men, I think I'll throw up.'

Why weren't they saying what they had? It was impossible to tell, but it was hard to avoid the conclusion that they didn't have anything much, and that certain parties couldn't bear to admit it.

They burbled on for a while about their bit of newspaper with a date on it, and about how they were going to go on digging in case anyone else had died of Spanish flu. The logic here, as in so much of this situation, escaped me. You've got seven deaths recorded in the company diary, you've got seven grave markers, you dig, you get seven coffins – so what more is there to dig for?

Halpern gave Duncan another opportunity to allow her lip to tremble. He asked, 'Is it possible to get any indication for viewers of the state of the coffins?'

Duncan said, 'No, I'm afraid not. Most of us in death are accorded privacy.' Again her voice fell, and the tears seemed to well in her eyes as she continued, 'These seven young men haven't been given that. We've been given a very great gift, which I know everybody treasures, in being allowed to do this work. We would not violate that gift, and to allow filming in the tent,' she concluded, in an intensely dramatic whisper, '*would be a violation.*'

Halpern asked mildly, 'Has there been any filming or photography in the tent?'

Duncan stared. Smith jumped in and said, 'Photographic references for scientific purposes were made all the way up to the end . . .'

Duncan recovered herself to chip in, 'And this is with the full support of the Governor of Svalbard. It is important to have scientific documentation.'

The questions dwindled away; there wasn't much point asking them, if you didn't get any answers. Everyone looked at each other; after a long pause Duncan said, 'If there are no further questions, I'd just like to say two further things. One, this team is elated. Absolutely *elated* . . .'

Smith butted in with a tribute to the Necropolis crew, which was more than well deserved. When he was done Duncan said, 'Thank you, Dr Smith. The last thing I want to say is that we are elated. But I want you to know that we have never forgotten that these were seven young men, and that all the work has been done with great respect and dignity.'

Webster then presented her with a customized T-shirt sporting an illustration of a flu virus beneath the legend, 'Get A Grippe!'

There was a bit of joshing about among the scientists at this sartorial quip, and some random milling around. At some point as the conference broke up, Duncan asked Halpern, 'Did the respect and dignity come across?'

Halpern contained himself and said, 'I think that was pretty clear.'

The team went for a meeting at the *sysselman*'s office. When they got back, they found that the sodden walls of the pit were collapsing into the hole; they decided to call it a day.

'So,' said one of Halpern's people, 'it's all over bar the recriminations.'

I took a ride on the MS *Langoysund* up Tempelfjord to the joint face of the Tuna-Von Post glaciers. The Lars and the Longyear are babies by comparison; the face of these two where they carve into the fjord is three miles across, 130 feet tall, and breathtakingly lovely.

The fjord is lined with titanic, jagged ochre-grey cliffs, a bleached Arctic version of Monument Valley, wreathed that morning in scarves of milky cloud. As we approached the glacier the water became strewn with chunks of ice, gleaming white and blue, until there was a constant scrape and clunk of these mini-bergs beneath the hull. Just yards away from the ice wall the boat hove to, and we were served a tot of whisky with a chunk of glacier in it.

It was rock hard, many thousands of years old, full of tiny bubbles. I can't describe how, but it definitely tasted different; maybe it was just the air I was breathing, the absolute frozen purity of it. With the sun out and the sky radiant, the light off the glacier was dazzling; seals swam by to have a look at us, and the air was full of a faint but constant cracking, splintering sound, as ice split and melted in the water. In its eerie, unearthly way it was, quite simply, one of the most beautiful places I've ever been to.

Svalbard's glaciers are frozen to the ground and to the sides of the valleys; they're not plastic and mobile like a normal glacier. They tend therefore to get steeper, carving ice off the front and packing snow up on top, until the mounting pressure from above forces them suddenly to surge. In 1936–7, one glacier lurched over six miles; it was moving about thirty-eight yards a day, and even faster than that in the mid-section.

It would, I think, have taken something at least that substantial to move Kirsty Duncan into any admission that her project had gone less than swimmingly. When I got back to town from the Tempelfjord, I bumped into her in Longyearbyen's little cluster of shops, and did my utmost to get at least some sense of perspective from her on what had happened in the cemetery.

I said that if science was easy, we'd be on Alpha Centauri by now – and sure, the virologists could work on those samples in their laboratories for months – but right now, their primary goal had been genetic material from the 1918 flu virus. To find that you needed bodies in permafrost, and these weren't. So Duncan kept saying she was thrilled and elated, when *she hadn't found what she came to find* . . .

'No, that's not right, Pete. It's really discouraging from my point of view. I *did* get what I came to find . . .'

But . . .

'No, let me explain. The whole point of this project was to get tissue samples. These bodies, you're right, were not buried in the permafrost, but they were buried in the active layer. That means that they are buried in permafrost . . .'

Black was now white, and white black – I couldn't believe what I was hearing. She ploughed on, 'It does freeze and thaw, but it does remain frozen for part of the year. What allows preservation is either extreme cold, extreme dry, or in some cases extreme wet. Here you have extreme . . . extreme cold. It's not . . .'

She was floundering. The whole point about preservation of viral material was that it needed *not* to be repeatedly frozen and thawed, as had surely occurred here. Precisely to that end, I said, she'd turned down Alaska and Iceland because permafrost wasn't guaranteed there.

'That's right.'

So you came here . . .

'And we didn't find it in the permafrost. But we did find it.'

She cut a tragic figure. For five years, she'd pushed towards these moments in that chilly little Arctic cemetery with a steely determination. At first alone, and then clinging to control of a fractious team whose members changed and bickered and ran her down behind her back, she'd done everything the right way. For all her hammy guff about respect and dignity, they had indeed proceeded with all due regard to the ethical niceties; they had indeed conducted their dig in a correct and safe fashion. It just hadn't worked out – but she was damned if she was going to acknowledge it.

Up at the cemetery, I found Rod Daniels packing his equipment away. He said the samples, after the disappointment of finding the coffins where they did, were better than he'd hoped for at first; they were at least taking home a fair amount of material. Therefore, he said, 'We'll try to go for virus isolation. But with what we've got, and where they've been in the active layer, I'd say our chances are zero.'

The Huset did an Arctic buffet – all you could eat for about £16. You could eat char tartar, reindeer heart, reindeer tongue, seal stew, whale steak and whale carpaccio, either marinated in brandy, or with parmesan. If you were so minded, you could wash all this down with a bottle of '82 Château Margaux for £325, or a glass of 1939 Armagnac at £15 a time.

Someone weighed up the menu and said casually, 'Norway wears its pariah status as a nation lightly, doesn't it?'

I ate the lot. The carpaccio was rancid, and the seal tasted like someone had slow-cooked a load of old car tyres, but the whale steak had a rich, flavoursome heft to it – if good beef tasted of fish, that'd be whale – while the reindeer tongue had a pleasant, rubbery, mildly smoked and greasy tang to it. For musical accompaniment, a group of locals – the women in little black numbers, one of the men in tweed with elbow patches and a deerstalker – gathered round the piano to perform their repertoire of Abba songs.

The last day I was there was Esther Oxford's birthday. Elliott Halpern's crew clubbed together to buy her a little gift, a souvenir jar of Svalbard coal; that night in the Huset, they asked Pastor Hoifodt to present it to her. Travelling by helicopter, the Pastor had come back a little earlier from the Miners' Day festivities in Barentsburg; his more than cheerfully gregarious demeanour now suggested he'd been obliged while he was there to share a vodka or two with the Russians.

He gave Oxford her gift with much good grace, and said contentedly what a great idea these little souvenirs were. With so much coal about the place, he said, 'All we've got to pay for is the jar and the label. We've been thinking about bottling reindeer shit too.' While we contemplated this bizarre addition to the memento industry, he spread his

arms wide and said, 'We could pay students to gather it.'
Well – that'd be a summer job with a difference.

I flew home the next day; four weeks later, Esther
Oxford's piece ran in the *Independent*. Unsurprisingly, her
story was in essence a defence of her father against the
touchy-feely emotionalism of Kirsty Duncan – a defence
which foundered somewhat on Oxford's peculiar idea that
although they'd found their seven bodies (and the pit was
collapsing anyway) they should have carried on digging. For
what?

Esther Oxford's account of the Svalbard team's attempt
to find the 1918 virus had, however, one altogether more
serious failing – because she somehow omitted to mention
the rather important point that, in Washington, DC, there
was a man who found the virus two years earlier anyway.

7 THE LANGUAGE OF LIFE

It started with government cut-backs, a large quantity of dead dolphins, and the pickled eye of an English chemist.

Born in 1766, John Dalton was primarily a teacher; he was also a self-taught experimenter with such an interest in the earth's atmosphere that over the course of his seventy-eight years, he recorded more than 200,000 observations about it in a thick stack of notebooks. Given this interest, he moved naturally to the study of gases; from that study, he developed the atomic theory that lies at the root of modern chemistry. Published in 1808 as his 'New System of Chemical Philosophy', it's for this that Dalton is best known; less well known is the fact that he had red–green colour blindness, a condition known in his honour as Daltonism. And what, you will naturally ask, does any of that have to do with influenza?

Until 1995, Jeffery Taubenberger had never had anything to do with flu either. Then thirty-three years old, Taubenberger had moved to Washington, DC with his German parents when he was nine. He'd grown up and gone to medical school there, doing a combined MD and PhD that allowed him to pursue basic science while he qualified to become a doctor; it was a course designed for people minded to follow a career in medical research.

His interest lay in developmental immunology; how the primitive cells of your bone marrow differentiate into the mature cells that make up your white blood cell system.

Lymphocytes and macrophages, toiling to provide you with defences against disease, are held to derive from a basic stem cell – but how does that starter pack decide what it wants to turn into? If it has the latent ability to develop in a number of directions, how does it grow until it's committed to performing just one function, and how does it decide which function? Whatever the process, it has to occur through gene regulation – that is, the switching on and off of genes – but which genes, and why?

This was Taubenberger's principal research interest – an interest he maintained while he undertook a residency in pathology at the National Institutes of Health in Bethesda, Maryland, just across the District of Columbia's northern border. Then, in 1993, his boss Tim O'Leary recruited him and a colleague to start a new lab at the Armed Forces Institute of Pathology (AFIP).

Part of the Walter Reed Army Medical Campus, a substantial compound in the north-east corner of Washington, the AFIP is housed in a handsome concrete bunker on the corner of 14th and Alaska. President Dwight D. Eisenhower opened it in 1955: 'I dedicate this building to the conquest of disease so that mankind, more safe and secure in body, may more surely advance to a widely shared prosperity and an enduring and just peace.'

The Institute started life as the Army Medical Museum in 1862, set up by order of Abraham Lincoln to combat 'diseases of the battlefield' in the armies of the Union. These armies had grown from a regular corps of 16,161 soldiers at the start of the Civil War to a fighting force of 214,903 men by the end of 1861; they'd be over three times that size before the conflict was ended.

The biggest enemy these men faced was not the shells

and bullets of the Confederacy, but infectious disease; two-thirds of Civil War casualties resulted either directly from disease, or from infections arising from wounds and the surgery upon them. It was a field in which so much progress was made in the next half century that ironically, before the autumn of 1918, the United States Army was the healthiest army in history.

Today, the pathology division of the AFIP spends most of its time acting as a consultant, giving second opinions on tricky cases that come in from all around the world. Most often, they'll be infectious diseases or cancers – so if a woman has a breast biopsy taken, for example, and the hospital in question isn't sure of the diagnosis, it'll go to Washington for a second work-up. Basically, the place is nothing but pathologists, sub-specialized into departments for the breast, brain, eye, skin, and so on. They work free for the military, and for a fee to civilian contributors; they handle tens of thousands of cases every year, on the basis that they get to keep a representative sample from any case you send them.

Taubenberger was invited to join the AFIP at a time when molecular pathology, as a field of study, was beginning to grow rapidly; new technologies meant you could not only look at ever tinier pieces of organic creation, but manipulate them too. To keep pace with all the advances now being made, once a week he and his group have a journal club; each week, one person picks a paper out of the literature and presents it, and then it's discussed and criticized. You can present your own work, or someone else's, and in 1995, Taubenberger presented a piece of work from *Science* which had really caught his imagination.

It was about John Dalton's eyes. Dalton wasn't a physician, but he was fascinated with the anomaly he had – his
inability to distinguish between red and green. He tossed
around a raft of theories as to why his vision was distorted
in this way, and settled eventually on the notion that the
vitreous humour, the liquid filling his eyeballs, must be blue
in his case. Carrying his potent curiosity beyond the grave
with him, Dalton was sufficiently intrigued about it that
before he died in 1844, he asked his personal physician to
examine his eyes when he was gone.

Dalton's doctor took one eye out, cut it open, poured
the vitreous humour into a wash glass, and saw that it wasn't
blue, but clear. With the other eye, however, he did something
else. Instead of cutting it in half (Taubenberger says admir-
ingly, 'It was incredibly clever. I don't know if I'd have
thought of it') he took his penknife, cut a little nick in the
back of the eyeball, held it up and looked through it.

It was clever, maybe, but it was also inconclusive
because again, Dalton's doctor could see no colour distor-
tion. He could determine that the problem was post-retinal
– that it wasn't a mechanical or physical problem of the
eyeball itself – but more than that he couldn't say, and that
was an end of it. Still intact, Dalton's eye was pickled in a
jar, kept by the academic society that bears his name, and
forgotten about for a century and a half.

Forgotten about, that is, until the gene defect for red–
green colour blindness was worked out. It's a deletion from
part of a gene that codes for a protein in the retina, and the
work that Taubenberger presented to his journal club in
1995, the little slice of historical–pathological detective work,
was the proof that Daltonism is a justly named condition.

An English group had got permission to take a tiny sliver of tissue from Dalton's eye. They'd extracted DNA from it, they'd looked for the mutation in that particular gene, and sure enough, John Dalton had the classic red–green colour blindness deletion.

Taubenberger loved it. A slight, lively, infectiously enthusiastic man, he told me, 'This was really cute. And my first thought was, Hey – we must have somebody famous whose tissues are here. We could do something like that. Then I started thinking about it, I had a session running through different ideas with my boss – and what came out of it was the 1918 flu. We thought that would be a really great project. Here was something that killed tens of millions of people, and no one knew a bloody thing about it.'

They had other imperatives than curiosity, of course. From the Civil War onwards, the forerunners of what's now the AFIP had started collecting tissue samples; doctors would go out to the battlefield and bring back surgical biopsy or autopsy specimens, up to and including whole organs and amputated limbs. In one sense, it was part of the Victorian passion for collecting things; many museums were started around that time, founded in a general cultural view that if you sought after knowledge, you needed concrete databases built up in which to find it.

In another sense, however, those early pathologists were showing great foresight; they collected their specimens not only to study them there and then, but with the aim in mind of maintaining them for future study too. As a result, the AFIP now has an archive containing literally millions of tissue samples from surgical and autopsy pathology going back 100 years. It covers all aspects of human disease, and it covers animal disease too; the Institute maintains a veterinary pathology group to do for animals what Taubenberger and his colleagues do for people.

Maintaining two large, spanking-new warehouses filled to the rafters with bits and pieces of people and animals, however, is not a cheap exercise. For sure, in the global scheme of the United States' defence expenditure, it's nothing – in the local phrase, it's 'budget dust' – but none the less, from Reagan through Bush and continuing with Clinton, the mood of these American times has been to brush off every possible piece of budgetary chaff and lint from the supposedly bloated Big Government.

Sparked by the case of Dalton's eye, the idea of trying to track down something as dramatic as the 1918 flu virus was, therefore, plain bureaucratic good sense. Taubenberger said, 'Why would anyone care about tissues collected eighty years ago? So I wanted a project that would highlight the utility of the Institute maintaining all these samples. Everyone was bending over backwards to see what part of the Government they could cut away next, so I wanted to make my own little contribution, and point out why it would be prudent to keep this place in business.'

Clearly not a man low on ambition, he wanted to show what his own division could do too, never mind the AFIP as a whole, because over the previous few years they'd developed their techniques for getting nucleic acids out of antique or degraded pathology material to a high and rare pitch of precision.

The reason they'd done so was, quite simply, that they'd had to. Taubenberger said, 'Most people who work

199

in molecular pathology have the luxury of being in a place where they actually have patients. So you can take a biopsy out of somebody and freeze it, or extract DNA from it directly in the fresh tissue state, and you can do a lot with that. Whereas we, unfortunately, practically never get fresh tissue.'

What they mostly have, instead, is tiny pieces of tissue fixed in formalin and then embedded in paraffin wax blocks. When they want to look at it, they put it on a microtome – in essence, a microscopically accurate version of a salami slicer – and that takes an incredibly thin section off the tissue. For molecular pathology, when we say thin, that means something of the order of five to eight microns – five to eight millionths of a metre – which is a good deal thinner than a human hair. It's about the thickness of a single red blood cell.

You set this phantasmal wafer on a piece of glass, dissolve the wax, dye the tissue with whichever dye will stain the cell features you're interested in – the nuclei or the membranes – and preserve it by cementing another piece of glass over the top of it before it goes under the microscope. Then you go hunting for a diagnosis – or, in this case, for fragments of an eighty-year-old virus.

As a field of study, pathology really came into being in the mid-nineteenth century, though obviously the notion of studying tissues and cadavers to determine the causes of disease had been around a lot longer. At the great medical school in Bologna, the physician Taddeo Alderotti established procedures for post-mortem dissection in the thirteenth century; notions of anatomy in the Western world date twelve centuries further back than that, to the Greek physician Galen.

If you wanted to look at symptoms and structures more closely, however, you needed magnification. Credit for the invention of the first microscope probably goes to the Dutch father-and-son lensmakers Hans and Zacharias Jannsen, whose devices employing compound lenses were first reported at the start of the seventeenth century. Another Dutchman, Antoni von Leeuwenhoek, was a businessman who started grinding lenses and making microscopes as a hobby; he ended up making over 400 of them. He was the first man to see and describe single cell organisms – he wrote to the Royal Society in London to announce his discovery in 1683 – and among much other study, he was also the first man to see red blood cells and spermatozoa.

It was only in the nineteenth century, however, that pathology was firmly established on a scientific basis. The father of cellular pathology was a German, Rudolf Virchow, who put microscopes to use to show how tissues and organs are made of cells, and how changes in cells either cause disease, or result from it. The advances of the past century, however, have been exponentially more rapid.

Another German, Ernst Ruska, built the first prototype electron microscope in 1931 (he won the Nobel Prize for his work fifty-five years later, two years before he died) and commercial models were on sale by 1935. By 1950, you could look at something just two nanometres big – a nanometre being one thousand-millionth of a metre. This meant that instead of merely knowing a virus existed, you could actually look at it up close and in detail; you could look at individual proteins on the surface of the thing.

After the electron microscope, the new field of molecular pathology is the next revolution. As we learn more and more about the genes in the human body we can, for example, now examine the genetic malfunctions behind tumour growth. Tumours have specific gene changes that result in their difference from normal tissue, and you can tell a lot about them by looking at these genetic alterations. The same applies to infectious disease; viruses and bacteria all have their DNA or RNA, and once you know something about the gene structures involved in that, you can start using it to help you with diagnosis and treatment. To see how Jeffery Taubenberger and his team applied these techniques to hunting down the 1918 flu, however, we need first to understand at least a little of the basic grammar involved in the language of life.

The language of life has four letters – A, C, G and T – and the basic plan for every living thing on earth is spelt out in these letters. They represent adenine, cytosine, guanine and thymine – the four nucleotides that make up the steps on the spiral staircase of DNA. DNA itself is a double-stranded molecule, with a backbone of sugars and phosphates; the four nucleotides are strung along the two strands in a sequence of base pairs, like rungs on a ladder. The arrangement is extremely specific; A and G always go together, C and T likewise, and the pairs are ordered in groups of three.

The instructions for the business of organic creation, therefore, come in words of three letters. With four letters available, that gives you sixty-four possible combinations, all of which are used; sixty-one combinations code for amino-acids, and three others code for the word STOP. Along the two strands of DNA, one set of letters and words is the 'sense strand', and the other, the 'anti-sense strand', is a mirror image of the first; when DNA replicates (to put this in exceedingly crude terms) these two strands split apart, proteins read the instructions, and start making a new copy.

We're in the zone of miracles here. The human body has 100 trillion cells (give or take) and every one of them has its personalized instruction manual; if you laid out the DNA from a single cell in one continuous strand, it'd be six feet long. That DNA, however, is just a blueprint; genes don't actually *do* anything. In Taubenberger's phrase, 'They're not the building; they're just the plan.'

Proteins do the construction work; they might be enzymes with specific functions, or structural proteins that make up the skeleton of a cell, but, as Taubenberger puts it, 'They're what does stuff.' So when the DNA is unzipped into two single strands, a protein called the DNA polymerase comes along, reads the A-T/G-C instructions, and copies them off until you get a new string of amino-acids as ordered by the genes in the blueprint.

Whatever you're studying – flu, fruit flies, yeast, oak trees, people – if you know the specific sequences of the genes involved, you can start knowing which bit does what and why. Knowing something, however, isn't the same as doing something with it; you then have the practical questions of how to get hold of this material, on its nanometric scale, in such a way that you can actually work on it.

With flu, the problem is compounded by the fact that it's an RNA virus; the blueprint's single-stranded and, in semantic keeping with its sinister *modus operandi*, the flu genome only packages the anti-sense strand. To get on in life, it has to hijack our cellular material and make complementary sense strands twisted to its own purposes. So to work on it (to get hold of the mirror-image sense strand that flu cooks up out of us when it's infective) you have first to copy flu back into a DNA version. But even if your object of study is DNA-based in the first place, until the early 1990s it was still hard to amplify enough material to manipulate easily.

The polymerase proteins that read and copy the nucleotides on the separated DNA strands have been understood for decades. Watson and Crick published the structure of DNA in 1953; thereafter, the component elements of the copying process were isolated, purified, studied, and their functions identified. As a result, we've been able to copy DNA in a test-tube for years. You took the piece you were interested in, you added enzymes and nucleotides, you threw in some salt to help it all work, and there you had the ingredients to turn one bit of DNA into two.

The trouble was, you had first to heat it to boiling point to get the two strands of DNA to come apart. Then you had to cool it back down before you could put in the enzymes that set the genetic photocopier working. Then, if you wanted to make four bits from the two you'd now got, you had to heat it up to boiling again, split the double strands another time, cool it back down, add more enzymes, stop, wait and start all over. It was tedious, it was prone to contamination because you had to keep opening the test-tube to sling new stuff in, and on top of that the enzyme was extremely expensive.

In the late 1980s, this problem was solved by a group at a small firm in California called Cetus; the technique they came up with is called Polymerase Chain Reaction (PCR), and their leader Kerry Mullis got the Nobel Prize for it. Their original idea was simple and elegant. They knew there are bacteria living in geysers and hot springs; organisms that are perfectly happy living in water that's practically boiling. So if they're functioning contentedly at 90°C all their lives, they must be able to do everything – including copy their DNA – at those temperatures.

Mullis's team isolated the DNA polymerase from these quirky life forms (from a species called *thermus aquaticus*, or TAQ) and made a protein called TAQ polymerase. The crucial advantage is that it's not destroyed when you boil your samples, so you take your starting sliver of DNA, you add the bases, the salt and this particular polymerase, then you close up the test-tube. Now you can boil and cool it as many times as you want, and every cycle you're doubling your DNA.

It makes the business of reproducing DNA massively more efficient; run the cycle twenty times, and you'll go from one bit to more than a million. Do it twenty-five times, to be precise, and one piece of DNA becomes 33,554,432 pieces – enough material to enable you readily to go to work on it. You can determine its sequence, you can do something functional with it, and without PCR, says Taubenberger, '*None* of what we do here would work. The patient care, the research on flu or breast cancer – it all depends on PCR. It's revolutionized our lab, and every other molecular biology lab in the world. It's the most important thing that's happened since Watson and Crick determined the structure of DNA itself.'

It meant the Nobel Prize for Mullis, and the 1918 flu for Taubenberger. First, however, it solved the mystery of a serial dolphin killer.

*

Catching Cold

In 1987, there was a big die-off of bottlenose dolphins along the Atlantic coast of the United States. It began around New Jersey and moved steadily south, reaching Florida in the spring of 1988. Tens of thousands of dolphins died – it's not known precisely how many, but it's thought around half the dolphin population along the Atlantic seaboard perished that winter – and nobody knew what was killing them.

The prime suspect was red tide, or algal bloom. Strictly speaking, this is not caused by algae at all, but by a single-celled creature called a dinoflagellate; the point is, it produces a toxin that turns the water red and kills animals. In a report to Congress about the dolphins dying, red tide became the official view.

At AFIP, however, one of the veterinary pathologists had expertise in marine mammals, and he obtained necropsy samples taken from dolphins when they'd washed up dead and dying on the beaches. From the look of the samples under the microscope, it seemed to him their condition wasn't compatible with red tide deaths, and that a viral infection was more likely; they looked like what you'd get in a dog with a bad case of distemper.

He speculated that the dolphins were dying of an unknown morbillivirus, the family of viruses that causes distemper in dogs, and measles in humans. Meanwhile, in 1988, there was a die-off of seals in Lake Baikal in Siberia, and again in the early nineties in the North and the Irish Seas; in 1991, dolphins in the Mediterranean fell victim too. It was curious, because none of these animals – seals, dolphins, or porpoises – had ever been known to fall prey to morbilliviruses before. In Rotterdam, however, Ab Osterhaus now managed to culture such a virus from them;

this wasn't red tide, but a new infectious disease in marine mammals. Then in 1993, thousands more dolphins started dying in the Gulf of Mexico.

No virus had been cultured from the samples the AFIP had from the first die-off in 1987; the tissues were too degraded. But with the problem clearly still out there, the veterinary pathologist came to Taubenberger's group and asked if they could look at these old tissues. Could they, he wondered, develop a molecular test for the presence of unknown or novel morbillivirus from his samples?

'After we stopped laughing,' said Taubenberger, 'we said sure, we'll give it a try. We were laughing because these were dolphins that had washed up on the beach dead. These were really necrotic, stinky-smelly dolphins whose tissues were just rotten, in really bad states of preservation.'

Worse, like flu, morbilliviruses are RNA viruses. 'We thought, there's *no way* we're going to isolate RNA from this kind of tissue. But it turned out we could. We were able to isolate tiny fragments of morbillivirus RNA from the vast majority of those animals, to sequence it, and to compare it to the known sequences of other morbilliviruses.'

It turned out there were two related viruses (or possibly two strains of one virus) and that in the different die-offs sometimes one was present, sometimes the other, sometimes both. Funded by the Environmental Protection Agency, Taubenberger's group worked out the epidemiology of the outbreaks on this molecular basis.

In the process of figuring out that mystery, they developed a precocious set of tools. Taubenberger said, 'The work served as a template for perfecting techniques to find and extract RNA from highly degraded tissues, which is the term I'd use in a formal interview. In the laboratory,' he grinned, 'the term you'd use is crap.'

So now they had the tools to do the job; as often happens in science, one of the reasons that Taubenberger's team found the 1918 flu virus was, quite simply, because they could. PCR, as applied to the hunt for morbillivirus RNA in decomposing dolphins, provided them with equipment that could find viral needles in molecular haystacks. The fear of government cutbacks provided the motive to put that equipment to ground-breaking use – and John Dalton's eye provided the inspiration as to what that use would be. So, on 14th and Alaska in 1995, the hunt for the Spanish flu began – and no one in the flu community knew the first thing about it.

The AFIP's tissue repository is a couple of miles north across the DC border, at Forest Glen in Maryland. It's housed in two featureless grey warehouses and looks like any small, nondescript block of light industrial plant or storage space; it gives no indication that behind the breeze-block and corrugated-tin walls, stacked in cardboard boxes or fixed on glass slides, lie bits and pieces of some 2,600,000 people.

It's a new facility, built to bring most of the samples the Institute holds together in one place – they've come from as far afield as Germany or the Philippines – and it's run by a friendly, unassuming man named Al Riddick. Riddick, one gathered, had felt slightly uncomfortable about the way he'd been presented in some of the media coverage on Taubenberger's work as a muscular, balding man with a gold chain round his neck, spending all his working hours in a barn full of body parts.

He was in fact a quiet man who saw little sensational about his work; by job title he was the Warehouse Materials Manager, and the bulk of what he did was simply to file, store and preserve the Institute's samples. These were mostly indeterminate slivers of tissue, bearing no visual connection to human beings.

About sixty million samples were held on glass slides and stored on robotic carousels; some ten million more were embedded on paraffin blocks, varying in size from thumbnail to palm. 'Wet tissue', the third mode of preservation (actual, tangible pieces of human being, like a liver or a kidney) was a good deal more rare; ordinarily, said Riddick, the doctors would use up anything they had in that condition. If they didn't, the leftovers usually went on slide these days; wet tissue and paraffin blocks were bulkier items to store. They were held in Building 509, a climate-controlled tin barn packed with high-density storage shelves; you cranked the shelves back and forth, then walked in where you needed to go.

Forest Glen is home to the AFIP's older samples; fresh material stays for ten years in the basement at 14th and Alaska before shipment over the line into Maryland for permanent storage. When it comes over, Riddick's staff check that it's in a maintainable condition, then file and shelve it. Apart from eating up space, wet tissue presents an environmental problem, with the stink of the formalin; it's costly to filter it, and big fans run continuously. They're set along the base of the walls, because formalin's heavier than air; if they stop running, said Riddick, 'You clear the building. Over two parts per million, you get out.'

Apart from that potential to get a tad odorous, however,

the new facility was better by far than anything Riddick had
had to cope with before. He'd started working for the AFIP
in 1976; he said, 'When you first come and see bits of brains,
it's a little strange. Then after a while, you're just going to
work. But the place we had then – we were in an old
dealership garage downtown – you wouldn't believe it. There
were good restaurants in the area,' he laughed, 'but storing
stuff – well! Some days the paraffin blocks'd fuse together,
it was so hot in there. We had *huge* exhaust fans trying to
keep that air clean.'

Other times he'd had floods, or seen it so cold that the
blocks got brittle, so the move to Forest Glen made Al
Riddick a happy man. It had made his job a lot easier, and,
without bragging about it at any time, he was also quietly
proud that Taubenberger's flu project had shown that the
job was done well. Speaking of the work his nine-strong
staff did, he said, 'All day you write numbers and brush
dust. So it's important these guys know what it is they've
done, when something like these cases comes up – it's a
reward for them. I force-feed them credit for that.'

They were working their way backwards through history, loading everything they had into a database. All the
slides were logged; with the paraffin blocks, when Taubenberger's request came in, they'd not got as far back as 1918.
'It was just like any other order,' said Riddick, 'five or six
routine pages. Our job's to service the pathologist; we had
no idea of the significance of it. We just look at the numbers
– so all we knew was, it was old. I understand he wasn't
even sure if we had it at all. I do remember he asked for a
number of cases, and we had to do a physical search. You
always doubt you'll find it, when there's 2,600,000 cases in

here. Then from one case you might have one block, or a hundred. But we pride ourselves on being able to find things; finding something that old was important to us.'

The box Taubenberger wanted was right at the back of a shelf, way high up; marked 6-1490, it was filled with smaller, pale brown cardboard boxes of assorted shapes and sizes. Each bore a faint pencil scribble denoting the size of the wax blocks it contained – one inch by one inch, two by two, one by three, and so on. Holding the box now, Riddick said it would have survived three or four moves and seen some pretty poor storage conditions in its time – then, as I peered towards it, he laughed. 'Open it up,' he said, 'it won't bite.'

I fished out two dice-sized, flat-topped, slightly pyramidical blocks of wax. Riddick studied them and said he wasn't a histotech, but it might have been liver or spleen. It was just a little brown smear on a creamy-white surface. 'It's incredible to think,' said Riddick, 'that 1918 stayed in something like this for all that time.'

He said of Taubenberger, 'I met him when a camera crew came. I was real impressed. I was thinking he'd be some rangy, professor-looking guy, but not at all. And I can only wonder what he must feel inside, knowing his kids can look in a library book some day and see what he's done.'

First of all, Taubenberger had to find out if the repository had any samples at all. He put in his order to Riddick; Riddick came back with around 100 autopsy cases from soldiers who'd died in the 1918 pandemic. Out of those cases, tissue was still available on wax blocks from seventy-seven men; on their first go-round, Taubenberger's team randomly selected twenty-eight cases, and most of them were useless.

Most of the men had died of acute bacterial pneumonia, the co-infective aftermath of the initial viral infection. Flu replicates incredibly rapidly in the respiratory system, peaking from twenty-four to forty-eight hours after the onset; it's then shed from the body pretty fast. Even under modern circumstances, if you try to culture flu from a patient five or seven days after the onset of infection, you're not likely to have much luck – so in tissue eighty years old, from patients who'd succumbed to the secondary bacterial infections, the virus was long gone.

Clinical histories for the patients who'd died of bacterial pneumonia showed courses of illness lasting ten days to two weeks; Taubenberger needed to find someone who'd died a lot more quickly. It was a curious feature of the Spanish flu that some victims did pass away horribly fast, with that massive haemorrhaging of the lungs, and of their original twenty-eight cases, it looked as though seven seemed to meet that criterion. They set to screening the samples from those seven more closely – and this is where PCR comes in.

The ten genes sitting on the eight gene segments in the flu virus blueprint are pretty small to begin with – only about 13,000 base pairs between them, compared to 3.4 billion in the genes that run you or me. (And in case you think having heaps of base pairs in your genome makes *homo sapiens* something special, be advised that the lungfish, a Syrian butterfly, two species of lily, an onion, a pine tree, a toad, and two kinds of amoeba – to name but a few – all have much bigger genomes than we do. More scary is the fact that HIV can do what it does with only 9,750 base pairs.)

In the flu virus, meanwhile, it goes without saying that

you can only get hold of those 13,000 base pairs in coherent and comprehensible form if the virus is intact. If it's crumbled to fragments in a slice of lung eight decades old, on the other hand, that leaves you hunting pieces as small as 100 base pairs. The quantity of material's so laughably tiny that if you can't make copies of it, you certainly can't work with it – and that's assuming you can find it in the first place.

To do that, you need to know the A-T/G-C sequence at each end of the molecule you're looking for. Then you make a primer – a short bit of DNA that's the mirror image of the sequence at each end. You boil your target DNA, it unzips, the primers bind to it, the polymerase comes along and sits on the primer, and it starts adding bases from there to make copies of the thing you want to study.

The trouble with the 1918 flu was, no one knew the sequence, whether it was human, pig, avian, or what. On the contrary, the sequence was precisely what Taubenberger was looking for, to find out why it was so bad. This quandary was solved by first assuming, on the antibody evidence from 1918, that Spanish flu was indeed an H1N1. That narrowed the field; if we'd not known whether it was H1 or H15, Taubenberger's team would probably still be looking for it today.

Even so, H1 strains alone can still be incredibly varied; the haemagglutinin gene changes wildly within one host species, never mind across different species barriers. Hundreds of different H1s have been studied down the years, but as a result of that, a large number have had their sequences determined and placed in different databases round the world.

Taubenberger's team lined up all the known H1

sequences and looked for areas of the gene that were conserved across the bulk of those sequences – that is, where different strains from different hosts all have, if not exactly the same structure, at least a very similar one. Then they designed their primers to bind at two end points, with the idea that whatever sequence copied off from between them might turn out to be useful.

Their first efforts, then, were with these universal primers – tools that would amplify whatever flu strain might be there. It wouldn't tell them much about the virus, but at least it would tell them that they had it. Then, if they did find something, they could design more targeted primers on the basis of that new sequence. Using the four letters in the language of life strung along these carefully designed little chemical sticks, they could poke and prod the flu virus into talking that language back to them and telling them what it was.

The bulk of the benchwork was done by Ann Reid, a handsome, big-boned, silver-haired woman from Cincinnati. Thirty-eight years old, a mother of three working four days a week from six in the morning to two-thirty in the afternoon so she had time to marry her work with her children, Reid had come to the task of slinging PCR primers at phantom shreds of lung tissue in a fairly roundabout way.

She'd done environmental science at college, a master's degree in European politics, and fetched up working for three years on telecoms policy at the Organization for Economic Co-operation and Development in Paris. She hated it. She said, 'I hated the fact that you'd do a study, you'd take an issue and think really hard about what the best answers were, you'd present it to twenty-four member countries, and none of them gave a *hoot* about the facts because they all had a political agenda.'

Thinking she'd go back into science, she got into medical school back home in the States; then she decided, when she started having children, that she didn't want to miss their childhood. In 1986 she took a lab job at Walter Reed instead, when molecular biology was just starting to take off. It was difficult to hire staff with the necessary technical skills out of college, because the skills in question had barely started to be taught; people like Reid pretty much learned them on the job.

She moved to the AFIP in 1988. Tim O'Leary was trying to establish a group there who could apply the new molecular disciplines to the Institute's pathology work; he wanted to see if they could use PCR to access viral and bacterial DNA out of formalin-fixed tissues, or detect transgenetic events like the mutations involved in cancer. Reid's colleague Amy Krafft had done the heavy loading on the dolphin project; when Taubenberger then mooted the flu idea, Reid picked up the techniques Krafft had developed and started applying them to the young soldiers' lung tissue.

She said, 'I think we knew it would be paid attention to, if it were possible to do it – and that, frankly, is why we were willing to try. If we hadn't thought there'd be a major impact if it worked, we wouldn't have spent a year and a half beating our heads against that wall. Because it took a very, very long time for it to happen, and a lot of resources. My full-time job was working on a project that did not work *at all* for well over a year, and there aren't too many places that would allow that. Most scientists are expected to have a paper out every six months or so, so to have something that had no signs of succeeding – it had to be a big pay-off, to make that kind of investment.'

They kept going, she said, simply 'because it was so important. We felt this was the only possible way to get the answer to what caused the 1918 pandemic. And the more we read about it, the more we learned about it, the more we thought this really *should* be possible. But I think, frankly, we just got lucky that there was a case with enough virus in it to work.'

After more than a year with no joy, Reid went back to Krafft for help. She was wondering if there was something wrong in the way she was going about her RNA hunt; she asked Krafft to have a go, because she'd developed a lot of the techniques to start with – and on 23 July 1996, Amy Krafft got a positive.

'That case,' said Reid, 'hasn't given a beautiful positive every time we've used it. It was really sort of serendipitous that that particular day, that particular slice of that block . . . well, who knows? Something just made that particular prep absolutely spectacular. It's been our gold standard ever since.'

The viral fragments emerged from an army private named Roscoe Vaughn. On 19 September 1918 he'd gone into hospital at Camp Jackson in South Carolina with a fever, a cough and a headache, and he'd died in five days; he was twenty-one years old.

His clinical course was fairly unique; that's why Taubenberger reckons they struck lucky with him. He'd died of pneumonia of the left lung. If you lose a lung slowly, you can compensate (it's actually possible to lose an entire lung and not be greatly troubled), but if it happens fast, the shock to the system can be too great. So what probably happened is that massive bacterial pneumonia set in on top of the flu in Vaughn's left lung, the lung filled with fluid and inflammation, and that killed him – but the right lung, meanwhile, was two or three days behind in the progression of the disease. The flu had only just moved in and started multiplying there when he died, leaving a snapshot of the virus still setting up shop as Roscoe Vaughn passed away.

I asked Reid how that July day had felt, and she gave a great big sigh. She recalled a previous occasion when they'd been trying, not just with 1918 cases, but also with others from the Asian flu pandemic of 1957, and a positive came out; thinking they'd found a 1918 case at last, they'd run to the databank to compare it with existing strains, and found it was only a '57. 'Well,' said Reid, 'bad word, bad word.'

It was, at least, the first time they'd got flu RNA from an old wax block – it just wasn't from one of the blocks where they'd really wanted to find it. 'That,' said Reid, 'was the first really thrilling day – but it turned out to be a cheap thrill. So when we got this other one, we refused to get excited until we'd actually sequenced it. Then we put it in the databank, and we knew – we had 1918. And I'm sure other scientists have days that are their most thrilling days in science, but I don't think anything could ever beat that. After all those months and all that prayer, to have it finally work – it was just fabulous. And the thing is, from the outside now, I suppose it could look pretty tedious; we're basically just repeating that same sequence of experiments with each new set of primers I design to find different parts of the virus, and I realize that might look very routine. But every time you get another chunk of it, it's the first time anyone's ever seen that before. And then, every time, it might be the part that made it lethal.'

The first part of the 1918 virus that Krafft and Reid brought to light was a piece of the gene that codes for the matrix protein, a structural element of the virus inside the lipid coat. They sequenced it, and it turned out that even though that matrix gene is highly conserved from one isolate to another, this one didn't match any known matrix gene exactly. It was definitely a flu virus, and it was definitely one that had never been seen before.

Apart from anything else, that meant it wasn't a contaminant; no one had sneezed it into a test-tube by mistake. They did have the advantage that their lab had never worked with flu before; others labs that have done have the constant problem that PCR is so sensitive, you can have the tiniest piece of DNA floating about on a dust molecule and if it lands in a test tube, it can start getting amplified. So at least, said Taubenberger, 'being a novice flu lab, anything we got was *likely* to be 1918'.

Once they were sure of what they had, they started designing primers to find other genes. From this first case, at this stage of the project, they got nine fragments of viral RNA from five different genes; the haemagglutinin, the neuraminidase, the nucleoprotein and two matrix proteins. The haemagglutinin was the one they really wanted; when they first published the results of their work in *Science* on 21 March 1997, they only had about 15 per cent of it, but it was enough to start arriving at some pretty interesting conclusions.

In keeping with the standard nomenclature of the flu

trade, they proposed that the 1918 strain should be christened 'Influenza A/South Carolina/1/18 (H1N1)' – and the first thing to say about it was that it didn't look anything like what had happened in Hong Kong. They'd analysed the sequences they'd got so far with software packages rather wonderfully called MEGA and PAUP (Molecular Evolutionary Genetics Analysis, and Phylogenetic Analysis Using Parsimony), then rummaged about for comparable sequences in the files of the National Center for Biotechnology Information using another tool called BLAST (a Basic Local Alignment Search Tool). The results suggested that the 1918 haemagglutinin wasn't from a bird flu; it was mammalian, either human or pig, or a mixture of both.

More specifically, the haemagglutinin gene didn't have the cleavage site mutation that makes H5 and H7 strains so deadly in birds, so that theory now looked shaky. But then, said Taubenberger, that mutation had never been seen in any other H1, not even avian H1s, so maybe this wasn't so surprising; maybe H1 viruses just don't do that.

They were going to have to look for some other explanation. 'The bottom line,' said Taubenberger, 'is that a hell of a lot's known about the biology of flu, but after sixty-five years of study, there are still a lot more questions than answers. Because,' he shrugged, 'life is complicated.'

So are people, and they found the reactions of some people in the flu community more than a little disconcerting. Maybe they should have expected it; no one knew who they were, and their paper in *Science* was an earthquake. For flu people, it was as if a complete stranger had arrived on the doorstep and casually announced that he'd cornered the market in gold dust.

The paper, said Taubenberger, 'was like throwing a bomb. The flu world's not a big area of science, and there's not a lot of scientists in it . . .'

Should there be?

'Yeah. But there aren't. It's a pretty small, tight community, and we put a lot of noses out of joint. You know – who the hell is this guy Taubenberger? What business has he got working on flu? I mean, this was the Holy Grail of flu work. The whole reason they discovered the flu virus in the thirties in the first place was to try to figure out what had happened in 1918. And now my group had come out of the blue with it. So we're not very popular with the flu community.'

We were speaking in April 1998, a year after Taubenberger had first published. He said, 'I think we've won over a lot who do think we know what we're doing now. But we're still not popular with some of them.'

Ann Reid was blunter. Their work, she said, and the publicity attendant upon it, 'caused jealousies and difficulties. You know, I didn't get credited, you didn't get credited, all that stuff, which is ugly and unpleasant. And this'll sound hopelessly naive, but we really feel that we do good science. So if people want to talk to us about the good science that we do, then we're happy to talk about it. But the flu world is *very* political, and we were very naive about that when we entered into this. It was not automatically accepted as science. It took some time before we could get the work published, and that was certainly a problem we never anticipated. We thought, my gosh, if we get sequence from the 1918 flu, it's going to be published [she clicked her fingers] like *that*.'

It wasn't; in some quarters it was rejected, and Reid had no idea why. She said, 'It was a big surprise. But I think the flu community had a hard time with this work coming out of here. We have really tried not to get into that at all; it's not like we scooped a bunch of flu experts who were working on the same thing, because they didn't have any samples. But then, they didn't have the techniques to work on the samples if they did have some. That's really what made us successful – not that we knew so much about flu, but that we knew so much about working with really cruddy old material. We *knew* we'd have to go for very small pieces. We *knew* we'd have to make a primer degenerate and still have it work. It was the techniques that made this work – that and having the archives, obviously. And now we have a pile of gold here.'

Casting green-eyed glances at the AFIP's viral gold, flu people raised two particular criticisms. Firstly, Taubenberger said, 'How did we know that what we had in the South Carolina case was the lethal form of the virus? To use Rob Webster's term, were we really looking at the bastard? Then secondly, maybe the sequence wasn't real because the process of fixing tissue in formalin had induced mutations in the structure of the gene. That one didn't worry me at all, because we've done all this other work with other specimens, other viruses, other genes, where we know what the structure is, and when you look for it, you never see mutations. But the first criticism was a valid one. OK, you've got a healthy twenty-one-year-old who gets sick with flu at the height of the fall wave of the 1918 pandemic and dies five days later – that's pretty good evidence. But it is only one case.'

The answer – easier said than done – was to find another

case to confirm what they'd found in the first one. Before that, however, they had to figure out what to do with the material they already had. The problem was, it was just this one tiny shred of lung tissue; it was a really limiting amount of material. After the first paper was published, obviously they wanted to move on towards obtaining the complete sequence of all ten genes, but with what they had, while they might get a couple of them to read out in full, the likelihood of finding the whole lot was slim.

They concentrated on the haemagglutinin; they had the full sequence of that by the summer of 1997. To be sure they'd got it right before seeking publication, however, ideally they needed to do it a second time, starting all over again from scratch; they wanted to double back through every step for every little piece of the sequence, to check absolutely that they'd spelt the gene out correctly. The trouble was, they'd used up half the tissue from the Carolina case just getting that one gene the first time. Taubenberger said, 'We could use up the rest of the tissue and say, OK, haemagglutinin is good and that's the end of the story, thanks very much. But maybe this was the only piece of 1918 anywhere, ever – so we had to try something else.'

He put a moratorium on generating new sequence, and they tried instead to find a way of increasing the number of copies of RNA still left in the tissue. There are chemical ways to do that, they spent all the summer of 1997 trying them, and it didn't work. They packed it in, and had a look instead at the other cases in the repository.

So far, they'd picked twenty-eight at random out of what Al Riddick had found them; now they went back to the other cases they hadn't screened yet. One of these was

Private James Downs, thirty years old, who'd died in a delirium just three days after he fell sick at Camp Upton, New York. By an odd stroke of coincidence, he'd died on the same day as Roscoe Vaughn at Fort Jackson, and he too had fragments of the virus still present in his lung tissue.

They got the positive on Downs in September 1997. By then, however, another potential source had turned up. As a young man in 1951, Johan Hultin had gone to Alaska with his colleagues from the State University of Iowa, and they'd disinterred the mass grave of seventy-two Spanish flu victims at Teller Mission. Forty-six years later, he'd read about Taubenberger's work in *Science* and, though he was now seventy-two years old, he wrote to Washington and offered to dig that grave up once again. It was, said Hultin, 'unfinished business'.

8 $3,000 AND A SHOVEL

If Taubenberger's paper in *Science* in March 1997 was a bolt
from the blue for the flu community in general, for the
Svalbard team it called into question the whole purpose of
their project. Where was the point in going to the Arctic, at
considerable expense, to dig up bodies that might or might
not bear traces of the virus, when Taubenberger had found
it already in a suburban warehouse?

In April, a few weeks after Taubenberger published,
the question of whether to proceed was considered at the
group's second meeting at the CDC in Atlanta. It was decided,
for entirely valid reasons, that they should, one of those
reasons being supplied by Taubenberger himself. Invited to
the meeting to talk about his findings, he explained how
little material he had to work with at that point; it wasn't
looking likely just then that he'd come up with more than
one or two genes' worth of sequence, so if Svalbard produced
more samples that could only be good.

At Mill Hill, John Skehel said, 'Any information is good
information.' The more people working to figure out 1918,
the better; they could either confirm or enhance what
Taubenberger had done, or determine that the virus in Norway had some tell-tale variation from the virus in the States,
or both. Furthermore, the thoroughness with which the dig
at Longyearbyen was being prepared would surely yield

224

more than just the virus anyway; they wanted information about the bacterial co-infections as well.

There was good reason to proceed – and, logically, to invite Taubenberger to join them, since the addition of his team's proven expertise made nothing but sense. As Charles Smith tells it, however, Taubenberger asked one other critical question at that April meeting. As a member of the team, how much did he share with them, and how much was his own work? The principle they settled on, reasonably enough, was that any work with specimens of your own, wherever they came from, was yours alone. Any work with specimens generated from Svalbard, on the other hand, would naturally be shared by all.

Taubenberger asked whether anything remained of the samples the Iowa team had exhumed in 1951; as far as anyone had been able to ascertain, none of that material had been preserved. He then asked whether, besides pursuing the Norwegian source, the group should consider returning to that Alaskan site.

They decided they shouldn't, said Smith, for three reasons. Firstly, because there'd already been an intervention with the Alaskan bodies, they'd presumably been thawed, and wouldn't be in as good a condition as was hoped for on Svalbard. Secondly, the group didn't think the bodies in Alaska had frozen as quickly as they would have done on Svalbard in the first place. Thirdly, what you had in Alaska was a native community, and that made it extremely difficult to get permission at all the appropriate levels. Besides, at that point in April, said Smith, they'd progressed so far with Svalbard that it didn't make sense to get diverted with looking elsewhere.

Taubenberger went back to Washington; a couple of months later, the CDC pulled out of Duncan's project. Publicly, the reasons given were carefully neutral; they were just too busy. In Atlanta Nancy Cox said, 'It's a resource issue. Hong Kong had really taken over our lives, and there's only so many things you can be involved in productively. Plus, when we first got involved, there weren't so many other scientists on board; by the time we left the project there were, and it was clearly going ahead whether we were there or not. Whereas all the other things we have to do – routine surveillance, the H5 investigation – those are things we're uniquely qualified to do, and if we don't do them, they won't happen.'

They're also, frankly, more important than 1918. Understanding that virus may tell us a lot, but with current strains of flu killing 20,000 people in an ordinary year in the United States alone, it's more immediately pressing to deal with strains of the virus that are running around now than it is to dig up an old one, even the biggest and baddest old one.

Publicly, then, the CDC had too much on their plate to back Duncan as well, but there was something conveniently disingenuous about that stance, when we know every flu scientist on earth would give limbs to get 1918 RNA in their labs. Nor was it hard to gather that, privately, the CDC didn't want to back Duncan anyway. They thought her team was unwieldy, and they were also profoundly uncomfortable about her relationship with the media.

Though still on Duncan's team, Taubenberger felt the same. He said, 'I work for the Government. The policy of the United States Government is that any work funded by the taxpayers like mine is free and open – that is, if anyone from the media calls me up, I'll talk to them. But there were lots of concerns brought to my attention that the Spitsbergen group was trying to limit access, and that made the Institute very nervous.'

Duncan, of course, said her team was entirely open to the media; certainly, she herself gave interviews freely and profusely, as she did for me in Toronto. During that first interview, on the other hand, she refused to tell me the names of anyone else on her team, which, apart from being pointless when it was perfectly easy to find out, did strike me as rather bizarre. Her stated reason was that she didn't wish to give out people's names without their prior permission; no doubt it was just a side-effect that any journalist with a deadline to meet would have to stick to writing about her.

With these misgivings in the air, it's no surprise that when Johan Hultin turned up in Taubenberger's mailtray offering him a second shot at Alaska, he jumped at it. So far, the hunt for the 1918 virus hadn't been a race; no one else had known Taubenberger even existed, let alone that he was out of the blocks and half-way round the course already. Now, however, Hultin was giving him a chance to break the finishing tape before Duncan's team had even put on their spikes.

Johan Hultin is a remarkable man. If you climb a mountain that's never been climbed before, you get to name it – so there's a summit in the Karakoram called Old Codger's Peak, because Hultin climbed it when he was sixty.

He also claims a world record for a skiing ascent, having been inspired to tackle it after reading an article in *National*

Geographic. It took him two years to put it together and two months to do it, but at the age of fifty-eight (with the assistance of some camels) he duly got himself 25,000 feet up a mountain on skis.

He also has a great interest in archaeology. In his native Sweden there are a number of old labyrinths, some many centuries old, and the Government seeks to preserve these stone mazes as part of the nation's cultural heritage. Hultin knew of one in particular, on a Baltic island, which had been decreed to be in too poor a state of repair for restoration to be attempted.

Off his own bat, therefore, he got in touch with a chemicals firm, and worked with them to develop a new glue for bonding granite to granite. Then, in the summer of 1997, he arranged for a group of his old schoolfriends to have a rustic reunion, to be spent repairing this abandoned island maze. Unfortunately they ran out of glue, so in the summer of 1998 he went back with more of it to finish the job. But then, finishing things when you started them clearly mattered to Johan Hultin.

He stands tall, at least six foot four; though seventy-three when I first met him in 1998, he also stands straight as a redwood. He's a little hard of hearing, and he speaks and moves slowly – with great courtesy and thoughtfulness – but his grasp when you shake his hand is firm as a vice. He is, chuckles Taubenberger, who's come to admire him enormously, 'a Scandinavian *Übermensch*. He's an incredible man.'

He grew up in Stockholm and went to the United States in 1949 to study immunology at the State University of Iowa. They'd been working on flu there ever since Richard Shope isolated the first swine virus in 1930; Hultin went to work on it too, and that winter of 1949 they had a visitor from NIH.

Hultin happened to overhear a discussion between this visitor and one of his professors about 1918. The gist of it was that they'd done everything possible to try to determine what that virus had been, and only one avenue remained – somebody had to travel into far northern climes, and find flu victims buried in permafrost. 'I heard that,' said Hultin, 'and my God, then I knew. That was the subject for my PhD. That was *it*.'

He talked to his professor and asked what he thought about his taking on that challenge; his professor backed him, and he started on it right away. Among his multiple interests, it happened that he'd already been in Alaska the summer before, working with a palaeontologist there on the early evolution of the horse; they'd been collecting metatarsal bones, the small bones of the foot. Now Hultin wrote to ask him how he could get mission records from settlements in northern Alaska and on the Seward Peninsula, a blunt knob of land sticking out towards Siberia in the centre of Alaska's west coast.

It was well documented that the suffering of the native peoples of Alaska during the 1918 pandemic had been as terrible as that of the people in Labrador. Native Americans were badly hit wherever they lived – their mortality rate was four times as high as that among urban white Americans – but Alfred Crosby's account of what happened in Alaska makes particularly chilling reading.

In the week ending 12 October, seventy-five people died in Seattle; 108 people died the following week, 160 the next.

Alaska's Governor Thomas Riggs Jr asked all the steamship companies to check their passengers and refuse passage north to anyone who might have the flu – but it didn't do any good. When the *Victoria* left Seattle for Nome, on the south coast of the Seward Peninsula, her crew and passengers had all been examined and passed fit. No one fell ill on the voyage, all were quarantined for five days on arrival, all mail and freight were fumigated, yet within days 300 people were sick (half the white inhabitants of Nome) and twenty-five of those were dead within a month.

In Alaska's larger settlements, with higher proportions of white population and at least some level of health care provision, the death rate wasn't significantly worse than elsewhere in the United States. In the aboriginal villages, however, the pandemic was devastating; among the Eskimos in Nome, 162 people died in eight days. Upriver from Anchorage, all bar two of Susitna's 250 people fell sick; no one could hunt, cook or cut firewood, help took eight days to arrive, and twenty-nine died in a month. On Kodiak Island, cut off by storms for two months, forty-seven people died out of 550.

Aleut societies simply ceased to function. At Hamilton, across the Norton Sound from Nome, an evidently exhausted and exasperated schoolteacher wrote in his diary, 'They refused to help themselves, but preferred to sit on the floor and wait to die. I did everything for them; furnished wood and water, split kindling, made shavings, built fires, cooked food and delivered it to them, and even acted as undertaker and hearse driver. Apparently the native had no regard but rather fear for their dead. Frequently I had to rescue corpses from the dogs which began to eat them.'

At one settlement, when a number of Eskimos were gathered into a single large building to be cared for, some thought they'd been locked in a death house, and hanged themselves. Others, fleeing in panic, spread the flu from village to village, cabin to cabin. Rescuers breaking into log houses and igloos would find entire families dead; too sick to make fires, those not taken by the virus had frozen to death.

At York, south of Wales on the westernmost point of the Seward, a young boy fell ill and died. The boy's father brought him to Wales for burial; two days later he was sick himself, and within days the whole village lay prostrate. There was no help; everyone in York had died, and Nome was 160 frozen miles away. The final toll in Wales was 170 dead out of 310 people; five of them were infants born during the pandemic and promptly killed by it. As for York, it's not even in my atlas any more.

By January, the Alaska Bureau of Education was feeding entire native populations; hundreds were orphaned, and whole swathes of the state had been reduced to charity dependence. Burying the dead was a nightmare; fires had to be lit to thaw the ground. Trying to cope, Governor Riggs spent so much more money than the state actually had that, technically, he was in breach of the law. But, he said, 'I could not stand by and see our people dying like flies.'

Hard-pressed too, Washington gave him little support; when the third wave struck in the spring of 1919 and more people started dying, Riggs, despairing, his state bankrupt, fled from his travails on a two-week bear hunt. In six months, nearly one in ten of Alaska's native people had died, and the territorial government had fallen $90,000 in debt. Riggs

231

wrote, 'I doubt if similar conditions existed anywhere in the world – the intense cold of the Arctic days, the long distances to be travelled by dog team, the living children huddled against their dead parents already being gnawed by wolfish dogs.'

In November, at an Inupiat village called Teller Mission on the Seward, Spanish flu arrived by dog sled with the mail man. The Lutheran missionary Oluf Fosso fell ill, the village teacher got pneumonia, and the local interpreter died together with his wife and child; of the settlement's leadership, only the pastor's wife was left standing, with her four-month-old baby to care for. For three weeks, Clara Fosso was the only fit person in the settlement; her husband lay delirious, driving dogs in his sleep. With only four hours of light each day, in temperatures tumbling to −35°C, she hauled fuel to keep half a dozen stoves lit, struggling to feed the people and the dogs.

Around her in the mission house, the sick lay moaning. Corpses were strewn in the igloos round about, with no one fit to bury them; dogs broke into one house and left only a bloodied mess of human bones. When rescuers finally came to help the survivors face the grisly task of burial, they had seventy-two bodies to inter, from a population in and around the mission of about 150; the Fossos had forty-six orphans to care for.

The dead were buried in a single mass grave. Thirty-three years later, this was where Johan Hultin would dig for the 1918 virus.

Otto Geist, the palaeontologist, sent names and addresses to Hultin in Iowa. Through 1950, he wrote to all the missionaries; by the end of the year, he had a series of hand-written death records from different mission logs, and he'd narrowed his search to three places. In each of these there'd clearly been a mass death; he had the names of the dead and the dates of their passing.

He'd also written to the military, for temperature records and the permafrost line. Oddly, nearly half a century later, Kirsty Duncan would decide against looking in Alaska, on the grounds that she couldn't be sure where continuous permafrost lay, but Hultin didn't have this problem in 1950. He set his three sites against a military permafrost map and thought they all looked promising.

He planned to travel in the late summer of 1951. He didn't have any money, so during the previous winter he'd applied for a grant from NIH; compared to today there were pots of money available, and he was certain that funds would come through. He had locations, death records, everything, but the months went by and he heard nothing back. Increasingly frustrated, he approached an Iowa congressman to find out what was going on and was appalled to learn that one of the members of the evaluating committee had taken his work and run with it.

He'd talked the military into equipping an Alaska expedition. They had transports and diesel generators to power freezers to store the bodies that Hultin had tracked down. He said, 'I was astounded. I was angry, and I was really disillusioned, because I'd admired that man a long time, and he'd stolen my stuff.'

When this news came in, the University in Iowa put up money immediately, and the team flew to Alaska the next day. Hultin travelled with his professor of virology, and a pathologist to do the autopsies; they met Geist in Fairbanks as soon as they arrived. The other three stayed in Fairbanks; Hultin went ahead with a bush pilot in a light plane to scout out the ground. He said, 'That man could land in the damnedest places, you wouldn't believe it. It was a tremendous adventure.'

The first cemetery was in Nome, and it didn't take long to see it was hopeless. Since 1918, the river had changed course on the alluvial plain there, coming through the cemetery and thawing the permafrost; he knew he'd be wasting his time. He moved on while, funnily enough, three weeks later the military landed in Nome, unloaded all their personnel and equipment, and started to dig. Hultin said, 'I could have told them there was nothing left. No soft tissue, no lungs, just bone. So they thought Hultin was wrong, they packed up,' he chuckled, 'and went home to get criticized for wasting taxpayers' money.'

His next site was the hamlet of Wales, the westernmost populated place in North America; on a clear day you can see Siberia from there, fifty miles across the Bering Strait. The villagers had to clear driftwood off the beach so the plane could land; looking back now, Hultin sighed and said, 'I was twenty-six. What an adventure!'

Wales was no good either. A single large cross marked where the bodies lay; it stood on a bluff over the beach and it was clear that since 1918, the sea had eaten into the bluff until it was getting close to the burial site. Hultin did a test dig – not at the gravesite, but nearby – and again it was clear that it wasn't worth asking permission to dig there.

A storm blew in; with the wind tearing at ninety degrees across the beach, Hultin and the pilot were stuck. Eventually the pilot got them out by careering down the beach, then hauling the plane through a right angle into the wind and the water when he was ready to take off. Hultin shook his head with a smile and said, 'I distinctly remember the waves hitting the wheels.'

His third and last chance was Teller Mission. The beach there was gravel; they couldn't land on it. The pilot found a place to set down, they crossed an inlet in a whaleskin boat, tramped six miles across the tundra, and when they arrived Hultin thought the gravesite looked good. He talked to the locals and found three who'd survived from 1918; he had these three speak to the village council to tell them what had happened, then he spoke himself. He explained that if they gave him permission to exhume the bodies, it might be possible to make a vaccine in case a virus like 1918 should ever come among us again. The people on the council understood about shots – they'd been inoculated against smallpox – and permission was duly granted.

Hultin started to dig. He said, 'The others had been waiting in Fairbanks for over a week now; I had to get on. I started to dig a rectangle three feet by six; this was in June and the ground was soft for about a foot down, so I cleared that off. Then I lit a driftwood fire and let it burn down; that melted a couple more inches, and in that way I worked my way deeper and deeper. I needed a big space to keep air channels going to the fire; the sides started to melt, and it was hard to keep it going. I worked sixteen hours a day; there was no darkness. I kept digging until I found the first victim.

'She was a child about six years old. She was beautiful, with her black braids. She was well preserved, and I knew

235

there'd be many, many more. I telegraphed Fairbanks, and when the others arrived we opened a much larger hole, six feet by ten, all four of us digging. We found many bodies well preserved, with good lung tissue, everything ideal. The pathologist did post-mortems; we observed a sterile technique, because we didn't want to contaminate the samples with any virus from ourselves, obviously, and we didn't want to catch anything from them. We had masks, gloves and sterile instruments; we didn't move the bodies, we took samples of the frozen lung right there. It had ice crystals in it; it wasn't solid, but near enough. We sealed the samples with dry ice in Thermos bottles; we'd got the dry ice from fire extinguishers. We took specimens from four bodies, closed the hole up, then went rapidly back to Iowa, still with the fire extinguishers. We were flying in DC3s, there were a lot of stops, and I had to keep filling the bottles with dry ice. But when we got back, they were still in good shape – still frozen.'

Hultin worked on the samples every day for six weeks. No limit was set on the number of eggs he could use; he tried ferrets, mice, guinea pigs, he had a technician full time, he tried everything he could think of. He felt, he said, 'so focused on this thing. It wasn't just my PhD or my career – I felt everything was on the line.' His professor helped him, making sure he did everything right, and he couldn't get a whisper of the virus. He got bacteria like pneumococcus and Pfeiffer's, and that was interesting, but it wasn't flu. There was no live virus; he shrugged and said, 'Well, it's easy to understand today how fragile it is. But we knew none of that then.'

As for finding it in fragments, there was no PCR in

1951; it wasn't possible, and it couldn't occur to them that it might be. Hultin's wife Eileen said, 'For decade after decade, he's always told anyone who'll listen that he was the right man in the right place at the wrong time.'

'Oh,' said Hultin, 'it was disappointing, disappointing. I used up all the material, and I got nothing from it. So,' he sighed, 'I never finished my thesis. I went on to medical school, and I became a pathologist. But all the time it was in the back of my mind that sooner or later, someone would be able to find it. Once PCR came along, someone would be able to analyse it – and sure enough, Taubenberger did it. So far, he's the only one. So I read *Science*, I wrote to him, and I told him I could get him more material. I offered to go and get it myself.'

I asked him why, at the age of seventy-two, he would want to go back to the frozen wastes of the Seward Peninsula to do that grim and difficult job himself. He said firmly, 'Because I failed once, and that really impacted me. I'm not used to that.'

The letter arrived in Taubenberger's mailtray in July and sat there for two weeks; Taubenberger was off work while his wife had a baby. In the letter Hultin explained who he was, and what he'd done forty-six years before; he enclosed a photocopy of the passage from Crosby's book about the Iowa team's attempt to find the virus, along with photographs from the expedition, to prove he wasn't some crazy type just making it all up.

Hultin explained that though he was in his seventies now, he was in good shape, and he was willing and eager to try it again. He said he'd do it at his own expense and contribute any samples he might obtain to the AFIP. So would Taubenberger be interested?

When Taubenberger got back to work the answer was, obviously and immediately, that he'd be very interested indeed. He called and asked Hultin when he could go; Hultin said, 'I think he expected me to say "Next year sometime." I told him, "I cannot go this week. But next week, I will."'

Hultin didn't tell him why he couldn't leave straight away. Now retired and living in San Francisco, that week he was finishing work in the Sierras on a replica Scandinavian log house. It stood three storeys, he'd built it entirely with hand tools, it had taken him twenty-nine years – and he wasn't going to mention it because, he said, 'Jeff might have thought he was dealing with a nut.'

At the beginning of August, Hultin took a commercial flight to Anchorage, rode a freight plane from there to Nome, then found a bush pilot to take him to Teller. Home to 265 people, the settlement's called Brevig now, and it's got a landing strip, so it's a shade easier to get to than it had been in 1951; they had to wait a day for a heavy fog to clear, then Hultin walked back into the mission with nothing more on him than a duffel bag and a set of sketches to show what he was hoping to do.

He went first to Brian Crockett, the pastor at the Lutheran church. Crockett had heard the story of how Hultin and the others had come to dig before, and the village elders remembered giving him permission to do it. Crockett said, 'Not just anyone could have walked in here and done this, but he could.'

Hultin met with the village council, and they agreed to let him conduct a second exhumation. Brevig's Mayor,

Gilbert Tocktoo, said it took a couple of hours of discussion, but they could see that if he found any samples of the virus, and if that helped find a way to stop it ever spreading again, then it had to be worth it.

Hultin started digging the same day he was given permission, with the help of four local young men. They worked from nine in the morning until midnight; Hultin slept on an air mattress in the village school. On the afternoon of the third day, six feet down, they found the first body; it was rotted, which Hultin suspects was due to the previous exposure in 1951.

The fourth day, another foot deeper, they found more bodies. Three were little more than skeletons, with some soft tissue remaining, but not much; between them, however, lay a woman who was still remarkably well preserved. She'd been maybe thirty years old, and she was obese; the layers of fat had protected her from decay. Hultin sat on a pail and looked at her; he knew her lungs would be in good shape. In the mass grave, her name could not be known; he christened her Lucy, after the skeleton three million years old that had been found in Ethiopia in the 1970s. The name Lucy comes from the Latin word for light; if the first Lucy had shed light on human evolution, now Hultin hoped this Inupiat woman might shed light on 1918.

Using rib cutters and scalpels, he took tissue samples from three other bodies; from Lucy, he took both lungs. He fixed the samples in preservatives supplied by Taubenberger, and reburied them to keep them frozen; then, in the wood shop at the village school, he built two new replicas of the original crosses at the gravesite, one standing five feet tall, the other nine feet. While the site was being restored he retrieved the samples and made them up into four packages; using Federal Express, UPS and the regular postal service, he mailed them to Taubenberger on different days to guard against loss or accident.

Three weeks later, Taubenberger called to tell him that Lucy's lungs were full of fragments from the 1918 virus. They were mostly smaller pieces than those contained in the two sets of tissue samples he'd now got from the archives – around 100 base pairs, as against 150 in Vaughn and Downs – but there was so much of it that in the next couple of years, his group would be able to sequence the entire genome of the Spanish flu.

Hultin had paid the young men who'd helped him $900; with his travel costs, he estimated he'd spent $3,200 altogether. Of his decision to fly to Brevig and dig again he said simply, 'You can see the temptation, can't you? I knew where to go, and I could go and do it myself. So I did.'

Twelve months later, the Svalbard team would spend a large sum of money to little purpose; meanwhile, this extraordinary man had already done the job with little more than $3,000 and a shovel.

When Taubenberger called him in San Francisco to tell him he had RNA in Lucy, Hultin was ordering two engraved brass plaques to go on the larger of the new crosses he'd built for the gravesite. The one along the crossbar reads: 'The following 72 Inupiat Eskimos are interred in this common grave. Pray, honor and remember these villagers, who lost their lives during the short span of five days in the influenza pandemic, November 15–20, 1918.' The second plaque, on the upright, lists their seventy-two names.

Hultin returned to Brevig in September 1998. On the bleak, flat tundra by the chill and spray-flecked waters of the Bering Strait, he fixed the plaques to the crosses.

By then, he'd tracked down his thesis supervisor from his university days in Iowa; now retired and in his eighties, he was living in Arkansas. Hultin wrote to him to let him know that he'd finally completed his PhD; he said, 'It was a good feeling to finish the job.'

Neither Hultin nor Taubenberger told anybody what they'd done. From the beginning, Taubenberger had told Hultin about the Svalbard project; Hultin's reaction was that if Svalbard produced more genetic material from 1918, well and good; if more people got more samples from different sites, anything that might reveal about evolutionary drift in the pandemic strain would be valuable.

On the other hand, coming on the back of Taubenberger's *Science* paper, Svalbard was beginning to generate a great deal of media interest; according to Taubenberger, Hultin didn't want any part of that. Moreover, 'He also knew that at the time, I was still willing to participate in the Spitsbergen group, but I told him there were problems with it. It was so large, people seemed to have different agendas, and they didn't really all get along with one another – it was a very discohesive group. So Hultin thought it'd be much better to have a very tight collaboration, just he and I.'

As with public explanations for the CDC's withdrawal from Duncan's project, this also is carefully incomplete stuff. It's impossible not to believe that Hultin wanted to get his hands on 1918 first; he'd already tried once, and he clearly meant to see it through. As for the suggestion that he's media-shy, he's not; he's justifiably proud of what he's done, and he keeps all his clippings.

Similarly, Taubenberger can only have seen an opportunity to get the 1918 genome all to himself. So if Brevig came up blank, no one would know about it, and he'd still be on board with Svalbard; if Brevig came up trumps, on the other hand, he wouldn't need Svalbard. They could do what they wanted, and good luck to them; he'd have the gold dust already.

If this sounds sneaky, remember – it had been agreed in Atlanta that if you got samples somewhere else, that was your business. Besides, science is a cut-throat trade; success means reputation, and success and reputation added together mean funding. Asked if science was competitive, Taubenberger told me emphatically, 'Sure.' He shrugged and said, 'Scientists are people, right?'

The Swedish adventurer–pathologist and the American molecular pathologist kept quiet; Taubenberger and Reid went to work on what the former now described as a lifetime's supply of RNA, looking first to generate complete haemagglutinin sequences out of Lucy and Downs to confirm the one they'd already got from Vaughn. Then they could answer the criticism that Vaughn was only one case, and that his flu RNA might conceivably not be the killer strain; they had three cases now, all of whom had died rapidly at the height of the pandemic, and all three turned out to have very nearly the same H sequence.

Out of 1,800 base pairs, just a couple were different here and there. This was the best of all possible worlds; since they were fractionally different they couldn't be a contaminant, but since they were otherwise the same, all coding for a previously unseen version of the protein, then these were indeed the sequences for the 1918 H1. The next question was, when to announce it?

In December 1997, the Svalbard group met at NIH in Maryland to review the results of the GPR scan and make their final decision on whether to go ahead in Longyearbyen. Taubenberger said nothing about Alaska; he said only that he had three positive cases now, and was continuing to work with the samples he had. The group agreed to meet again in February at Mill Hill – and that was when he and Hultin lobbed their bomb.

Charles Smith tells the story in tones of the deepest, most mournfully bitter anger. On the evening before the meeting began in North London, he said, 'Kirsty walks into this little guest house there, and she's in shock. She's clearly, clearly upset. She takes me aside and she says, "I finally got through to Jeff. He's not coming. He dug up the Alaska specimens. He's working on them." So I asked Kirsty what had gone on, and she said Hultin had gone up, got permission from the village council, and done it with a pickaxe using some local youths. And I felt sick, because I thought that would jeopardize our project.'

Two months later in Toronto, I asked Duncan why Taubenberger wasn't on her team any more. She said, 'I . . . um . . . you haven't met him?'

I said that I had.

'Oh, you *have*. He's *lovely*. I have the *greatest* respect for what he's done, I really do.'

But you don't want to talk about why he's not involved any more.

'There are just some issues that . . . no. As I said, he's a *lovely* person.'

Duncan had spent five years putting together a project to find the 1918 virus in frozen bodies in the permafrost. If Taubenberger was a jolt, Hultin had to be a body blow; it seemed reasonable to ask how she felt about it.

She said, 'I can't comment on his work, because I don't know the details of what was done. What I can say is I'm very proud of the way this has been handled. I am pleased about the way the permission was handled, I asked permission from the Governor of Svalbard . . .'

You followed the proper channels. But how do you *feel*?

She paused a long while, then said she didn't know a lot about what Hultin had done. She said, 'I can only comment on what I've done. I find the project very difficult, as I've said, but at least I can be proud of the way I've handled it.'

But when you learned that one of Taubenberger's cases was from Alaska, that surely must have given you a dark moment?

'Well . . . there's been many along the way.'

But surely none so bad as learning that someone else had already done what you wanted to do?

'I guess, from a scientific point of view, more information is good information . . .'

I don't think you're answering the question, Kirsty.

She had the grace to produce a big peal of laughter, and then to ask with dramatic irony, 'How can you say that to me?'

Again I said, you must have had a dark moment. You must have thought, I've done all this . . .

'It's disappointing. But I believe in my heart of hearts I've handled it properly. It's taken a long time, but it has to. It *has* to. I have to go through those channels . . .'

Which implies you think Hultin didn't do things correctly.

'No, I wouldn't say that. Because I don't know.'

If Duncan wouldn't lay charges against Hultin and Taubenberger, others around her had no qualms about doing so, Charles Smith most pungently among them. In terms of both ethics and safety, he said that the way Hultin had got the samples in Alaska, and what Taubenberger had done in accepting them, 'is not the right thing to do. It simply gives science a very, very bad reputation. I'm really concerned about the ethics involved. There are certain ethical standards that have to be met, and I couldn't believe they were met on this. I said to Kirsty, this could not have been done with informed consent. There's no way he could have done that with informed consent. And you can't accept a specimen that may not have been obtained with the proper legal, medical authority or consent. So what concerns me about this work is not that someone else got results – it's that the work was done in such a way that it's really a black mark on the pathology community.'

There are two issues here – standards of safety, and of ethics. The first involved allegations against Hultin that he'd been reckless; that he could have unleashed live, infective 1918 virus. It was a possibility that the scientists involved in the Svalbard dig all readily admitted was exceedingly small, but against which they were none the less taking elaborate precautions.

Hultin, knowing full well the accusations laid against him, and remaining affably sanguine in the face of them, said calmly that he understood why the Svalbard project would want to take those precautions. He told me, 'I have to put myself in their place. They don't know if it's dead or alive there, so they have to approach it that way. I'm the only one who *knows* it's dead in Alaska, because I'd been there. And I wouldn't have tackled it if I had any suspicion the virus was alive – I couldn't have afforded it. I spent $3,000 of my own money, OK – but I don't have a million, do I? But anyway, what is the probability of it being alive? I've heard it said that someone put a number on it, that it's one in ten to the power of ten (that is, one chance in ten billion), that it's *that* unlikely. So would you be concerned at that level? My wife was concerned, of course – so I told her, if it was dead in 1951, forty-six years later it can only be deader.'

Taubenberger said, if they were to find more cases in Svalbard, that might certainly have some utility. But when they talked of the risk (or the dream) of live virus, 'I think the chances of that are zero. So why bother spending all that money over something you know isn't going to be there? All the people involved in it will tell you, it isn't going to be there. Yet they're doing it anyway, and it just seems silly to me.'

Asked about the possibility of Duncan's people turning up live virus in Longyearbyen, Jan de Jong in Rotterdam said firmly, 'No, no, no. That's not possible. Live virus will not survive that long. Perhaps in liquid nitrogen – but Spitsbergen, I think, is not made of liquid nitrogen.'

So was Hultin reckless in Alaska?

'That's nonsense.'

One might question instead whether Duncan's team weren't planning recklessly to spend a large sum of money guarding against a non-existent risk. Asked if it wasn't just a waste of good research dollars, Taubenberger said, 'I don't know. It's not for me to say. It's not my money. Well, some of it potentially is, because Webster's got NIH funding, so that's kind of interesting. But I think they really want to go to Spitsbergen because they want their own samples. It's a human thing. *I want my own . . .*'

Certainly, in some quarters on Svalbard, the stench of sour grapes seemed pretty potent to me. The quality of Taubenberger's work was more or less grudgingly admitted by some; only John Oxford, to his credit, was unequivocal in his praise. Though he'd tried himself to do the same thing with archive samples at the Royal London, he swallowed being beaten to it with the best of good grace. He thought Taubenberger's work was superb, and he'd kept in touch with him; he said, 'I didn't fall out with him. Kirsty did, after he went in with Hultin – but I'm still discussing other samples with him, because he's the world expert now. He's amazing. It's like a shooting star coming out of the firmament; I was totally flabbergasted when I saw what he'd done, full of admiration, and I have been ever since.'

As for Hultin, 'I rather liked him. He's a real one-off. I felt my nose put out of joint a bit, when we heard he'd gone off to Alaska like that – but we cracked open a bottle of champagne in my garden the other day, and had a really nice afternoon talking about it. He said he had unfinished business, and I can appreciate that. He didn't need us, so off he went.'

*

If Hultin's work hadn't been reckless, had it been unethical?

Hultin said, 'This issue of respect for the dead. To Kirsty Duncan – whose determination and focus I admire very much, by the way – I can only say I'm so sorry it's been portrayed as a race, but I didn't set out to compete with them. I didn't know about them until Taubenberger told me, and by then I was already on my way. And if they find more material, that's good. But respect for the dead – well, I'm sorry, but I've got permission from the people there, some of them descendants of those victims. Then I've put everything back in proper order. I've made two new crosses for them, and I've found all the victims' names. With the help of a lady in Nome I've got their proper spellings, because the missionaries in 1918 didn't get them right in English. So those seventy-two people have their names properly recorded on those crosses now . . .'

It was very clear that he felt he had indeed done everything correctly, and it was very hard to see how you could say that he had not. He would not rise to the charges against him, however; he simply described what he'd done, speaking mildly, and leaving others to say what they may. As he spoke, however, his wife cut him off. Like her husband, she was an entirely charming person; she could not, however, let him go undefended, and she spoke for him with a fierce and angry pride that was impressive to behold.

She proclaimed any charges that he'd been reckless, or that he'd not respected the dead, to be false and vicious. 'My husband has done something for the good of humankind,' she said, 'and these people have *maligned* him. I can get *really* ticked off about it. I'm half-Welsh, so I can get pretty feisty – but it really makes my blood pressure *soar*.'

Hultin by now was quietly, deeply chuckling. 'Eileen,' he said, turning in his chair to reach up his big hand and touch her cheek, 'you're beautiful when your blood pressure rises.'

9 MARVELLOUSLY HUMILIATING

Scientists – particularly those dependent on an ever-diminishing pool of public funds – operate in a fiercely competitive milieu. The shorthand summary for the way the system works is 'publish or perish'; to secure grant funding, you must forever be adding to the sheaf of literature that demonstrates your diligence, drive and invention. Combine this with the fact that the successful scientist is impelled as much by ambition as by curiosity, and the environment gets a weighty emotional charge to it.

Bickersome squabbles are par for the course. Petty jealousies, overweening self-regard, desperate insecurities both of tenure and of personality – all these are intensified by the ever-nagging quest for funds. You publish or you perish; there are no prizes for coming second. The result is a world in which, all too often, impressively large brains come housed in depressingly small minds; a world in which proving other people wrong wins brownie points, while admitting you're wrong yourself can carry a burdensome price tag.

This isn't to say that those involved can't be good and genial company, or that they don't recognize and applaud each other's achievements. But as Noël Roberts of Roche puts it, 'A lot of scientists are so committed to what they're trying to do that it's not a job, it's their life – and if someone encroaches on their life, they defend it. So some people are very tooth and claw about it.'

There is almost certainly no other way for it to be; the spats and eccentricities that come with science are the way it ever was. You have to be a singularly focussed individual, not to say downright peculiar, to want to spend your time rootling among the molecules in the first place, and if the funding system that helps maximize that on-the-brink oddness may look mad to the outsider, it remains hard to think of a better one.

Competition is the spur that drives these people, just as it does sportsmen or politicians or anyone else. Unlike football games or elections, however, the prize on offer in the contests fought by scientists over a subject like flu is the greater health and happiness of humankind. If they don't scrap and claw their way towards a better understanding of it, humanity doesn't make progress – on the contrary, we must live all the time under the threat of the next pandemic. So if egos get puffed up or trampled *en route* to a solution, that's just the game, and if they want to carp and snipe and grumble while they're playing it, good luck to them. Did you never complain about anyone you work with? And are you doing something that might help to save millions of lives?

When work gets duplicated, therefore, or money gets wasted, that's part of the process. When different people race to achieve the same result, it's not necessarily a bad thing anyway; any result must be confirmed elsewhere or, as John Oxford nicely puts it, 'I'd always be right, wouldn't I? And I might not be. Everything has to be put to the test – that's the whole point.' As for money getting wasted, we have to accept that most of what scientists try to do doesn't work; that's another part of the point as well, that finding out what *does* work isn't easy.

Indeed, given the threat flu poses, it's easy to argue that these people should have more money, and certainly not less. There *is* a lot of money spent on flu, in terms of annual vaccine production – which, it should be noted, Cox and Hay and the rest of them do usually get more or less right – and the surveillance system, while it still has worrying gaps, is improving, most notably with the dozen new labs the CDC's been helping to set up in China. Basic research on flu, however, what some call 'blue sky research', remains one of science's poor relations.

Obviously, flu has to be kept in perspective. Cancer, heart disease, HIV, hepatitis, global warming – it doesn't take long to run out of fingers when you start counting the threats humanity has to deal with, and that scientists can work on. Jeffery Taubenberger says, 'There's an infinite variety of research to be done, so of course scientists think funding should increase – but research is expensive. Science is a luxury of a rich society, and we do spend a lot of money on it, but clearly you can't fund everything. The NIH is probably the biggest source of funding for bio-medical research in the States and right now, their funding rate is something like fifteen per cent of the grant applications that get submitted. So there's a lot more science being proposed than can ever be funded.'

Hence the intense competition; hence also the problem that anything risky or anti-dogmatic will very likely have a hard time finding backers. Taubenberger doubts, if he'd gone to the NIH for funds at the start of his project, whether he'd have won their support (he's currently funded by the Veterans' Administration and the Department of Defense), which only goes to show how much blind luck can be involved in picking the right horse at the scientific races.

'The only way to really sort this out,' says Rod Daniels, 'would be to have a world Government, and that will obviously never happen. So at the moment you've got the Americans doing stuff, we're doing stuff, other people are doing stuff, and there's a lot of repetition out there. You need some of it, to confirm your results, but it's not an ideal environment for conducting research. Research should be conducted openly, but there's so much secrecy going on; you almost don't dare talk to potential colleagues, and you're always fairly concerned when you submit grant applications about who's going to read them. Do they give you a true review process? Or do they trash your ideas, then go away and do them themselves? Because you've got to get there first, every time.'

Like it or lump it, that's the nature of the beast; as long as they're scrapping for money it's not going to change, and if they did have pots of money, it probably wouldn't change anyway.

With refreshing candour, Taubenberger says scientists are children. 'Scientists,' he says, 'are people who refuse to grow up. You know how kids are incredibly curious; the first thing they do when they start talking is to ask, Why? Why, why, why? Because they want to know. And eventually the parents say, Shut up. So I think what happens is, most people get it drummed out of them – but the scientist is someone who refused to grow up, and kept asking that question. So it's incredible that I get paid a decent salary to come in and do thought, all day long. It's like playing in a sandbox, you know?'

Where the comparison falls down is that when children ask why-why-why, they expect someone else to give them the answer. When scientists ask why-why-why, on the other hand, they want to find the answer themselves, they want to find that answer before anyone else does, and they want to be famous for it – which, justifiably, Jeffery Taubenberger will now be. Ann Reid and the rest of Taubenberger's group, on the necessary combination of luck, brilliance and plain hard work, are the people who'll sequence the genome of the 1918 flu virus.

Moreover, they may well get an answer as to why it was so bad, because, in the summer of 1998, they found a positive case of flu RNA in the archives from the first spring wave of the Spanish flu. If they can tell from this what genetic mutation occurred between the mild and the deadly variants of that H1N1, we shall have the solution to an eighty-year-old mystery.

'It's fun,' said Taubenberger, 'but it's serious too – and we feel we're making progress. We know a lot more than anyone else has ever known, and it's an incredible honour, and an incredible thrill, to be reading sequence from a virus eight decades old that no one on earth has ever looked at. We're the first people ever to have seen it. Sometimes you get lost in the day-to-day function of it – is this really a G here, or should it be a C? You get locked in that nitty-gritty – then you stand back a bit and think, *Damn*. We're looking at a virus that killed forty million people.

'So it's like a murder mystery – someone interviewed me and put it that way, and I like it. You're trying to solve an eighty-year-old murder, the trail's cold, you're looking for clues, and you're trying to bring the murderer to justice. That was the phrase he used, and it's a little over the top, OK, but it's what we're trying to do. We're trying to find the killer, so it's intellectually satisfying, but it may also be useful for mankind. I wouldn't want to downplay that altruistic aspect either, us working for the good of humanity, but to be perfectly frank, that's not why people do science. I don't want to sound like a complete bastard, but people do science because they're driven to it, because they're curious – and the good of humanity's sort of a nice benefit.'

So the next question is, just exactly how much of a benefit does understanding 1918 really bring us? Because, by definition, won't the next pandemic strain be a new variant we've never seen before, and not actually like 1918 at all?

The answer is, we don't know. 'It's incredible hubris,' says Taubenberger, 'to suppose that you actually know what influenza viruses are about, even after all this work. But if we can take the best possible outcome from this – something specific about the gene structure of the virus which gives us a clue as to why it behaved the way it did – then we could use that as a screen for new viruses. As new flu viruses emerge, we can look for those genetic features, and if you find a virus that's got them, hey, heads up. This is Bad Virus.'

The likelihood of such a virus emerging is impossible to quantify. If the proponents of viral recycling are correct – it's not the fashionable dogma of the day, but few are willing to write it off entirely – then maybe old strains of flu pop back out from some unknown state of latency, in which case something very much like 1918 may be out there as I write, just waiting for its moment.

Alternatively, if total randomness is the key to flu's evolutionary survival strategy, then it must be possible for it randomly to reappear sporting at least some characteristics from 1918, if not all of them. Rod Daniels muses about each strain in turn having an elastic limit; in 1918, in 1957 and again in 1968, each strain comes in and knocks us down, then seems slowly, fitfully to attenuate in virulence as – presumably – it becomes better adapted to us, and we to it. To be a successful parasite, after all, it's not in the virus's interests to kill off large numbers of the host; it wants to settle down and get along with us.

That means it's seeking an equilibrium, so the rate of evolution might slow as it tends to find one. In finding that balance, it'll work through all the viable permutations it can – then it'll start trying out old ones again. In the H3N2 that's been around since 1968, therefore, there were a lot of changes in the early years – then, as with a strain that cropped up in Mississippi in 1985, old configurations started reappearing, in a kind of reverse mutation. 'It had flipped back one move,' said Daniels, 'almost as if it had got into a stasis situation, and was doing just enough to maintain itself in the population.'

The longer it's around, however, the more people will acquire immunity, which is why, sooner or later, flu will always pull out the big gun. Sooner or later it'll manage a reassortment event, and cook up a viral newcomer that can rip through us all. That doesn't mean the next one has to be an H1 like 1918; it might be an H2 like 1957. That sub-type disappeared in 1968, so anybody born in the three decades since then is a sitting target, which is why Rob Webster won't let young people work with it in his lab. Be it H1 or H2, however, the point is that if minor mutations can reoccur, why not major ones?

In short, we don't know the statistical likelihood of another virus appearing like 1918; we only know that it *could* happen. 'The problem is,' says Taubenberger, 'it happened once. So whatever conditions allowed it to be as nasty as it was can obviously happen again – because they already did. And a lot of people ask me, What's the chance of another pandemic like 1918? The answer is, I've no idea. But if you ask me what the chance of another flu pandemic of *some kind* is, I'll tell you. It's one hundred per cent. And I'd like to be ready, wouldn't you?'

Johan Hultin's final word on Taubenberger's work is more dramatic yet. With the RNA from Lucy, he says, 'Jeff's not running short of material now. He's just running short of time.'

In seeking to understand what happened in 1918, Taubenberger (and whoever may come after him) have two problems to confront. Firstly, the sequences now unfolding in the AFIP represent a singularly isolated isolate; we want to understand its evolution, but there are great constraints in what we can compare it to. The first swine and human strains of H1N1 weren't isolated until the early thirties, and in that gap from 1918, flu would have massively mutated even within the one subtype.

Moreover, when flu viruses were first discovered, they were grown in so many eggs and passaged through so many ferrets and other animals, that they may themselves have altered considerably from whatever form they first bore in pigs or people. Really solid flu sequences, sequences whose genetic accuracy you can fully trust, only go back about ten years, so comparing 1918 to other strains of flu involves a lot of guesswork.

Having said that, on the evidence of the haemagglutinin sequence, it does look so far as if 1918 lies somewhere near a common root for human and swine flu strains, and if good sequence can be got from the earlier, milder 1918 strain, Taubenberger should be able to place it that much better.

The second problem, however, is that having the sequence isn't at all the same as having the actual virus. Having the blueprint is nothing like having the building; having the recipe is nothing like tasting the meal. That's why, no matter how unrealistic it may have been, so many of those involved in the Svalbard expedition harboured their fervent dreams of live virus.

John Oxford says, 'You will not get a full explanation of its virulence just by looking at the genetic sequences. You won't. Look – I bought one of my children a book of stamps last Christmas, a 1953 Coronation series from Africa. It was perfect, all these countries people have never heard of these days, Tanganyika, Rhodesia – *perfect* stamps. Elephants, flowers, locals, everything. But you couldn't reconstruct a picture of Africa from that stamp book, could you? You have to *go* there. And the sequence is like that stamp book.'

This, of course, begs the question of whether we *want* anyone getting hold of live 1918. Taubenberger doesn't want it; his lab couldn't work on it, and there are only two facilities in the United States with BSL4 clearance that could – at the CDC in Atlanta, and in the military equivalent at Fort Dietrich near Washington. Taubenberger does readily concede, however, that only having the sequence and not the thing itself may well be a problem.

Even with the whole sequence, he says, 'We still might not be able to point to one gene and say, That's it. It might be many different factors. So we'll give our best shot to analyse it and say, this is what we think it means, this is where we think it came from, and this is what we think the implications are for the biology of the virus. But that, in a sense, could be the end of our work. Once the sequences are out there in the literature, people like Webster, Cox, Oxford, Skehel, they can take them and do their own stuff. I mean, it's not like I necessarily want to work on flu all the rest of my life. Right now I want to work on 1918, because it's unbelievably bloody interesting . . .'

But actually, what he'd really like to do some day is settle down to composing classical music.

Meanwhile, in confrontational mode on Svalbard, Rob Webster asked me, 'What d'you want? As the public, what d'you want to know? Because I don't expect to be able to tell you why that virus ever killed. If Jeffery comes up with a total sequence, we will not know why it killed.'

So what will you know?

'It will allow us to see whether the currently available antivirals will be any bloody good when one of these things appears again. You can tell that with great certainty. And you can design a vaccine that would cope with it, and prepare that vaccine. Is that enough for you?'

I'd settle for that.

In their hunt for funds to arrive at such an outcome over the past two decades, the flu community was greatly hampered by the fall-out from the swine flu affair of 1976. In January that year, a new contingent of recruits arrived at Fort Dix in New Jersey; in a cold damp winter a number of them reported sick, and several were hospitalized. There'd been an earlier outbreak of respiratory disease at Fort Meade in Maryland; samples had been sent to the Walter Reed Army

Medical Center in Washington, and the culprit was identified as an adenovirus. This would ordinarily cause mild, flu-like symptoms, and is a regular repeat offender in the crowded confines of military bases; at Fort Dix, the camp doctor assumed at first that he had adenovirus on his hands as well.

Dr Martin Goldfield of the New Jersey Department of Health thought it looked more like flu; he asked for specimens, and eleven out of nineteen proved positive. Four were the then-prevailing strain of H3N2, a strain first isolated in Victoria, Australia; five were harder to type, and two samples didn't respond to any reagents the New Jersey lab had at all. These seven were sent to the CDC in Atlanta.

Meanwhile, more soldiers were turning up sick. On 4 February, Private David Lewis reported ill with flu and was sent to bed; presumably he didn't feel too bad, because that night he got up to go on a routine five-mile march. During the march, he collapsed; he was dead with pneumonia a few hours later.

In the next few days, the New Jersey public health labs found two more specimens they couldn't identify; one of these came from Private Lewis. By then, the CDC had shown that the first five uncertain strains were regular H3, but that the other two were something unknown. By 12 February, they'd typed them instead as H1N1 – an H1N1, what's more, that was closely related to the swine flu first isolated by Shope in 1930, which was itself thought to be related to the 1918 killer.

The CDC flu staff contacted their boss David Sencer that night; the next day they double-checked, and reconfirmed their results. On 14 February, national public health officials gathered for an emergency meeting in Atlanta.

It should be borne in mind at this point that in 1976, there was a widespread assumption (based in part on work by Edwin Kilbourne at Mount Sinai in New York, and almost certainly correct) that growing human populations, engaged in ever more travel, would offer flu more opportunities to mutate and evolve. It was thought that the timespan between pandemics, therefore, would probably decrease; from H2 in 1957 to H3 in 1968 had been only eleven years, and by 1976 flu people were beginning to get jittery.

At that time, somewhere from eight to twelve million Americans were vaccinated annually. It saved lives, it cut health care costs, and it was safe; in the previous five years there'd been only fifteen successful lawsuits, all of them settled for modest sums, the largest pay-out being $26,000. Moreover, the experience of the two previous pandemics had been highly instructive.

In 1957, though they knew H2N2 was coming, the Government wouldn't countenance undertaking the huge public health programme that mass vaccination would entail; medicine in the United States, after all, was a private business. The pharmaceutical companies, on the other hand, wouldn't risk producing large quantities of vaccine without financial guarantees until they knew it was needed. But the trouble with flu, of course, is that by the time you need vaccine, it's too late to start producing it – so H2N2 arrived, the vaccine makers geared up, H2N2 killed 70,000 Americans and moved on, and in its wake the manufacturers were left sitting on tens of millions of doses that they couldn't sell.

The private system proved not only hopelessly inadequate, but also dismally inequitable. Vaccine became near enough a black market product; big corporations and baseball clubs procured it for their workers and their players, while the poor took their chances.

Nineteen sixty-eight wasn't much better; 34,000 Americans died, while the costs in lost production and health care ran into billions on both occasions. In 1976, therefore, confronted with an H1N1 in New Jersey at a time when a feeling was abroad that the next pandemic was due, the instinct to recommend mass vaccination was understandably strong. In the two weeks after the first emergency meeting, moreover, 500 soldiers at Fort Dix had tested antibody-positive for swine flu.

Then as now, the logistics of confronting a potential pandemic were horrendous, as were all the moral, medical and financial implications. Assuming that the flu season began in September, and that the new strain would most likely take off then, the United States had six months to prepare 200 million doses of vaccine – if indeed the scientists and public health officials decided to take that option. Put at its starkest, obviously, you could vaccinate and then find that the flu never happened – but what if you didn't vaccinate, and then it turned out to be like 1918? 'Better,' said one scientist bluntly, 'to store the vaccine in people than in warehouses.'

On top of producing the vaccine, however, it would take eight to ten weeks to administer all the doses, and a couple more weeks for people to develop immunity, so if this was a bad strain, come September it would very likely start reaching people before the vaccine did, even if they started in the spring to go all out at making and delivering it. On the other hand, if they did go for it, at least a proportion of the people could be reached in time – say, 60 or 70 per cent. Then you'd have a good degree of herd immunity; you'd have a lot of people who'd be barriers to the virus.

At a press conference on 10 March, it was announced that the Fort Dix incident was real; it was also confirmed that, as yet, there had been no more new cases. Asked what the pandemic potential was, the scientists put the likelihood at anywhere from 2 to 20 per cent. As for the severity of it, it was impossible to predict, but who could say with any certainty that it would be mild? Only one thing was sure – vaccination would be milder. There'd be a few sore arms, a few fevers, maybe an unlucky heart attack or two, but nothing more.

All bar one member of the Advisory Committee on Immunization Practices said mass vaccination was the way to go. That single demur came from Dr Russell Alexander of the University of Washington School of Public Health, who felt, 'One should always be conservative about putting foreign material into the human body, especially when the number of bodies approaches two hundred million.'

His objection was noted, but not heeded. The three senior public health officials at the press conference – David Sencer of the CDC, Harry Meyer of the FDA, and John Seal from NIH – understandably agreed that if a pandemic came and people died, and it then emerged that they'd had a vaccine and they'd put it in the fridge, it would look truly awful.

Doubtless it was also a consideration that CDC's budget had been cut by Nixon and Ford; in the face of that, here was a chance to show what they were there for. Moreover, as Arthur M. Silverstein subsequently wrote in *Pure Politics and Impure Science*, his account of this affair, 'Consider the influenza virologist, normally confined to his narrow circle of fellow specialists, who must now have felt a secret thrill of anticipation at seeing his subject in the forefront and in newspaper headlines, and at finally being able to show the general public how important his science really was.'

Sencer wrote a memorandum for action which passed up through the bureaucracy to the White House; there was, he said, a 'strong possibility' of an H1N1 pandemic. He recommended vaccination of every single person in the United States – 213 million people – at a total cost of $135,000,000. He and those advising him wanted to stop another 1918, of course, and they wanted to show that they could do it as well. Also, however, they wanted to do something that had never before been attempted in history, with all the research opportunities that involved; Sencer's budget included $8,000,000 for monitoring, surveillance and research as the programme unrolled.

The memo was written on Saturday, 13 March; Sencer was in Washington with it two days later. David Mathews, the Secretary of State for Health, Education and Welfare, was won over that Monday: 'We had to assume a probability greater than zero, and that's all that we needed to know.'

Mathews immediately wrote a note to James Lynn, Director of the Office of Management and Budget, and Silverstein tracks the way language changed as the message moved up the system with a meticulous fascination. On 10 March at the press conference, there'd been a 2 to 20 per cent chance of a pandemic. On 13 March in Sencer's memo, there was a 'strong possibility'. On 15 March Mathews wrote, 'The indication is that we will see a return of the 1918 flu virus . . . the projections are that this virus will kill one million Americans in 1976.'

In five days, the possibility of a pandemic had evolved into a blunt prediction of a million deaths, and a strain antigenically related to 1918 had become the thing itself. Moreover, as Silverstein notes, politically the OMB knew, 'Any program that posed an urgent choice between spending money or putting lives at risk could have only one answer – spend the money.'

It was an election year, for the Presidency, for one-third of the Senate, and for the full House of Representatives. In the White House, the Sencer memo was seen as 'a gun to our heads'; on 22 March, President Ford agreed to vaccinate. Furthermore, keen to counter charges of indecisiveness laid against him by both Jimmy Carter, and Ronald Reagan in the Republican primaries, Ford said he'd announce the programme himself, thereby tying the authority of his office to its progress.

A meeting of scientists two days later backed the decision unanimously. On top of this scientific assurance, it looked like good politics; it upstaged the Democrats on a health issue, but it was popular with them too because it was more money for public health. The appropriations bill zipped through Congress, and Ford signed it into law on 15 April. Asked if there were enough eggs to produce all the vaccine, one of his advisers told him, 'The roosters of America are ready to do their duty.'

By June, it was fouling up already. One vaccine company grew several million doses of the wrong vaccine; assorted technical problems led the manufacturers to admit that they might only manage eighty million doses by October. In Britain, meanwhile, Sir Charles Stuart-Harris (one of the discoverers of the first human virus in 1933) said the Americans were being alarmist; it was reported in *The Lancet* that five out of six volunteers infected with swine flu were only mildly sick, and the sixth volunteer not at all.

Field trials found that the new vaccine didn't work in children unless you gave them so much of it that they were really sick anyway. In New Jersey, Martin Goldfield said the vaccine should be stockpiled, not administered; Albert Sabin, one of the pioneers of polio vaccination, backed off his previous support for the programme, and agreed with Goldfield. The *New Yorker* ran a glorious Oscars spoof titled QUAX BACK MAX VAX! Swine flu, 'a relatively unknown pathogen whose last starring role was in 1918', ran away with the honours for Best Disease, Best Symptoms, Best Virus, Best Potential Epidemic: 'Right now we're grossing a hundred and thirty-five million at the docs' offices.'

Problems arose over liability insurance; leery of a project this immense, the manufacturers' insurers threatened to pull out altogether. The Government was obliged to try to indemnify the insurers with public money – a precedent intensely disliked in Congress. One Congressional lawyer dubbed swine flu 'the tar baby', after the character who keeps coming back to dirty everyone who touches him.

It was now August, and there had been no more cases of swine flu; the unfortunate Private Lewis remained the one and only fatality. With the insurance issued mired on Capitol Hill, vaccine manufacturers had slowed or even stopped their production, and it looked as if the programme might quietly die. Then Legionnaire's Disease broke out in Phila-delphia.

There were 182 cases among the American Legion con-ventioneers, of whom twenty-nine died; among thirty-nine cases contracted by people passing the building that housed the disease, another five died. The CDC weren't able to identify the agent responsible for this new disease for some time, because the unusual bacterium involved doesn't grow in ordinary lab culture procedures. Congress, however, panicked that the outbreak was swine flu, and reactivated President Ford's bill to indemnify the insurers of his vaccine programme. When the CDC then said that whatever it was in Philadelphia, it wasn't swine flu, Ford – fearing his programme would be blocked again – held a press conference to blame Congress for leaving the American people unprotected against the imminent pandemic.

By now, it didn't look as if vaccine would be available in anything approaching nationwide quantities before November. While chaos reigned over the wording of the informed consent forms, and whether children were to be included in the programme or not, the first million doses were administered by 10 October. On 11 October, three elderly people then dropped dead at a clinic in Pittsburgh.

The fact that they'd all had serious heart conditions got lost in a media frenzy; looking for other vaccine-related deaths, the press started running a body count, and the vaccination programme lurched to a stuttering crawl, with nine states and the city of Pittsburgh stopping it altogether.

On 14 October, the CDC showed that these deaths weren't caused by the vaccine; the President and his family had their flu jabs on national TV. The programme stumbled on; through the next two months several million people were immunized weekly, until by mid-December about forty-five million had had their shots.

In the third week of November, meanwhile, a case of

Guillain-Barré Syndrome cropped up in Minnesota, shortly after the person involved had had their flu jab. Guillain-Barré is a neurological disorder in which the lining of your nerves disintegrates; it results in paralysis, with much associated discomfort. Most victims do recover, but about 5 per cent of cases are fatal, usually due to respiratory problems – in essence, you lose the ability to breathe – and another 10 per cent are left disabled to a greater or lesser degree.

Three more cases showed up in Minnesota in the last week of November, one of them terminal. The CDC started looking for more cases; by mid-December they'd found 107, six of them fatal, with more reports coming in all the while. The data were imperfect, but it looked as though vaccination left you five to ten times more likely to contract Guillain-Barré. On 16 December, the vaccination programme was halted for good.

Private Lewis remained the only person to die of the Fort Dix swine flu. By March 1977, on the other hand, 423 cases of Guillain-Barré had been reported, with seventeen deaths. In the next few years, nearly 4,000 claims were filed seeking $3.5 billion in damages; the CDC, meanwhile, was left sitting on ninety million doses of unused vaccine designed to ward off a pandemic that never materialized.

It was arguably the greatest public health fiasco in history. The incoming Carter administration fired Theodore Cooper, President Ford's Assistant Secretary of Health, and David Sencer lost his job at the CDC. The official report characterized Sencer as a 'wily bureaucrat'; the mess laid at his door was, of course, all the fault of the scientists, and as usual the politicians were blameless.

But what would you have done? Arthur Silverstein was

a Professor of Ophthalmic Immunology who observed the débâcle at close quarters; at the time, he was on secondment as an adviser to Senator Edward Kennedy's Health Committee. He wrote that 'The pejorative charge is made that scientific subspecialities such as influenza virology are ruled by closed cliques that are inbred and self-serving. This is basically true, but it is difficult to see how it might be otherwise.'

He then went on to defend those who'd initiated the vaccination programme on the grounds that on all previous evidence, they'd thought it would be safe; that the measures taken in 1957 and 1968 had been pitifully inadequate; and that doing nothing when the *threat* of a pandemic was certainly present would have been inconceivable. The officials responsible, he wrote, had therefore been 'erroneously indicted and convicted . . . but far worse, a misperception of what had happened in 1976 could cripple governmental efforts to cope with the next massive influenza pandemic, which will surely come sometime in the future'.

Certainly, morale at the CDC nose-dived; it took years for the flu community to recover their credibility, and it's only since H5N1 blew up in Hong Kong that people have started realizing that we really ought to listen to them again. With hindsight, meanwhile, it's pretty hard to blame someone like David Sencer for crying wolf, when we know how many millions of people the wolf might eat. In short, the 1976 swine flu affair shows both how fundamentally unpredictable the flu virus is, and how immensely difficult it is to know what to do in the face of it.

As the Reverend Daniel Bell Hankin sonorously intoned from his Stoke Newington pulpit in January 1890, 'There is something marvellously humiliating in the simple fact that the commerce of the world has been seriously disarranged by an epidemic . . . the projects of kings have been overturned, and their personal plans and wishes thwarted.' We were humbled, said Hankin, and deservingly so, by 'myriads of tiny microbes, invisible to the naked eye, and yet more powerful really than all our armies'.

So should flu researchers have more money? That depends on whether you're prepared to gamble that the next pandemic will be like the '57 or '68 varieties, rather than being another 1918. Given the history of flu pandemics, certainly that would seem more likely, especially since we have antibiotics now. Even so, it seems a fairly major gamble – and that's assuming you think a 'lesser' pandemic (just a million or so deaths in a year) is an acceptable event every thirty years or so.

Whenever it comes, and however severe it may be, the one thing that's sure is that it'll whip round the world faster than any previous pandemic. Every adult inhales 10,000 litres of air a day, so if flu's about, it's always the case that you stand a good chance of getting it; air travel, however, means you now have a chance of getting it from anywhere in the world as quickly as tomorrow.

For example: In 1979, a jet with fifty-four people on board was grounded in Alaska for three hours with the ventilation system turned off. One passenger had flu. Within a few days, so did thirty-nine of the others. Now, fly that jet to its destination, disembark those passengers . . . and where our pandemic preparation time used to be months, in the modern world it's down to days. In the past, if a flu strain emerged in China, it had to work its way out through

Hong Kong and on to ships, or along the Trans-Siberian railway, but today, with China opened up to an increasingly crowded urban world woven intimately together by ever more plane flights, it can girdle the planet in a week. As far as flu is concerned, we are indeed a global market.

According to the British Ministry of Health's report from 1920, in Paris alone the Spanish flu killed nearly 20,000 people in five months. In Lyons, one doctor wrote, 'I have lost in these five weeks more young mothers than I saw die in the previous ten years.' In the worst three months in Spain, 128,000 people died of flu and its attendant complications; one-third of those who died were between twenty and forty years old. In South Africa over the same period, the figure was nearer 140,000.

At least 85,000 died in the Philippines, and around a quarter of a million in Japan; in Kabul, it's thought 10,000 people died in a month, and in some rural districts of neighbouring Persia (now Iran) one out of every five people died.

Nowhere in the world is safe. Australia instituted a strict maritime quarantine, and got through relatively lightly as a result, but the virus found a way in all the same; it just arrived a couple of months later than elsewhere. With a woeful insouciance on the part of the Auckland medical authorities, New Zealand, by contrast, let a merchant ship come into dock – though it was known that Spanish flu was aboard – because the ship was carrying a few high-ranking politicians. In the next couple of months the country was ravaged, and the Maori population decimated.

In the United States, meanwhile, thirty-seven out of

forty-eight life insurance companies were cutting or cancelling their dividend payments; at the end of October 1918, the number of death claims submitted to Equitable Life was 745 per cent higher than at the same time a year before.

One small town in Arizona made shaking hands a criminal offence. People put potatoes in their pockets, or tied a cucumber to their ankles; a woman in Oregon buried her four-year-old daughter neck-high in onions.

One doctor reported mahogany spots spreading on the faces of some victims 'until it was hard to distinguish the coloured man from the white'. Another doctor at Fort Devens wrote that the disease left its victims' lungs looking more like redcurrant jelly than breathing apparatus.

In Atlanta, a midwife called Mattie Varner would later recall, 'They were dying just like leaves off them trees.'

Clifford Lovins, a textile worker in Douglasville, said, 'Man, they sure did die. My mom and my oldest sister had it, and there were five of us boys and all of us come down with the flu but one brother. Well, it got so bad they had to stop the mill. This sister of mine died a week and four days before my mother did. Oh, there was a lot of them that way.'

In England, Manchester ran out of coffins. James Niven, the city's health officer, described visiting a school where the children were falling sick: 'They simply dropped on their desks, like a plant whose roots have been poisoned.'

During the months after the pandemic in Central Africa, people would come on villages of 300 or 400 families entirely unpeopled, 'the housing having fallen in on the unburied dead'.

In Chicago, a father driven mad by the flu announced

that he had found a cure, and promptly cut his children's throats.

And yet we think today of flu as if it were nothing; we talk of 'having the flu' when we have nothing of the kind, confusing it with the common cold and other lesser respiratory infections. We get worked up about rabies or Ebola, when these kill no one we know; when, in England, they kill no one at all. But flu, ordinary flu, kills thousands every year – and only eighty years ago, it killed some 200,000 British people, and forty million around the world.

In the aftermath, the Ministry of Health's report concluded, 'The problem of influenza is still unsolved; its solution will be one of the great events in the history of medicine.' So, eighty years on, are we any nearer to beating flu?

10 PLUG DRUGS

It was the beginning of December 1998, and the Pacific trade winds had been blowing steadily out of the north-west across Hawaii for several days. At a remorseless thirty-five miles an hour, gusting to sixty in the valleys, they bent the palm trees and rattled their hard leaves all through the day and the night. Localized power failures came and went as lines blew down, trees were flung across roads, tiles flew off rooves, and grounded window washers fell behind on their high-rise cleaning schedules. In Honolulu, the First Hawaiian Bank postponed the installation of a two-ton Christmas star atop its 438-foot office tower.

It was, said the weather people, 'a semi-rare occurrence'; it might happen once a year, if it happened at all. Surfers were delighted; beaches facing the wind were a pounding roar of spray, with twelve-foot waves common. For the 'top recruiters' from BeautiControl, on the other hand, it was rotten luck; an end-of-year jamboree at Kapalua on Maui to reward their feats of salesmanship was, literally, being blown out of the water. Whale watching and snorkelling jaunts were cancelled, as was the Atlantis Submarine Adventure; even the Pineapple Plantation Horseback Ride was called off.

In a broad corridor leading to the Ritz-Carlton hotel meeting rooms, felt-tip scribbles on flow charts announced the demise of entertainments; for three days, the best part of 200 virologists and physicians filed past this litany of cancelled pleasures, and assembled in a windowless conference hall to discuss weightier matters. In a very paradigm of incongruity, the Ritz-Carlton was hosting an International Symposium on Influenza and other Respiratory Viruses at the same time as the perks trip for the cosmetic company's sales force. It is to be doubted, however, if the likes of BeautiControl could ever dream of the kind of money that Roche and Glaxo-Wellcome hope to make from their plug drugs.

The story begins with an Australian called Graeme Laver, a spirited character with a throaty chuckle and a deep, wrinkled tan. Now seventy years old, in 1947 Laver had started work as a technician for Alfred Gottschalk, the man who discovered neuraminidase at the Walter and Eliza Hall Institute of Medical Research in Melbourne. Australia has a rich pedigree in this field (at the same institute, McFarlane Burnet won a Nobel Prize for his work on flu), and John Oxford, who's worked there himself, says simply, 'If it comes from Australia, it's probably good science.'

Oxford describes Laver's style in the lab as somewhat like that of a brilliant cook. As a student Oxford would ask him, 'How much of this should I put in? Five milligrams? Ten?' And Laver would grin and tell him, 'Just a pinch.' If Laver's achievement started out as good science, however, the end result has dramatic practical import.

In the fifties, Laver went to London to get a PhD in organic chemistry; as an indication of the kind of character we're meeting here, the way he went home in 1958 was to spend nine weeks driving a Standard 8 across Europe, through Turkey, Iran, Afghanistan, Pakistan and India to

Bombay, and then on by sea. Once back, he went to work at the John Curtin School of Medical Research at the Australian National University in Canberra, and he's been there ever since.

It was from there that, with Rob Webster, he showed how the H3N2 that swept round the world in 1968 had been caused by a reassortant hybrid. To do it, they'd taken samples from birds in Canada and the United States, on the Great Barrier Reef, and in southern China. Any difficulties involved in heading into China in the aftermath of the Cultural Revolution to take swabs off the rear end of ducks would not, after all, give much pause to a man prepared to drive from London to Bombay.

In the seventies, as knowledge of flu's workings advanced, the main focus of researchers' attention was haemagglutinin, the protein spike with which the virus first attaches to the host cell. The way haemagglutinin goes about its business – docking with the target cell, then mediating the fusion of cell and viral membranes – was fathomed by Don Wiley at Harvard and John Skehel at Mill Hill. In the words of Laver's colleague Peter Colman, 'Haemagglutinin is a hell of a molecule, with these wonderful gymnastic things that it does. It's a truly beautiful and spectacular story in structural biology that Skehel and Wiley worked out.'

Neuraminidase, by contrast, was 'sort of a boring old enzyme'. On the other hand, there weren't many people paying it much attention. As Laver puts it, 'Skehel and Wiley had solved the structure of the haemagglutinin, and we were good friends, and also rivals – so I thought, Bugger it. They've got that, so we'll do the neuraminidase. I told someone I was going to go and crystallize it as a joke, to get one up on them – but there you go. At that stage, it was pure science. It wasn't with any thought of drug design at all.'

If you imagine haemagglutinin as the grappling hook with which the terrorist first gains access to the building, you can think of neuraminidase as the cutting tool which lets him escape from the wreckage when he's finished breaking the place up. Both proteins lock on to the same receptor site on the host cell, but for different reasons; the receptor to which they bind is a molecule called sialic acid, lying on sugar chains on the surface of the cell.

On arrival at the cell, the haemagglutinin binds to the sialic acid, and the fusion of virus into cell gets under way. It's a remarkable process, but it does have one major design fault. If haemagglutinin sticks to sialic acid on the way in, what's to stop it sticking to it on the way back out again?

Cue the neuraminidase. As newly budded virus particles start heading off from the disintegrating host cell to find new targets, the neuraminidase binds to the sialic acid as they leave and then dissolves it. The virus is set free to go forth and multiply, and you're free to start feeling ill.

In the seventies, no one knew what neuraminidase looked like; then in Canberra in 1978, Graeme Laver produced crystals of it. Getting crystallized influenza protein involved growing the virus in 1,000 eggs, sucking off fluid full of new virus particles, then concentrating and purifying it until he had 100 billion viruses in a couple of millilitres of creamy-white goo. Laver then used a specific protease (in effect, a molecular axe) to split the heads off the neuraminidase spikes, sifted them apart from the rest of the virus in a centrifuge, and there it was – a host of tiny, plate-like crystals.

Putting it like that makes it sound easy, which of course it wasn't, and as Laver has subsequently written, some people scoffed at the very notion that he even thought he'd pulled it off: 'All you've got are salt crystals. Don't be such an idiot!' Moreover, as he blithely admits himself, 'Having got them, I didn't know what to do with them.' So he called Peter Colman.

Colman was in Munich at the time; Laver told him what he had, and asked if he thought he could use X-ray crystallography to figure out the structure of the neuraminidase. They thought, if they could do that – if they could visualize the molecule in three dimensions – they could see how it changed from one flu strain to another, and maybe see some clue from that as to why certain strains are particularly virulent.

Now fifty-five, Colman is a small, trim figure with his hair turning a polished silver; at the Ritz-Carlton he wore a collarless shirt and round spectacles, and looked more like a movie director than a scientist. Originally a physics graduate from Adelaide, he'd gone to the United States in 1969 to do post-doctoral work in protein crystallography, and it was only then that he began to deal with matters biological.

The science (and the art) of X-ray crystallography is a further step on from the electron microscope in the study of minutely tiny matter. It allows you to magnify an image of your object 100 million times – an order of magnification which electron microscopes could manage with certain images, but not with protein molecules. It gives you a complete atomic picture of your target protein, but to do it, of course, not any old crystal will do.

The neuraminidase that gave them the best material to work with was an N9 that Laver and Webster had discovered in a strain from sea birds on the Barrier Reef. Colman returned from Munich to Australia and went to work at the Commonwealth Scientific and Industrial Research Organization in Melbourne. The CSIRO is a large and many-tentacled body set up originally to conduct applied research for agriculture and industry, working on anything from the wool and dairy trades to metallurgy and building materials; blue sky research on neuraminidase crystals wasn't really in its remit, but Colman went ahead anyway.

Laver supplied him with protein and crystals; growing decent crystals to work with involved some pretty extraordinary adventures. At one point they had neuraminidase growing in orbit on the space shuttle, because crystals grow more perfectly in gravity-free conditions; that project stopped when the *Challenger* exploded. Undaunted, Laver flew to Moscow to ask if he could use the Mir space station instead.

As he tells it now, the Russians were somewhat surprised. 'They were used to dealing with government delegations, not some guy who comes in off the street and wants to use their space station.' Nevertheless, they agreed; they'd never done anything like it before, but in three months flat they designed and built the equipment for growing crystals on Mir. It went up in June 1988 with two Soviet cosmonauts and a Bulgarian.

For a while, the Pentagon got itchy; one expert in technology transfer solemnly opined that the ramifications of the Australian experiment were 'absolutely awesome', threatening the national security of the United States. Laver managed to calm the Americans down, the crystals grew in space for three months, then the Russians made a hash of bringing them back to earth.

Laver said, 'First the re-entry vehicle, with two Afghans in it, went into the wrong orbit and they nearly lost it. These two poor cosmonauts were whizzing around up there without any water, without any air, with the neuraminidase crystals sitting on the seat next to them. They almost died. At the last minute they brought the re-entry vehicle down with a big bang in the Gobi Desert, and we got some crystals back. They were battered, and covered with hairs . . .'

With *hairs*?

'Well,' grinned Laver, 'have you ever been in a Russian lab?'

The crystals were still good enough to be used by a pharmaceutical outfit in Alabama to improve yet further our understanding of the protein's structure because by that stage, Peter Colman had already figured it out. The structure had been solved in 1982, and it was a sufficiently notable advance that when it was published the following year – five years after Laver first called him in Munich – it made the front cover of *Nature*.

Laver says now, 'I'd want to stress that at that time, getting the structure was a real achievement. Techniques have developed so you could do it in a few weeks today, but back then it took months and years of intensive work.'

More importantly, it wasn't just significant as a piece of pure science. The minute they could see what the protein looked like, they could also see that there might be a way to disable it. They hadn't done it with this in mind, but if ever there was an argument for more money to go into basic research, this was it, because what they found themselves looking at was the first real possibility of a drug that might reliably beat flu.

The analogy Laver uses to explain what they'd done is the transformation of a skein of wool into a jumper. The skein's a tangled single strand; it's only when you get the jumper knitted that you can see what shape the wool is meant to have. Similarly, before Colman did his X-ray crystallography, neuraminidase could only be understood in one dimension, as a single line (a polypeptide chain) with 469 amino-acids strung along the length of it. It was known that most of these constituent parts of the protein changed from one flu strain to another, and it was known that a few of them didn't – but which amino acids went where, when the chain was folded into its real shape (into the molecular equivalent of a jumper) was impossible to tell without seeing the molecule in 3-D.

As soon as Colman produced that 3-D image, they could see where those unvarying parts of the protein fitted in the overall structure. What leapt out at the Australians was the realization that the 'conserved' parts of the neuraminidase were clustered together in the 'active site' – that is, the piece of the molecule that binds to the host cell's sialic acid, then cuts the virus free so it can infect other cells.

What they were seeing was a cavity in the structure of the molecule, a cleft which they found to be identical in every strain of flu they looked at. The rest of the neuraminidase might vary but for the virus to function, it seemed pretty certain that this one piece of it had always to stay the same – and the import of that was obvious. If you could make a drug to plug up that cleft, the virus wouldn't be able to get free from a host cell, and you could stop an infection in its tracks. Moreover, the antiviral agent you devised to do that would work against every known strain of flu and, at least theoretically, against any new strain that might occur in future, including any pandemic reassortant. In short, they were standing on the brink of one of the earliest exercises in what's now called 'rational drug design'.

At the time, no one was thinking too much about flu; HIV had arrived, turning the field upside down, and the rest of the world with it. We're starting to forget now the doom-laden climate of fear and moral hysteria into which we were plunged by that virus in the eighties, but it was a time when advertisements set their warning copy on dark tombstones, and footage of haggard, lesion-spotted victims haunted the news programmes and documentaries. If having sex could kill you – slowly and painfully – then how many of us were going to die?

Today, the World Health Organization estimates that well over thirty million people are HIV-positive (two-thirds of them in sub-Saharan Africa), so it's quite bad enough, but if HIV had emerged ten or fifteen years earlier, we'd have been in even worse trouble. Happening when it did, however, the spread of HIV coincided with (and helped to spur) the development of new techniques like PCR; these gave us the ability to clone, express and amplify different bits of the virus, and to study them independently. An unprecedented flood of money poured into this research and transformed our approach to designing antiviral drugs.

Beforehand, there'd been a common wisdom that you couldn't have an antiviral agent that wouldn't also be a cytotoxic agent – that is, in destroying the virus, it would destroy the host cell too. In the assault on HIV, however, as we looked at each separate gene of the virus, we started designing drugs to attack specific viral proteins, rather than the entire organism. These weren't scorched-earth drugs that killed cells as well as their parasites; they were toxic for the virus, but not for us.

To get this to work without unhappy side-effects, the molecular targeting has to be exceptionally precise. Several pharmaceutical companies now produce HIV protease inhibitors; a protease is any enzyme that breaks down proteins (as in the process of digestion, for example) and there's a lot of them about. We have one that's critical to determining our blood pressure level; it's very similar in its function to the HIV protease, so if you want to knock out the latter without destabilizing the former, the chemistry's got to be right on the button.

We can now be that accurate; we can't eliminate HIV, but we can suppress it, so if you're lucky enough to live in the West rather than Kampala or Gaborone, it's now possible to cope with the disease for many years. Meanwhile, the concept of genetic specificity of action in antivirals clearly applies to other diseases than AIDS. Hepatitis, mutant cancer genes, influenza – we can start going after a whole lot of them.

What Laver and Colman had arrived at in the case of flu was a pioneering example of this idea, in which an individual protein is purposefully targeted. Neuraminidase inhibitors – 'plug drugs' – became possible the moment Colman first saw the conserved active site in his 3-D images, a year before we even knew what HIV was.

In truth, the Australians weren't the first to try this route. In 1969, two chemists named Meindl and Tuppy had synthesized a compound in Vienna that they thought might disable neuraminidase, and various versions of it were tested in animals. By 1977, however, it hadn't worked, and it looked as if the compound would end up unused on the shelf.

It was commonly called DANA – and with the 3-D structure of the neuraminidase in front of them, the Australians were able to improve on it. Forming a company called Biota in 1985, they passed the drug discovery process to a chemist called Mark von Itzstein at the Victorian College of Pharmacy. Itzstein's would be the lead name on another cover story in *Nature* in 1993, ten years after the first one, when they published the news that their plug drug really looked as though it could work.

Putting it crudely, they'd taken DANA, re-engineered it in one crucial aspect, and that had made all the difference. Overall, DANA had a nice fit with the active site cavity it bound into, but in one particular place, it didn't sit in the cleft as tidily as it might have done. The Australians took out the misfit molecules and swapped them for something bigger that slotted in more snugly; in chemical terms, they replaced a hydroxyl group with a guanine. Thus modified, the drug now blocked the cleft 10,000 times more tightly – and this in turn meant that where DANA didn't work in animals, Biota's inhibitor did.

At the time, pharmaceutical companies weren't much interested in flu. How do you make money from a drug for a disease you can't readily diagnose, and which comes and goes before half the victims would bother taking a drug anyway? Laver went to one company after another, and they all told him there was no market for what Biota had, absolutely none.

Then Colman approached Glaxo; they came on board, and suddenly things changed. 'As soon as Glaxo started having some success,' chuckled Laver, 'they all jumped in. There are four major companies all designing their own inhibitors now, and those are just the ones I know of; it's become known as the neuraminidase inhibitor industry. I'd sent my crystals to all these people, and they'd all said no thanks. Now they're all clamouring for them.'

Biota went in with Glaxo, now Glaxo-Wellcome. Their drug, brand-named Zanamavir, is administered as a powder from a 'puffer'; you inhale it directly into the site of infection in the respiratory tract. In California, meanwhile, another small firm called Gilead produced a different version that could be taken in tablet form; Gilead in turn secured backing from Roche.

At least two other major companies are pursuing different versions of the plug drug, but Glaxo and Roche are ahead of the game, and their respective drugs were the stars of the show in Hawaii. Glaxo's clinical trials had started in 1994, when Professor Fred Hayden of the University of Virginia was the first person to give a neuraminidase inhibitor to a human being; now Hayden was co-chair of the meeting in Maui.

All the data presented on the drugs there were promising. They got you better at least a day and a half quicker than would otherwise be the case, they reduced the risk of complications, and if you took them prophylactically, it looked as though you wouldn't get sick in the first place. They had minimal side-effects, and, even better, there was little evidence to date that the virus could work out a way around them. As a result, it looks likely that both will be registered for use before the millennium is out.

Even so, an air of due caution remained among the doctors and academics there assembled; given all we know about flu, after all, it would be the most overweening hubris to say we've actually beaten it. Peter Colman said bluntly, 'That'd be silly. That'd be *really* silly.'

Imagining a day when humanity has finally conquered disease is for the writers of science fiction; in any foreseeable future, we're not going to do it. On the contrary, our sometimes reckless pursuit of progress often opens doors to new diseases even as old ones are apparently defeated.

An overseas aid body once approached Rod Daniels for advice on a proposal for multi-tier farming. You'd have chickens on the top level, pigs in the middle, and fish underneath; the top two would rain faeces on the animals below, and the system would thereby help to feed itself. Don't do it, Daniels told them; what flu could cook up in an environment like that doesn't bear thinking about.

In this cautionary context, one conclusion arrived at in the Ministry of Health's report on 1918 still makes valid reading today: 'In the seeming conflict between man and his microscopic competitors, there can never be a time when man is securely master of the universe. Intoxicated by the victories achieved over the plague (in Europe), over the enteric group, over typhus (in Western Europe), and over smallpox, we are too apt to suppose that the campaign has ended in our favour . . . That we have just passed through one of the great sicknesses of history, a plague which within a few months has destroyed more lives than were directly sacrificed in four years of a destructive war, is an experience which should dispel any easy optimism of the kind.'

The Pacific was a good place to recall that sombre reflection; many of the islands in that vast ocean suffered grievously in 1918, their isolated populations helplessly vulnerable to the deadly new virus. In Tahiti, they have a proverb that says, 'The palm grows, the coral spreads, but man departs', and never could it have felt more true; in the capital Papeete, trucks rumbled through the streets around the clock, laden with bodies for funeral pyres that burned for days on end.

The island's French Governor refused to ask for American help on the grounds that it would have been too demeaning, but if he'd changed his mind he couldn't have called for help anyway, because both Papeete's radio operators were sick, and Tahiti was entirely cut off. In Western Samoa, meanwhile, before Spanish flu arrived on a ship from New Zealand, there had been 35,000 people; by the time it was done, one in five of them was dead.

If something like 1918 comes again, will we be better off with the plug drugs to hand? Some of those gathered on Maui had reservations, notably the public health officials who feared that a medical profession grown accustomed to having an effective flu therapy on the shelf would also grow less committed to the surveillance and vaccination system. Certainly, those controlling the finances of our hospitals won't look kindly on doctors spending money getting isolates and sending them up the system, if they think all you've got to do now is prescribe Zanamavir and go home. If surveillance gets patchier, however, the vaccine based upon it could become less reliably protective, or, if people think there's a wonderdrug out there, they might not bother getting vaccinated in the first place.

The importance of the surveillance system was summed up in an aside over breakfast from Alan Hay. Remarking (mildly, and without rancour) on how certain names in his trade tended to crop up again and again, he agreed that certainly those people were important. 'But the guy in Croatia no one's heard of,' he said, 'who somehow kept sending me specimens even when they were beating hell out of each other – he's important too.'

While that man in Croatia keeps watch, along with countless unheralded others in 100 laboratories in eighty different countries, many private companies and public health bodies are seeking better ways of making vaccine. Apart from the new drugs, much of the Maui conference was devoted to these efforts.

That's because, while the inhibitors look good, any notion that they're *so* good that people no longer need vaccination would be reckless. Fred Hayden, very much an advocate of the efficacy of the plug drugs, none the less told the closing session, 'We have to stress that immunization is the touchstone. Antivirals are useful in treatment, certainly in elderly homes, and maybe in a pandemic – but vaccination remains the key.'

The way we make vaccine has not changed in its essentials in fifty years. There are technological add-ons these days (like engineering your candidate strain so it grows faster) but basically you culture the currently circulating virus in eggs, concentrate it, purify it, inactivate it with formalin, and inject it. On an industrial scale it's still a remarkable process, but it's long-winded and cumbersome, and gearing it up to confront a pandemic would take a lot of time and resources; almost certainly, for too many people, it would take too long.

Growing virus in eggs is also imperfect because, when you put it in an egg, you force it to adapt to that avian environment, so Ab Osterhaus argues that growing virus in mammalian cells (in dog kidney cells, usually) could be developed on a large scale to give a better, more cost-effective alternative. You need a big vat, a high density of the appropriate cells, a seed virus out of the surveillance system, and off you go. In a pandemic, obviously, you'd need a lot of big vats, but the resulting vaccine should be nearer to the virus in terms of mirroring its genetic structure, and the antibodies you'd produce should tackle it more precisely.

Fred Hayden felt another development holding out much promise was 'cold-adapted vaccine'. Instead of using inactivated virus, this uses a live, attenuated virus that only grows at the cooler temperatures in your nose (relative to the rest of your body) so it doesn't spread to other sites in the respiratory tract. It's easily administered in a nasal spray, so you don't have to throw away millions of used needles. It provokes no symptoms, or at worst only minimal ones, but it does stimulate solid and lasting immune responses, particularly in young children.

It's a strategy the NIH and others have been working on for thirty years, and which Hayden now believed was on the brink of becoming a major advance. 'The data with children,' he said, 'are compelling. This vaccine could really make a difference in terms of the impact of flu on the general population. School-age children are the primary means of the virus's dissemination in the community – they spread it among themselves at school, they bring it home to their families – and this vaccine clearly protects them.'

Because it's easy to make and take, therefore, we might usefully be able to vaccinate many more people than the traditional high-risk groups, but after what happened in Hong Kong, would it work against H5?

H5N1 presented vaccine researchers with particular difficulties, to the extent that, a year on, there was still no absolutely proven product to defend against it. For a start, the containment conditions required to work with such a pathogenic virus make it awkward to handle, and the fact that it kills eggs doesn't help either. Moreover, if you do have something that looks viable, you can hardly start infecting people with H5N1 to see if it works.

Given these constraints, a small company in New England called Protein Sciences devised an ingenious alternative. Instead of producing vaccine based on the whole virus, their product contains only the haemagglutinin. That protein's produced by a baculovirus, a virus found in caterpillars that happens to have a massively productive gene giving protection against ultra-violet rays in sunlight – so you strip the coding sequence out of that gene, insert the sequence that codes for haemagglutinin instead, leave the virus to go about its business in insect cells, and it sits there churning out big quantities of the protein you've ordered it to make.

Protein Sciences first started cloning haemagglutinin from H3N2 in 1992; they got interested in H5 when the US Department of Agriculture came to them three years later, worried about the outbreak in chickens in Mexico. The commercial possibility that they might be able to market a poultry vaccine, however, was overshadowed by the onset of H5 in people in Hong Kong; an urgent call from the NIH in December 1997 set them working clean through Christmas, and at the start of February, 1,700 doses of bird flu vaccine for health care workers went off to NIH.

At first it didn't work too well; the protein was so pure that when they tried injecting it, it stuck to the glass vial, and next to none of it actually made it down the needle into the person being vaccinated. At that stage, however, they were trying to protect people with what was still an experimental vaccine, and they knew they were only giving a minimum dose so they could try to immunize the maximum number of people. They also knew that the vaccine was 100 per cent effective in chickens, so in people, it became a question of making the solution less dilute, escalating the dosage and rejigging the way it was delivered, with results that now look promising.

At CDC in Atlanta, meanwhile, another way to make vaccine against H5 has been explored; their work was presented by an Australian called Jackie Katz. They used a surrogate virus, a non-pathogenic strain of H5N3 from a duck in Singapore; they grew it in eggs, immunized mice with the resulting vaccine, infected the mice with H5N1 – and the mice lived. At which point you think . . .

'You think,' said Katz, 'that mice and humans are two very different species. But you do think it's a possible approach. And what we're thinking is, together with people at NIH and elsewhere, if we can do this for H5, maybe we should do it for H7, H9 . . .'

It was a constant refrain at the conference that what

we needed, if we really wanted to be prepared, was a complete panel of vaccine candidates standing ready against every foreseeable strain of flu, from H1 to 15, N1 to 9. Chairing the final discussion, Robert Couch from the Baylor College of Medicine said, 'I remember a meeting after 1968 when we said we really had to get a panel of seed vaccines ready for all the strains of avian flu that are out there – and then it just sort of died away. Maybe now it won't.'

He also said, however, 'We've heard about a lot of promising candidates. But the history of this business is a lot of them failing.'

Asked why a fully proven vaccine against H5 still hadn't been settled on, a year after the Hong Kong outbreak, the official line was that over time, the end of that outbreak had somewhat lessened the urgency – but, said Jackie Katz, 'If H5 was still out there, we'd have one.'

H5N1 came up early on the agenda. On the first afternoon Margaret Chan the Director of Hong Kong's Department of Health, got up to speak, and Rob Webster presented her with a signed plaque from all those who'd worked to beat the bird flu outbreak. Webster proclaimed, as he'd promised to do at their Christmas dinner a year ago, that what had happened in Hong Kong was indeed now an incident. None the less, he said, 'We have to keep watchful. We can't relax.'

Relaxation was out of the question because in fact the news from Hong Kong continued to be worrying. Webster and Nancy Cox from the CDC reported that H5N1 had appeared in two distinct forms, both deadly, and that it was definitely a reassortant. No one knew where the neuraminidase came from (or if they did, they weren't saying yet) but the haemagglutinin came from a strain isolated in geese in Guangdong, the southern Chinese province that lies around Hong Kong. The six internal gene segments, on the other hand, came from an H9N2 that's been circulating in domestic poultry throughout Asia since the early nineties.

It first showed up in chickens in Beijing and Hong Kong; it's not as lethal as H5 but it's debilitating, it stops the birds laying eggs, and if you get a bacterial infection on top of it you can lose maybe 40 per cent of your flock. An outbreak in 1996 caused an 80 to 90 per cent egg drop in Korea; just two weeks before the conference, Webster got an e-mail from Iran telling him it had turned up there too. More worrying yet, H9N2 had also now been isolated in pigs in Hong Kong, causing Webster to beetle his eyebrows together and say, 'The plot thickens, yes? There's quite a lot of concern, because now you have a virus with H5N1-like properties spreading into mammals. So we're watching. We're watching very closely.'

'If it becomes established in the swine population in China,' said Nancy Cox, 'that would be a real danger signal.'

As to whether any H5N1 viruses were still around, that was an extremely delicate political question. Asked at the end of her presentation whether they were, Cox replied carefully, 'We don't think they are . . . we don't believe they are.'

It was delicate, said Webster, because the H5 constituent of the Hong Kong virus was certainly still out there in geese. 'So it's a potentially fully pathogenic virus in China, and they really don't want to acknowledge that.'

That evening, while the delegates had cocktails and

canapés at a reception in the Aloha Garden Pavilion and the trade winds whistled past outside, Cox admitted they were treading on eggshells. Asked if the pandemic worry was now H9N2 instead of H5N1 she said, 'As well as. Not instead of.'

So H5N1 is still out there?

'We don't know.'

And you're going very cautiously . . .

'Absolutely. We all understand that when diseases occur in humans that have their source in animals, in any country, there's a potential economic loss to farmers, and there are repercussions that have to be taken into account. So it's understandable that there's caution in terms of discussing what's going on openly. In the United States we take a very aggressive attitude towards avian influenza that gets into domestic poultry, because you know what the potential for the virus is. There are other countries that don't have as extensive a surveillance system, and . . .'

She paused and said as carefully as ever, 'They take a different stance – and we have to work with countries the best way we can. The surveillance in China has been enhanced, but whether it's sensitive enough to pick up what occurred in Hong Kong is open to question.'

Of course, the next pandemic needn't arise in China anyway. Cox's WHO counterpart in Melbourne is Alan Hampson; on the surveillance front he was quick to point out, 'There's virtually nothing happening in India. We're only just starting to get groups up and running in Vietnam. There's virtually nothing in Indonesia or the Philippines, and those are huge populations. So China's unique in many ways, but it doesn't have to come from there, and wherever it comes from, it's going to come out pretty bloody fast.'

When it comes, it may or may not be an H5 like Hong Kong's, but Rob Webster's not taking any chances; he's had four shots of Protein Sciences' experimental H5 vaccine. When I told Bethanie Wilkinson, Protein Sciences' head of virology, Webster had done this, she raised her eyebrows. She said, 'Has he? That's interesting. Most people have been injected twice, so he must have gone outside the study. He must have decided he wanted more.'

The extent of Webster's concern had spawned several apocryphal stories about his efforts to protect himself, the best of them involving him and Ken Shortridge inactivating H5N1 with whisky, and then drinking it. When I asked if that was true he roared with laughter, and said contentedly that it wasn't. On the other hand, he said, 'I still don't think we're in very good shape for a pandemic.'

In New England, meanwhile, Protein Sciences were now dealing with an inquiry from NIH into what it might cost to produce a haemagglutinin vaccine to counter the H9N2 that had started turning up in pigs. It was, said Wilkinson, 'a good sign that they've asked us for a contract'.

And, I said, a worrying sign for everyone else.

'Yes. It's not panic time, but there is an awareness. They're trying to be prepared.'

The difficulties in confronting the pandemic threat with vaccine were most graphically illustrated in the swine flu fiasco of 1976. More recently, the Sydney strain of H3N2 has also shown how precarious our defences are. On the evidence collated out of the surveillance system, every year a new batch of vaccine is designed to guard against the prevailing strains of flu, and in 1997, at least to a certain extent, the Sydney strain beat the system.

There are three families of flu virus, labelled A, B and C. C is an oddity that needn't detain us – it's been dubbed 'a virus in search of a disease'. B does make people ill, so it's included in the vaccine, lately based on a strain first isolated in Harbin. Influenza A, however, is the villain of the piece; its greater mutability allows it to reassort across species barriers, and that's where pandemics most likely arise.

Prior to Sydney, as far as strains of influenza A are concerned, in recent years the vaccine has guarded against H1N1, the so-called 'Russian flu' that emerged in 1977, and against a prevailing strain of H3N2 that first appeared in Wuhan. Early in 1997, however, the Sydney strain cropped up in isolated cases in Korea and Japan; it got a name and a label when it took off that summer in Australia. By that stage, vaccine production in the northern hemisphere was well under way, but you'd normally expect a new, 'drifted' variant to take eighteen months to get around the world anyway.

Sydney moved much faster than that, causing marked epidemics in the winter of 1997–8. Since then, the vaccine's been remodelled to take account of it, but all the same, as I write this in the early days of January 1999, 45,000 Britons are reported to have missed out on their Christmas dinners thanks to Sydney. That number includes one of my brothers and his family, my best friend pole-axed in bed for five days, and the landlord and his family in my local pub across the road.

My local newspaper reports doctor call-outs running

at twice normal levels; the National Health Service is having a winter crisis of even greater severity than usual, with hospitals cancelling operations as they struggle to cope with the influx of flu patients, and refrigerated container units from lorries pressed into service as auxiliary morgues in hospital car parks to cope with the excess of bodies. Statistically, this isn't even an epidemic, yet it leaves me with the ironically apposite possibility, after a year spent travelling from Atlanta to the Arctic, from Holland to Hawaii, that I could get home at the end of it and catch flu in West Yorkshire.

Something like 100 million people around the world get flu every year, and while a better vaccine would stop people getting ill and save the costs in lost work and health care that entails, there's another, less obvious benefit. It's thought that of those who fall sick enough to see a doctor, something like 50 per cent are prescribed antibiotics. This is both expensive and worse than useless because, while having no impact at all on the virus, antibiotics help to promote drug-resistant strains of bacteria.

The arrival of neuraminidase inhibitors would also cut down on this wasteful and dangerous misuse of antibiotics. The plug drugs, however, only work if you take them early in an infection – in the first thirty-six hours – and the trouble with that is, unless it's a dramatically bad strain of flu, viral replication is well under way before you start feeling ill. So how are you going to know you've got flu in time to take the drug? And once you do feel ill, how do you know it's flu anyway, and not one of 200 other respiratory viruses?

A number of companies are therefore racing to produce a rapid diagnostic test kit; it may be that the winners make more money selling the kits than they will selling the actual drugs. The dream result for the pharmaceutical firms, three or four years down the road, would be for everyone to have a flu test kit in their bathroom cabinet as a matter of course. After all, the people of Western Europe and North America spend $8 billion every year on over-the-counter cold medicines as it is, because we really don't like having sore throats and runny noses; since we don't like having flu either, between the kits and the drugs, it's not hard to suppose that Roche and Glaxo look set to make a killing.

To that end, they need the test kits to ensure that people don't take plug drugs for every passing cough and sniffle, then complain (when they don't get better, because they didn't have flu in the first place) that the drug doesn't work. It's in this context that we can hope for these new antivirals to work in tandem with the surveillance and vaccination system, rather than somehow shouldering it aside. To be sure the drugs are used for flu and not for other viral impostors, the drug companies will need to keep an eye on what flu's doing – not least, to put it bluntly, because whenever the surveillance says flu's about, that's their marketing chance.

The other reason they'll need the monitoring system to continue functioning concerns the issue of resistance; indeed, on that front, Peter Colman argues that it's incumbent upon them to start running monitoring systems of their own. In trials to date, the resistance profile of the drugs has been encouraging; mutants have emerged trying to get round them, but either their adapted neuraminidase is unstable, or it's virtually inactive. Either way, the ability of the virus to replicate is massively diminished; the original theory that the virus needs that active site to stay the same looks sound.

All the same, a colleague of Colman's called Jenny McKimm-Breschkin from the Biomolecular Research Institute in Melbourne did offer one reason for caution. Researchers had expected, naturally, that when flu tried to get past a neuraminidase inhibitor, it would be the neuraminidase that mutated. Seeking to generate resistance on an experimental basis in laboratory strains of flu, however, McKimm-Breschkin found that the haemagglutinin mutated as well and that these latter mutations were at the receptor binding site. So why was it doing that?

Trying to beat the drug, the virus was changing the H so that its binding power became weaker; in effect, the virus had become dependent, addicted to the drug that was disabling it. Virus with a weakened haemagglutinin actually *needs* the neuraminidase to be disarmed, so the latter doesn't chop off the sialic acid before the former can bind to the host cell. Another way of putting it is to say that it's accepting the disability we've imposed on it; in a sense, it's trying to find a way to do without neuraminidase altogether.

This looks pretty clever, but there are several caveats here. Firstly, in infective terms, these mutants were still pretty useless. Secondly, they were artificial; these were lab strains grown in tissue culture, and whether wild strains would do anything similar in people is unclear. Thirdly, when we start talking about the virus's apparent ingenuity here, we come back to the philosophical difficulty of getting anthropomorphic with a bundle of molecules. As Colman put it bluntly, 'Flu's not clever. Forget this idea that the virus is clever. The virus is *clumsy*. It makes lots of mistakes when it's copying itself, the ones that have an advantage get selected, and that's why it's successful.'

For that very reason, no one's betting that sooner or later it won't evolve a strategy to get round the plug drugs. Graeme Laver said, 'This virus has learnt over hundreds of thousands of years how to change. It's learnt how to avoid antibodies, and it's going to learn how to avoid these drugs. It's having great trouble getting away from them, but given the nature of things, it probably will do it.'

As the virus competes with the drugs, the manufacturers will engage in intense competition with each other, part of which involves stumping up money to sponsor gatherings like this one in Maui. As one of them put it, 'Let's not be naive here. If we didn't pay for it, it wouldn't be happening.'

As the conference proceeded, a bizarrely genteel dance of mutually respectful watchfulness could be observed among the different interested parties. After key presentations, marketing folk would huddle in confab over the import of the data; professional chemists would seek idly to inquire of me which drug I thought looked better, and whether I might be making any recommendations one way or the other. Away from the academic and medical science, the marketing battle lines were being drawn up.

The conference was organized by a New York firm called the Macrae Group, whose boss Cathryn Macrae was one of those formidably charming people whose company you enjoy greatly but also carefully, in case you say the wrong thing and find yourself leaving the room with your head in flames. Part of Macrae's job was to secure sponsorship for the meeting from a sufficient spread of drug and vaccine firms to ensure that accusations of bias could not be levelled against any outcome of the proceedings, and towards the end of the final day, she asked me with a hint of concern whether the companies involved had behaved, as she put it, 'responsibly'.

Everyone I'd spoken with had indeed been polite and balanced about the merits of the respective drugs. That final evening, I then bumped into two men from Company A at the bar, who put the boot into Company B's drug without mercy. One of them said that of course the competition would be fierce; he said, 'It's my job on the line, isn't it?'

The coming battle for market share does at least mean that flu people will get more attention. Aside from annual meetings to decide the vaccine components, in the past flu specialists had only got together every few years or so; now, with the advent of the plug drugs, the development of new vaccine models, and the alarm bells still ringing in Hong Kong, they were going to start meeting annually. 'The field's moving so quickly,' said Fred Hayden, 'that having a meeting every four or five years is inadequate. And we have these advances now . . .'

I asked if I could therefore bring this story to an optimistic conclusion, and Hayden held me up abruptly. He said, 'If a pandemic hit today, we're not ready. The knowledge base about the threat is much enhanced. The theoretical tools, and in some cases the practical tools, are in place. But it's a question of quantity. If you look right now at what we have on the shelf that we could pull off and use, the fact is, there's very little.'

So the message out of Maui is simple. Firstly, the surveillance system remains vital, and needs continuing improvement. Secondly, we need a panel of vaccine candidates built up, and we need to stockpile sufficient quantities of the plug drugs; they're stable compounds, with a reasonable shelf life, so in theory this shouldn't be difficult. In practice, on the other hand, it costs money, and when I asked one of the drug companies' people whether he thought governments would spend that money, he snorted derisively and said he couldn't ever see it happening.

To fail to do it, however, would be remarkably short-sighted. Asked if there'll be another pandemic, Fred Hayden says the one thing that every one of these people agree on. He says, 'It's not a question of if. It's only a matter of when. It's an inevitability.'

Given that certain knowledge, there's one other point to be made. In Western Europe, in North America, in Japan and Australia and New Zealand, when the next pandemic comes we'll scramble into action, and with luck we'll fend off the worst of it. The drugs and vaccines with which we'll do that, however, cost money that two-thirds of the human race doesn't have.

When the next pandemic comes, at least four billion people will therefore remain wholly unprotected. If the mortality rate is as bad as 1918, that works out at eighty million dead people, with countless millions more falling painfully ill. In Africa and India and Russia, across great swathes of the planet, no one will go untouched; all who live through it will know someone who doesn't.

I talked about all these things with Rob Webster, then he smiled and said, 'I'm surprised you haven't asked me about Svalbard.'

It had taken longer than they'd hoped to get the lab work up and running in London, but while the conference was meeting on Maui, Rod Daniels in Mill Hill was running the first tests on one of the twenty-odd samples from Long-yearbyen that they thought looked promising. They had good brain tissue and some half-decent lung; John Oxford had told me he wasn't too optimistic about finding any fragments of 1918 virus in them, but Webster remained cautiously hopeful. In the meantime, everyone was waiting for the next news from Taubenberger.

The hunt for the 1918 virus was an extraordinary business, and it's far from over, but what happened in the autumn of that year hangs over everything the flu community is trying to do now. On Svalbard, I'd asked Noël Roberts of Roche if he thought the plug drugs could protect us against the next pandemic, and he'd said, 'I'd like to think so. I can't definitely say yes, until we know what the nature of that virus is – but fingers crossed, it's likely to be the case. Fingers crossed, we may have a defence.

'More importantly, though, this is only one specific story that reflects a bigger advance altogether. I think over the next ten years, there'll be many such stories. The concept of looking at a virus gene by gene, and finding out how to tackle each gene – it's revolutionized the way we can confront them. Things we haven't been able to treat for a long, long time will all of a sudden be treatable.'

Science, as John Oxford says, goes forward like an express train. There may be some odd people riding it, but it's on the right track – or that, at least, is the optimistic viewpoint. With luck and hard work, new drugs and vaccines will very likely be successful for those people and nations that can afford them, but we'd be wise, all the same, to remain both watchful and humble when we contemplate influenza. This tiny packet of molecules, so tiny that a million of them can fit on a pinhead and leave room to spare, contains in its shape-shifting genes an awesome power; somewhere in the world, it's killing someone even as you're reading this.

It's a stark lesson in fate and mortality, in the impermanence of all our lives – a lesson poignantly learnt by a young boy whose story Alfred Crosby told when he finished his history of the Spanish flu:

Francis Russell was seven years old in 1918 and lived on top of Dorchester Hill, from where he could see Boston and the ships with their zigzag camouflage in Boston Harbour. He bought thrift stamps at twenty-five cents each as his part in the Liberty Bond Drive, and had birthday cakes without frosting so that the Belgians wouldn't starve, and ate peaches and saved the stones and baked them dry and put them in the peach stone collection barrels to be used in gas masks. He watched the funeral processions pass by on Walk Hill Street, and watched the coffins pile up in the cemetery chapel, and watched Pig-eye Mulvey set up a circus tent that billowed in the wind to hold the coffins that kept coming faster than the grave diggers could dig.

Russell was chased away from watching one of the funerals as it passed; he walked home and on the way, at the age of seven, he had a fearful insight. He realized that 'Life was not a perpetual present, and that even tomorrow would be part of the past, and that for all my days and years to come, I too must one day die.'

FURTHER READING

The best work on 1918 is *America's Forgotten Pandemic* by Alfred W. Crosby; I'm particularly indebted to him for his account of flu on the troop transports. For specialists, the British Ministry of Health's 1920 *Report on Pandemic Influenza* is invaluable.

For the general reader, Richard Collier's *The Plague of the Spanish Lady* is based on hundreds of interviews with people who lived through 1918 world-wide, and has many extraordinary stories. Eileen Pettigrew's *The Silent Enemy* and *Black November* by Geoffrey Rice are both good on the pandemic in Canada and New Zealand respectively. The best fiction inspired by 1918 is Katharine Anne Porter's novella *Pale Horse, Pale Rider*.

The Reverend Daniel Bell Hankin's splendid 1890 sermon can be found in volume 112 of *The City Pulpit*. *Annals of Influenza in Great Britain 1510–1890*, edited by Theophilus Thompson, collects a wealth of contemporary accounts through four centuries. *Behind the Veil*, a 'reminiscence of influenza' published by Liverpool chaplain Thomas Lund in 1892, is a stunning account of what going through pandemic delirium is like; a cross between a religious tract and an acid trip.

Most people will already be aware of Oliver Sacks's *Awakenings*, on the aftermath of encephalitis lethargica. On the swine flu affair of 1976, Arthur M. Silverstein's *Pure*

Politics and Impure Science is excellent. More generally on disease in history and society, I found the following all useful: Blake, Robin, *Mind Over Medicine*; Karlen, Arno, *Man and Microbes*; Nikiforuk, Andrew, *The Fourth Horseman*; and Ryan, Frank, *Virus X*.